A CONCERT OF CHARISMS

Ordained Ministry in Religious Life

Paul K. Hennessy, C.F.C.

EDITOR

PAULIST PRESS
New York / Mahwah, N.J.

Cover design by Jim Brisson.

The Publisher gratefully acknowledges use of excerpts from "Canonical Implications: Ordaining Women to the Permanent Diaconate" (Washington D.C.: Canon Law Society of America, 1995).

Library of Congress Cataloging-in-Publication Data

A concert of charisms : ordained ministry in religious life / Paul K. Hennessy, editor.
   p. cm.
  Includes bibliographical references.
  ISBN 0-8091-3713-5 (alk. paper)
  1. Priests. 2. Monastic and religious life. 3. Catholic Church—Clergy—Appointment, call, and election. I. Hennessy, Paul K. (Paul Kevin)
BX1914.C66 1997
255—dc21
                                                              97–3222
                                                                 CIP

Published by Paulist Press
997 Macarthur Boulevard
Mahwah, New Jersey 07430

Printed and bound in the
United States of America

Contents

Contributors

DAVID J. NYGREN, C.M., and Miriam D. Ukeritis, C.S.J., are well known for their direction of the Religious Life Futures Project and the publications ensuing from it. Dr. Nygren, a noted lecturer and writer in the areas of planning and management, is professor of Strategy at the Haas Graduate School of Business, University of California (Berkeley). He is also a member of the Vincentian Leadership Team, Midwest Province. Dr. Ukeritis, once director of the House of Affirmation, has been until recently the director of the Institute for Leadership for Religious Organization at De Paul. She now serves on the Leadership Team of the Albany Province, Sisters of St. Joseph of Carondelet.

ROLAND J. FALEY, T.O.R., is a professor of Sacred Scripture at Immaculate Conception Seminary in Huntington, N.Y. He is the author of the highly acclaimed *Footprints on the Mountain: Preaching and Teaching the Sunday Readings* (Paulist Press, 1994) as well as *Bonding with God* (Paulist Press, 1997), a volume on the theme of *covenant* in the Scriptures. He served as minister general of the Third Order Regular Franciscans and executive director of the Conference of Major Superiors of Men.

DORIS GOTTEMOELLER, R.S.M., holds a Ph.D. in theology from Fordham University and was an official observer from the United States at the 1994 Synod on Consecrated Life. She is now in her second term as president of the Sisters of Mercy of the Americas. A noted lecturer and writer, she has also served on many boards and is a past-president of the Leadership Conference of Women Religious.

PAUL K. HENNESSY, C.F.C., is the president of the newly founded Blessed Edmund Rice School for Pastoral Ministry in the Diocese of Venice in Florida, where he also serves as professor of theology. A past-president of the Conference of Major Superiors of Men, he is a member of the Congregation of Christian Brothers. Articles by him have appeared in *Theological Studies, Horizons* and other journals.

JOHN W. O'MALLEY, S.J., is professor at Weston School of Theology. He authored *The First Jesuits* (Harvard University Press, 1993), which won many accolades and awards. His 1988 article in *Theological Studies* entitled "Priesthood, Ministry, and Religious Life: Some Historical and Historiographical Considerations" served as a catalyst for this volume.

PAUL J. PHILIBERT, O.P., is director of the Institute for Church Life and associate professor of theology at the University of Notre Dame. He edited Living in the Meantime: Concerning the Transformation of Religious Life (Paulist Press, 1994) and has written several essays on religious charisms and regular clergy. He coauthored *Seeing and Believing: Images of the Christian Faith* with artist Frank Kacmarcik (The Liturgical Press, 1995).

DAVID N. POWER, O.M.I., the 1996 recipient of the John Courtney Murray Award from the Catholic Theological Society of America for outstanding contributions, is professor of theology at The Catholic University of America. His books and articles in the area of sacramental theology are numerous. Especially pertinent to this volume is his classic work, *The Christian Priest: Elder and Prophet* (Sheed & Ward, 1973).

R. KEVIN SEASOLTZ, O.S.B., a monk of St. John's Abbey in Collegeville, serves as professor of theology at the abbey university. A noted canonist as well, he was a longtime member of the faculty at The Catholic University of America and serves as editor of *Worship*. His writings on ecclesiological, canonical, and liturgical issues have appeared in numerous journals, especially on topics touching Benedictine life.

Introduction:
The Parochialization of the Church
and Consecrated Life

Paul K. Hennessy, C.F.C.

For many Roman Catholics the word *parish* has become almost synonymous with *local church.* Catholic colleges, monasteries, health care centers, retreat houses, and the like are seen as *extras,* as somewhat tangential to "real" Catholic life. Parochialization—this movement toward the parish as center of the local church—has become increasingly pronounced in the years following the Second Vatican Council. In an address on parish planning and restructuring, for example, Bishop Howard Hubbard stated that his "assumption [is] that the parish community is the place where people receive the education, formation, support and spiritual nourishment they need to fulfill [the] call to shared responsibility, [the] call to exercise the priestly ministry of Jesus in our world today."[1] This statement clearly demonstrates how forceful the shift to the parish has become, and in this essay we will examine how it has affected and raised challenges for communities of consecrated men and women.

Parochialization has had a major impact on religious communities, especially those with ordained members for, as the number of diocesan clergy has decreased and the number of Roman Catholics in the United States has increased, not only ordained but also nonordained members of congregations have been increasingly called upon to administer parishes. This happened despite the fact that for centuries religious orders and congregations had a historic independence of diocesan structures because their charismatic calling was considered to go beyond geographic confines and at times necessitated confrontation with injustice and corruption, even within the church. In addition, many communities of consecrated men and women existed prior to the identification of diocesan boundaries. For these many reasons, therefore, their increased co-option into diocesan and parochial structures must be carefully evaluated.

It was not until the early Middle Ages that there was any widespread development in Europe of what we would today call "parishes." In the Roman

Empire, city and diocese were generally coterminous.[2] While even later the dioceses in Italy were still within the confines of cities, the same was not true in France and the northern lands, where dioceses were far greater in geographic dispersion. In these lands it became increasingly necessary for bishops to assign presbyters to care for persons in outlying areas. In some places, even earlier, where the feudal lords were bound to provide religious services for their serfs, clerics would be appointed by the lord. The Third Lateran Council of 1179 gave the bishop the right of institution, but the lord still had the power to supervise and appoint.[3]

The practice of ministering to persons within the confines of a parish or geographic area gradually developed even within cities. Since the earliest eras of Christianity, however, the mission of most religious communities of women and men was not so limited by geography. They were founded by charismatic individuals who saw a spiritual or corporal work of mercy to be addressed and who received approbation or even a mandate to do so. Their monasteries, missions, colleges and independent schools, retreat houses, hospitals and homes for orphans and the infirm, while subject to certain diocesan regulation, were seen as valid expressions of the church's mission and ministry independent of parishes. Most religious were easily transferred across diocesan boundaries. Even those religious communities founded as diocesan came into being to address needs that a parish alone could not handle.

Canon 515 of the Code of Canon Law of 1983 states: "A parish is a definite community of the Christian faithful which is established on a stable basis within a *particular church*."[4] Even prior to the Code and as a result of the reported usage at Vatican II, however, the term *local church* was and continues to be used more popularly, but with consequent ambiguity. One hears *local church* used to refer to the church within a nation, as well as an individual diocese, and individual parishes.[5] While ecclesiologists generally would prefer to use the expression *local church* to refer to the church within a nation, and canonists refer to a diocese as a *particular church,* much of the confusion has been caused by the use of the adjective *local* in the *General Instruction to the Roman Missal* (1969) where it refers to the diocese. "In the *local* church (*In ecclesia locali*) first place must clearly be given…to Mass offered by the bishop surrounded by his priests and his ministers…." (par. 74)[6] and in speaking of any eucharistic gathering, it calls it "a *local* assembly of the holy church" (par. 7).[7]

For many years the Eucharist was celebrated daily or on a regular basis in churches or chapels attached to houses of religious men and women. At times the principal celebrant was already a member of the community; in some places he was assigned by the diocese as a chaplain. In other situations it was the responsibility of the local community to arrange for an ordained person to come to celebrate. According to the mind of the *General Instruction,* each such assembly around the eucharistic table was an assembly of the church. In paragraphs 75 and 76 of this same document, it notes that every mass "represents the universal church in a definite time and place" (75). It continues, "Among the masses offered by certain communities, first place is given to the conventual Mass, which is part of the daily office" (76). Hence, within a *particular* church (a diocese), each approved institution was a manifestation of the church and was in no way inferior to a parish in the revelation of the entire church.

While the ministries of religious were integral to the mission of the church in a particular diocese, it became increasingly clear that to bishops, diocesan clergy, laity and at times even religious, the diocese was envisioned as having a cathedral church and many parishes. The houses and works of religious were seen as tangential. This trend became even more pronounced with the promulgation of the degree *Presbyterorum Ordinis* of Vatican II, which held the model of diocesan priesthood as the norm. Even more so than before, ministering to the faithful was seen, not in terms of seminary formation, mission bands, convent or private Catholic schools, houses of prayer and retreats, hospitals, universities and colleges, but as centered in parishes.

It should be noted that many of the structural regulations governing religious prior to Vatican II isolated them in many ways from a sense of belonging to a diocese. This was more true probably of women than men, but a sense of being isolated from the concerns of a diocese was fairly common. The life of worship took place within the chapel, and the ministry was in an adjacent institution. It created a mind-set that was hardly "catholic." Ordained religious frequently assisted in parishes on Sundays, but in many cases, the assignment was to a different parish weekly as "supply," as it was called. Nonordained religious began gradually to participate in the worship life of some parish in order to experience and form a wider assembly of people. The choice was made, however, based on more than geographic location, for example, style of celebration, the quality of preaching, the mix of the assembly and the eloquence of the homilist.

Religious, both ordained and nonordained, found their lives transformed by the church's response to Vatican II and the focus on parish. Along with the laity at large, they found the parish to serve as a magnet in searching to express the ideal of conciliar theology of a church gathered in baptismal solidarity. Positively, this added the presence of religious to the parochial Sunday assembly and extended social contacts between laity and religious acknowledging a "common universal call to holiness."[8] Negatively, however, this drew religious away from a strong point of internal liturgical solidarity with one another in local religious communities, perhaps contributing to some confusion about religious identity and certainly even more so about the meaning of *local church* for religious. The momentum toward the parish as magnet was strong and the transformation swift, and it is only in retrospect that we can begin to assess the consequences.

As one reads this volume, it will become clear that since the Second Vatican Council major transitions have taken place within the self-identification of religious communities. Competing with the pull of parochialization was the council's call to a renewal of consecrated life. The pertinent question asked of all was: "What would the founder want us to be doing here and now?" Religious orders were founded by charismatic individuals for rather specific purposes, for example, healing ministry, educational ministry, foreign missionary endeavors, ministry to the dying, and so forth. The call of Vatican II was to serve as a catalyst for a return to the original intentions of the founder(s) and an attempt to apply them to the present day. For those congregations or orders founded before the development of parishes or even dioceses, as well as those founded for apostolic mission beyond territorial boundaries, it raised some challenging questions about the charisms of religious life and the movement to parochialization. As one proceeds in this book, one will see that it continues to do so.

This volume, in fact, grew out of a recognized tension in orders and congregations of men who have ordained members and who have become increasingly involved in parochial ministry—by assuming the management of a parish at the request of a bishop or by assigning men to live in a diocesan rectory because of the shortage of diocesan clerics. The Conference of Major Superiors of Men (CMSM), the canonically recognized body for abbots, superiors general, provincials—the leadership—of communities of men, began to receive requests from its membership to study this question in the early 1980s. In many ways it was a natural outgrowth of a study on *clericalism* completed in 1985.[9] In 1988 John O'Malley, S.J., a contributor to this volume, wrote an essay in *Theological Studies,* in which he stated:

> ...the categories with which we usually think about religious life are inadequate to the historical reality, and that inadequacy is to a large extent responsible for some of the confusion in the Church today about religious life, especially about the relationship to priesthood and ministry of the "regular clergy," i.e., priests living in a religious order or congregation under a rule. This confusion, I further maintain, is harmful to religious orders and congregations, even those who do not have ordained members, and is also harmful in the long run to the Church as a whole.[10]

In 1990 the various regions of CMSM were asked to reflect upon the issue with facilitators who went to each regional meeting. It was decided as a result of these gatherings that indeed the "confusion" that O'Malley spoke of existed among the membership. Such questions as, "Are you a Franciscan because you wanted to be a priest or are you a priest because you were asked to be ordained by the Franciscans?" received quite different answers. There was an ambivalence about self-identification.

The national board of CMSM appointed a task force to study the issue and to request foundational funds. Because these funds were not easily forthcoming and because of personnel changes, the project languished for a couple of years. In 1994 the executive director Gregory Reisert, O.F.M. Cap., approached the present editor, who had just completed his term as president of the conference, and asked if he would direct the project and bring it to a speedy conclusion. Paul J. Philibert, O.P., a former member of the CMSM board, then recently appointed as director of the Institute for Church Life at the University of Notre Dame, agreed to act as a special collaborator. We met with some of the original task force, invited new input and succeeded in getting this volume ready for publication by Paulist Press. In his 1988 article, O'Malley stated that a study would benefit not only communities with ordained members, but also the entire church; hence it was decided very early on to make the volume available to a wide audience and to invite the participation of some women religious. It became increasingly clear as the volume progressed that something—perhaps unnoticed by most—was challenging the distinctive charismatic role that religious institutes have played in the church.

The first monograph in this volume appropriately comes from John W. O'Malley, S.J., of the Weston School of Theology in Cambridge. The distinguished author and teacher situates the problems in their historical context. In earlier years there was frequently an antagonism between religious orders and bishops, as well as a question as to whether consecrated life was compatible with priestly orders and hierarchy. Such appropriate quotations as the fifth-century one by John Cassian that "a monk ought by all means to fly from women and bishops" enliven O'Malley's treatment. The reforms of the Council of Trent were also a turning point in an understanding of ministry in the church. This chapter introduces us to the changes in theological reflection that have transpired from century to century.

In an essay written from a Western monastic perspective on ordained ministry by R. Kevin Seasoltz, O.S.B. of St. John Abbey and seminary faculty in Collegeville, we are brought back to the earliest forms of consecrated life. In only two periods, he points out, the Middle Ages and the nineteenth-century restoration of Benedictine life, did the monasteries become highly clericalized. Church law, not the *Rule of St. Benedict,* imposed a requirement for ordination on the abbot. He also develops in some detail the institution of classes of members in monasteries. This affected other religious communities as well. Seasoltz offers some interesting historical perspectives on the frequency of eucharistic celebration in early monastic life. This background is useful for the contemporary discussion on the same issue for religious women and men.

David N. Power, O.M.I., of the Department of Theology at The Catholic University of America, has the difficult task of examining the variety of theologies on both priesthood and religious life. The salient question, he believes, is whether in the years since the Second Vatican Council such theological development has taken place that "the retrieval of charism by religious bodies has affected the practice and understanding of ministry in general and ordained ministry in particular...." Relating ordination to many of the developments in the church, Power suggests that each group ask "Why ordination?" before proceeding with what has been done in the past. One will find that same suggestion repeated by other contributors to this book.

Scripture scholar Roland J. Faley, T.O.R., currently on the faculty of Immaculate Conception Seminary in Huntington, N.Y., reflects on both his own experience of priesthood as a Franciscan and the historical American setting for ordained ministers. Capitalizing on his experiences as superior general of his own community and executive director of CMSM, he asks some provocative questions about the focus of ministry for religious, whose traditional works never included parishes but who now find a significant number of their membership in such settings.

Doris Gottemoeller, R.S.M., president of the Sisters of Mercy of the Americas, does some "speculative theology" and reflects on the implications for women's communities if ordination for them to the diaconate and/or priesthood were to become a reality. Women have already become "parochialized" and in many cases called to the administration of parishes, away indeed from some of the founding charisms of the communities. A significant number have also moved to diocesan positions in chancery offices and can easily be immersed into a clerical culture. One wonders why the dialogue about the ordination of women seems to have taken place apart from the experiences of communities of men who are revisiting that very issue.

The canonical issues surrounding the relationship between religious communities and diocesan bishops is addressed by R. Kevin Seasoltz, O.S.B., this time as a canonist rather than a monk. The issues of exemption of religious from diocesan control has an interesting historical development. The relationship of jurisdiction to ordination is a stumbling block, not only within institutes made up of ordained and nonordained members, but also now in the wider church. The papal pledge to use women's gifts and talents in major positions in the church will not be achieved until these questions are answered. Indeed, in his recent apostolic exhortation *Vita Consecrata,* John Paul II states: "It is... urgently necessary to take certain concrete steps, beginning by providing room for women to participate in different fields and at all levels, including decision-making processes, above all in matters which concern women themselves."[11] This chapter also treats some contemporary moves in the revised rites of ordination to emphasize more episcopal control over religious men.

Miriam D. Ukeritis, C.S.J., and David J. Nygren, C.M., of De Paul University, the codirectors of *The Future of Religious Orders in the United States* study, revisit some of the data collected with specific references to the attitude of religious priests. One is initially heartened to see that among all religious, priests have the strongest understanding of what it means to be a religious in the church today. We recognize, however, that more data are needed to ascertain whether the identity comes from the priesthood or the consecrated life.

My close colleague and invaluable adviser in the direction of this task, Paul J. Philibert, O.P., of the University of Notre Dame, concludes the volume with some reflections on the situation in which ministry in the church finds itself. He indicates that much like the nascent Corinthian church, we are experiencing a rapid growth in new ministries. How we will cope with the need for new ministers—ordained or not—and how they are accepted in the faith community will say much about us as church. He then reviews the issues raised in this book and challenges leadership and membership to address these critical times in a faith-filled and courageous manner.

It may seem strange that a nonordained male religious would have an interest in editing this volume. From a lifetime of explaining what a "brother" is and noting the confusion on the face(s) of the listener(s), however, I became convinced many years ago that we have developed a massive mixture of charisms. The consecrated life in all its forms is certainly charismatic, but so too are the variety of ministries to which all disciples of Jesus are called. Priesthood is a ministry to which some are called by this community we call *church.* But, it is a *ministry,* whereas the various forms of consecrated life are truly *life-styles,* springing from our common baptism. It is my hope that through a reading of this volume, many years in gestation, we all may move closer to clarity—women and men from all walks of life, those called to special ministries in the name and image of the prophetic, kingly, and priestly one whom we call "Master."

The title of this volume reflects the ambiguity now experienced by clerics, religious and lay, or ordained and nonordained. A concert is dependent for harmony upon the intersection of many instruments and accomplished musicians being directed to the same end. One attends a concert expecting that all will work together melodiously. There are concerts, however, when because of lack of preparation, improper synchronization, acoustical deficiencies, inept performances or poor direction, cacophony results. There are also times when perfectly good performances are given in inappropriate settings—during a banquet when people wish to talk or when certain instruments developed for outdoor use (e.g., the bagpipes, the bass drum) are introduced into a confined banquet hall with earsplitting results. For centuries the distinct gift of consecrated life was regarded for its merits, even though there were various manifestations of the same gift. Likewise, the ministries of the church were also varied, all requiring some missioning, but only some demanding sacramental ordination. In the ordained ministry and in consecrated life, we have distinct charisms that are called to interface precisely and harmoniously to herald the reign of God. Perhaps at the end of this volume, the reader will recognize more clearly an appropriate path to true harmony.

NOTES

1. Bishop Howard Hubbard, "A Vision for Parish Planning and Restructuring," *Origins* 25, no. 42 (1996): 728. See also Dennis M. Linehan, "New Life for Parishes," *America* 174, no. 16, (1996): 3.

2. Karl Bihlmeyer and Hermann Tüchlé, *Church History*, (Westminster, Md.: The Newman Press, 1963), 2:105.

3. F. L. Cross and E. A. Livingston, *The Oxford Dictionary of the Christian Church*, 2nd ed. (London: Oxford University Press, 1974), 1033.

4. James A. Coriden, Thomas J. Green, and Donald E. Heintschel, *The Code of Canon Law: A Test and Commentary* (New York: Paulist Press, 1985), 415.

5. *The Jurist* 52, no. 1 (1992) is entirely devoted to a colloquium on the notion of "Local Church" that took place at the Universidad Pontificia in Salamanca on April 2–7, 1991. It is well worth reading.

6. *The New Order of Mass* (Collegeville, Minn.: The Liturgical Press, 1970), 153.

7. *Ibid.,* 83.

8. See the Dogmatic Constitution on the Church (*Lumen Gentium*) esp. chap. 5, in *Vatican Council II: The Conciliar and Post Conciliar Documents*, ed. Austin Flannery, O.P. (Collegeville, Minn.: The Liturgical Press, 1975).

9. The papers were published under the title *Who Are My Brothers?* ed. Philip Armstrong, C.S.C. (New York: Alba House, 1988).

10. John W. O'Malley, S.J., "Priesthood, Ministry, and Religious Life: Some Historical and Historiographical Considerations," *Theological Studies* 49, no. 2 (1988): 223.

11. John Paul II, apostolic exhortation *Vita Consecrata, Origins* 25, no. 41 (1996): 699, par. 58.

1

One Priesthood: Two Traditions

John W. O'Malley, S.J.

"Happy to meet you, Father! What's your parish?" This question is the almost inevitable initiation into a conversation about being a priest yet not being in a parish, about being a priest and at the same time being a member of a religious order. For many Catholics being a priest means by definition doing parish ministry under the diocesan bishop, and even for many priests in religious orders "real" priestly ministry means celebrating the Eucharist in a parish on Sunday morning. This identification of priesthood with parish and diocese is the result of a long tradition of thinking in the church that gained great impetus with the Council of Trent and reached a kind of climax with the Second Vatican Council and its aftermath. Books and articles about the history of priesthood deal almost exclusively with this tradition, reinforcing the impression that there is no alternative.[1]

But there is, of course, an alternative—the tradition of priesthood within the religious orders, the tradition of priesthood within the context of the consecrated life. That tradition is the subject of this book. The book itself is the result of lively conversations on the subject over the past decade, many of them directly or indirectly sponsored by the Conference of Major Superiors of Men. The subject is complex, for, besides its own specific complications, it is tied inevitably to all the other complex, confusing, and hotly debated questions related to priesthood in the church today.

The precise issue treated in this essay, however, is the relationship between the two traditions of priesthood—an issue that obviously cannot be dealt with without touching on many other issues. Nonetheless, our focus here is that relationship, no other, multifarious and distressingly complicated though it is.

The issue is not new in the church. During the first millennium it often took the form of ascetics propounding the thesis that the consecrated life was utterly incompatible with priestly orders and hierarchy. "A monk ought by all means to fly from women and bishops," said John Cassian in the fifth century, repeating what he took to be already an "old maxim of the Fathers."[2] The tone

9

of the discussion was sometimes angry and reproachful, almost always firm and eager to establish clear boundaries between the two ways of life. Since in the next chapter in this volume Kevin Seasoltz examines in detail the complex relationship between priesthood and the Benedictine tradition of monasticism that goes back to St. Benedict himself, there is no need for me to review it here.

Bishops, of course, had their own reservations and even antagonisms toward monks. By the early years of the second millennium in the West, in the wake of the Gregorian Reform, the antagonism took more public and aggressive form. At the First Lateran Council in 1123, for instance, the bishops turned the tables. They fired the first salvo in what would be the classic battleground from that time forward—where, by whom, and under whose authority is Christian ministry rightly performed. Canon 16 of the council reads in part:

> Following in the footsteps of the holy fathers, we order by general decree that monks…may not celebrate masses in public anywhere. Moreover, let them completely abstain from public visitation of the sick, from anointings and also from administering penances, for these things in no way pertain to their calling.[3]

In 1123 the bishops directed their salvo against monks because the mendicants and their successors, the principal target for later centuries, had not yet come into existence. Once the mendicants appeared in the thirteenth century, the conflict burst even more contentiously into the public arena with the bitter conflicts between "the regulars and the seculars" in the universities and in the great attacks on the pastoral privileges of the mendicant orders launched by the bishops in councils and synods.

The attack raged so severely and relentlessly at the Fifth Lateran Council in 1516–17 that Giles of Viterbo, the superior general of the Augustinians, was convinced that the bishops wanted to destroy the mendicants utterly and delete from memory their very name.[4] In his correspondence Giles relates his desperate and prolonged efforts to save what he could, running from the bishops to the cardinal protector, to the pope, and to the representatives of the civil powers. On that occasion the orders were saved through the intervention of Pope Leo X, who, like his predecessors and successors, saw them as allies in the papacy's ongoing powerstruggle with the bishops.[5]

The decrees of the Council of Trent, 1545–1563, do not reflect how persistently the bishops recurred to their now standard grievances against the orders or how much they wanted to bring the orders' ministries under episcopal control.[6] After Trent some bishops welcomed the orders, which now included newer ones like the Jesuits, into their dioceses as partners in a common task, whereas others tried to limit severely their activity and would have dispensed with their ministrations altogether if they could. The powerful and widely emulated archbishops of Milan—St. Carlo Borromeo (1560–1584) and his cousin Federico Borromeo (1595–1631)—worked toward an ideal of having practically all preaching in their archdiocese performed by diocesan clergy, but even their resources were too limited to allow them to attain it.[7]

In subsequent centuries the relationship between the two traditions of clergy continued to be marked by ambivalence and even raw antagonism, as Roland Faley shows later in this volume with telling examples from North America. Nonetheless, along with rivalry, conflict, jealousies, and petty and major graspings for power, there was in practice a division of labor that seems to have served the church well. The diocesan clergy ministered for the most part to the faithful, especially through sacrament and ritual in the parishes or their equivalents. It was for this task that they were trained. The regular clergy ministered to the faithful, especially through other instruments like schools, shrines, and retreat houses. Many went beyond the faithful in the pews to seek out the sick and the sinners and to work for the conversion of the pagan and the infidel.

This division of labor was distinctive of Roman Catholicism, for the Protestant churches had no equivalent to the religious orders and congregations. This meant, as well, that they had no equivalent to the many active congregations of women that sprang up, especially beginning in the seventeenth century, and that were, perhaps, even more distinctive of Catholicism. This ravishingly important phenomenon, however, falls outside the purview of our volume.[8]

VATICAN II

With the Second Vatican Council, the relationship between the two traditions of clergy reached, quietly and almost unobserved, a new crisis. As part of its sweeping and all-inclusive agenda, the council at a certain point realized that it needed to make a statement about priests, as well as bishops, in the church and especially to indicate for them the ideal in ministry for which they were to strive. The result was three decrees: *Christus Dominus* (On the Pastoral Office of Bishops in the Church); *Presbyterorum Ordinis* (On the Ministry and Life of Priests); and *Optatam Totius* (On the Training of Priests).

Although not among the documents that received the closest scrutiny and consideration during Vatican Council II, they were rightly greeted with enthusiasm upon their publication for being major improvements upon any official statements on the subject up to that time. *Presbyterorum Ordinis* was in several regards outstanding. In the first place, it sedulously tried to avoid identifying priesthood exclusively with the power to consecrate the Eucharist by giving equal importance and force to each aspect of the threefold ministry of word, sacrament, and governance—prophet, priest, and king. This was a radical departure from the extremely brief decree on holy orders at Trent, where priesthood was in fact narrowly described as "the power to consecrate, offer and administer his body and blood, as also to remit or retain sins."[9] Partly to fore-stall such a description, *Presbyterorum Ordinis* for the most part used, as in its very title, *presbyter* rather than *sacerdos* to indicate what it was talking about—an important distinction consistently ignored in English translations, where *priest,* with its denotation of somebody who offers sacrifice, carries the day.

Most important of all, the document defined the presbyterate as insti-tuted for *ministry*. It is almost impossible for us to recover what a dramatic shift in perspective such a definition betrays. The definition means that ordina-tion is not for the celebration of the Eucharist or for the hearing of confessions *per se;* it is not for the enhancement of the person of the minister by conferring upon him special "powers," but rather ordination is for the service of the peo-ple of God. We perhaps catch some glimpse of how radically the document departs from an earlier theology by noting that the word *ministry* plays an utterly insignificant role in the correlative document from the Council of Trent.[10]

Optatam Totius was basically a practical decree, but *Christus Dominus* and *Presbyterorum Ordinis* incorporated the best research and thinking then available on their respective subjects, although admittedly these were not sub-jects where research was particularly plentiful or profound. Diocesan clergy found the documents uplifting and encouraging, not least for their seeming promise of a more collegial relationship between priests and bishops. Priests in many religious orders found them confirmatory of the primacy they had given to various forms of ministry of the word from their founding years.

Not until some years after the council did members of the religious orders begin to detect perturbing implications for themselves in these docu-ments and in some of the ways the documents were interpreted and imple-mented, especially as they impinged upon the training of candidates for the priesthood. Was, for instance, a single "Program for Priestly Formation" appropriate for candidates from both the dioceses and the orders, with its implication that both would engage in identical forms of ministry? An alto-gether crucial question began to emerge—an old question, perhaps, but in new form and with new urgency—How do priests in religious orders and congre-gations fit in the ministry of the church?[11]

The three most directly pertinent documents of the Second Vatican Council are subtle and in many respects pliable in their rhetoric, yet they sug-gest that the specific difference between religious and diocesan priests lies in the fact that the former take vows of poverty, chastity, and obedience, whereas the latter do not. The ideals that these vows entail, however, are so vigorously enjoined upon diocesan priests in *Presbyterorum Ordinis* that, in the long run, the difference seems to be at most one of emphasis or to consist simply in the juridical fact of public vows, or perhaps life in community. The difference seems thus reducible to some rather vague particularities of spirituality that are, in fact, almost impossible to define.

The conclusion seems to follow that there is one priesthood, as the document firmly states,[12] but that priests can be animated by different spiritualities.[13] There are no further differences. Although *Presbyterorum Ordinis* concedes in its opening paragraph that its provisions are to be applied to "regular clergy" only insofar as they "suit their circumstances," the document seems to assume that they in fact suit their circumstances quite well. The topic sentence in that paragraph sets the tone for everything that follows: "What is said here applies to all priests."

Some things surely do apply to all, especially things that the documents state forthrightly and directly. First and foremost among them is the firm location of a priestly identity in *ministry,* a location doubtless pertinent to both diocesan and religious clergy. Yet it is in this very issue of ministry that perhaps the major problem lies. The difficulty with the documents in this regard is not so much what they explicitly say about ministry as how they frame it—and perhaps for that reason their radical implications for priests in religious orders were not at first grasped.

In other words, underlying the documents are certain assumptions that are not immediately obvious but that provide the basic design for priestly ministry as the council conceived it. That design consists essentially of four components:

1. Priestly ministry is a ministry by and large *to the faithful.*
2. It is a ministry that takes place in a stable community of faith, that is, *in a parish.*
3. It is a ministry done by clergy *"in hierarchical union with the order of bishops."*
4. The *warrant for ministry,* including preaching, is *ordination* to the diaconate or presbyterate.

This design clearly corresponds to the ministerial traditions and situation of the diocesan clergy—in theory since the early centuries of Christianity and ever more in practice since the Council of Trent. But does it correspond to the traditions and situations of the regular clergy? Not so clearly. In many instances, in fact, it runs counter to them.

As for the first component of the council's design for priestly ministry the Dominicans, to take an obvious example, came into being in the thirteenth century not to care for the faithful but to preach conversion to the Albigensian heretics. As for the second, many orders carried out their ministries principally in schools, third orders and sodalities, hospitals, soup kitchens and printing presses. They were, in fact, often forbidden to undertake parishes. As for the third, while they had to respect episcopal rights to regulate public worship and other matters in their dioceses, members of religious orders relied on their own superiors or chapters to decide when, where, by what means, and to whom they would minister. As for the fourth, at least in the Society of Jesus, the primary warrant for ministry was entrance into the order, for even the novices were expected to engage in all the "usual ministries" of the Society except, of course, the hearing of confessions. The novices and other unordained members preached, for instance, during mass and on other liturgical occasions.[14]

In the active orders, their constitutions, rules, officers and superiors, yes, even their so-called privileges, were not operative only for the internal discipline of their communities, as *Christus Dominus* by some historical sleight of hand seems to indicate.[15] They looked just as much, if not more, to effective ministry. The commitment to ministry affected the scope even of the vows traditional to religious life. For the Dominicans, poverty was not simply an ascetical principle helpful to the spiritual development of the individual friar, but a condition of effective ministry for dealing with the Albigensians' criticism of clerical wealth and corruption.

I have in several publications already elaborated on the relationship of ministry to religious life. Moreover, I consider my book *The First Jesuits* an extended case study of the question as exemplified in the foundational years of one major order. I will not, therefore, pursue these aspects of the question any further here.[16] I would, however, underscore that I think them of fundamental importance—the basic points of reference to which the discussion must always return.

I would also underscore, as I insisted in my article in *Theological Studies,* that we need to approach the question of ministry in religious life with a new method. We need to approach it as part of the history of ministry rather than exclusively as an aspect of the history of asceticism beginning more or less with Pachomius. The latter approach suggests that ministry is a kind of add-on to religious life. The former indicates that, at least beginning with the mendicants in the thirteenth century, ministry is constitutive of the identity of many of the new orders. Why not, in other words, do the history as from Paul to Ignatius rather than the traditional from Pachomius to Ignatius? Method, here as always, determines the outcome of the research!

What is crucial, in any case, is to move the discussion beyond the vagueness of spirituality and charism, where religious have often tried to argue their position. It must be moved to the more concrete ground of ministry—it must be moved to praxis, as David Power will argue in the third chapter in this volume. Such a move will impart substance and energy to words like spirituality and charism. Such a move will allow us to speak with clarity and will dispel the vagueness of the abstract theological categories that so far have been devised to explain the difference between the two traditions.

TRENT AND "PAROCHIAL CONFORMITY"

Perhaps I can at this point further illustrate the contrast between the two traditions by a few observations about the Council of Trent and its significance for the future development of ministry. Some critics of Vatican II have barely managed to conceal their sneer when they describe it as a "pastoral council," implicitly contrasting it with the presumably more robust "doctrinal councils" like Trent. While it is undeniably true that Trent issued a number of important doctrinal decrees, it issued a perhaps even larger number "about reform." For Trent reform meant, for the most part, reform of the ministry of bishops and priests or reform of their life-style in order to bring it more in conformity with the ministry they were to perform.

Trent was, therefore, very much a pastoral council. Indeed, the degree to which it descended to nuts-and-bolts provisions about ministry, most of which are utterly obsolete today, made it much more practical than Vatican II ever pretended to be. Few councils have been more concerned with the great central Christian mysteries than Vatican II, few more convinced of the power of ideas to effect change when appealingly presented. Few, therefore, have been more doctrinal. Ironically, given Vatican II's reputation for being a pastoral council, few councils have been, in proportion to the quantity of its decrees, less prescriptive about specifics concerning ministry.

If Vatican II was, therefore, just as doctrinal as Trent, Trent was in its reform decrees just as pastoral as Vatican II. We have been misled about this aspect of Trent because, besides a few recent social historians, scholars have concentrated their researches almost exclusively on Tridentine doctrine. But the impact and implications of Trent's pastoral decrees have been immense— still affecting us today and still pertinent for the relationship between the two traditions of priesthood we are discussing.

In that regard, I will look at Trent from only two of several possible perspectives. The first is Trent's focus on the parish, and the second is the significance of the norms and means Trent proposed for reforming or improving ministry. These perspectives allow us to rise above the confusing mass of detail and legalistic jargon in Trent's decrees *de reformatione* to see the ecclesiological and pastoral vision from which they flow.

Trent wanted principally to reform three institutions: (1) the papacy and the papal curia, (2) the episcopacy, and (3) the parishes under their pastors—through whom the laity would be reformed. The council was consistently frustrated in dealing with the reform of the first institution and finally had to abandon the project, but it was successful in dealing with the other two—bishops and pastors—which in any case are closely related to one another. The council made use of traditional legislation concerning bishops and pastors but created something new by marshaling it in such a thorough and coherent way.

The ultimate purpose behind the Tridentine legislation on these subjects was to transform bishops and pastors of parishes from collectors of benefices into shepherds of souls. In its doctrinal decree on the sacrament of orders, the council had practically nothing to say about ministry. But ministry was to a large extent the scope of Trent's reform decrees. Those decrees looked, in the last analysis, to a more effective ministry by bishops and pastors, a ministry located in the *parish.* As a fundamental step in the direction of such a ministry, bishops would have to reside in their dioceses and pastors in their parishes. The battle to put teeth in the legislation requiring episcopal residency was waged sometimes on the sidelines, sometimes at the center of the council during much of the eighteen years that it lasted. Further provisions followed, with this one as their indispensable premise.

Two features of these provisions need to be noted. First, in the course of the centuries, they were a slowly moving but massive force in transferring religious practice ever increasingly into the parish—almost as into its only legitimate place of exercise. Parishes existed well before Trent, and, as essentially urban institutions, they took on more importance as European cities revived from the eleventh century forward. Even by the sixteenth century, however, and well beyond, they were only one institution in a vast array of others where Christians might find their devotion and engage in the practices of their faith.

Among these institutions were shrines, monastery and manor chapels, the collegiate churches of the mendicants, and, as research in the past decade has shown in such stunning fashion, the various confraternities or sororities or religious "guilds" that flourished in the cities and towns of Europe. That research has revolutionized our understanding of how Christianity was practiced from the late Middle Ages well into the modern era.[17] Not only has it demonstrated how lively religious practice was and how well informed people were about basic Christian belief, but it also has shown how secondary was the role played by the parish churches. Of course, the situation differed greatly from place to place, from city to countryside, but very often indeed the parish church was where baptisms, marriages, and "Easter duties" of annual confession and reception of Communion were performed and registered, little more. They were juridical institutions. Religious devotion was sought and lived elsewhere—in institutions like the confraternities that to a great extent were managed by laymen and laywomen or third orders and sodalities under priests from the orders. It would be difficult to exaggerate the importance of these institutions or how they defined the practice of Christianity for serious adults in urban settings.

Although the bishops at Trent wanted to regulate such institutions better, they did not exactly want to squash them. Their focus, however, was on the parish, so as to leave the impression that no other instrument of ministry existed or was important. Moreover, after the council, zealous and ambitious bishops took the Tridentine legislation as a mandate to strengthen the role of the pastor and increase the level of practice in the parish. This led to what one historian has called the "parochial conformity" of the modern era—or the "parochialization" that Paul Hennessy has described in the introduction to this volume. It constituted a break with the earlier tradition of a much greater variety of institutions in which the faithful could practice their religion, a break with the more spontaneous and self-determining character of most of those institutions.[18] This conformity, so the argument goes, has led to lassitude and loss of engagement on the part of the laity.

The reform legislation of Trent paved the road toward Vatican II, which would, in its turn, frame priestly ministry as (1) for the faithful, (2) in a parish, (3) under the bishop. The kind of thinking inherent in the question, "Father, what's your parish?" was in fact also promoted by the Reformation, so that it received in the Catholic Church an indirect but powerful impetus from that seemingly unlikely source. With the destruction of shrines, the abolition of religious orders, and the dispersal of confraternities, the Reformation created an exclusively parish-based clergy and public practice, no matter what nomenclature for the phenomenon different Protestant churches adopted.

In Catholicism a much richer and more varied reality continued to hold sway. After the Council of Trent, the mendicant orders experienced a tremendous growth in numbers and influence, and they were joined by new groups like the Capuchins and the Jesuits.[19] Perhaps in no other field of ministry was their contribution more significant than evangelization of the "Indies" in America and Asia. Nowhere is the narrowness of Trent's focus more apparent than in the fact that, despite being held just when the evangelization of the newly discovered territories was at its peak in the mid-sixteenth century, the council bypasses it without a word. From Trent's decrees on ministry we derive a legitimate but astonishingly narrow perspective on where, by whom, and unto whom priestly ministry in the Catholic Church was in fact being performed.

TRENT AND SOCIAL DISCIPLINE

Besides this almost exclusive focus on the parish, there is a second feature of Trent's provisions on ministry that is pertinent to our topic. Trent would reform ministry by reaffirming some ancient canons, like the ones requiring or assuming bishops be resident in their dioceses, and by drawing up some new ones, which were generally just further specifications of long-accepted principles. Trent would thus accomplish its goal by reaffirming certain prescriptions for behavior and by instituting means to assure their observance through closer surveillance and, when necessary, through punishment for delinquency. Trent reformed by passing tough laws.

The Tridentine decrees might well have remained a dead letter, as they in fact did in certain countries for a long while, if they had not been taken up by persons like Carlo Borromeo, who made them a rallying cry for his activity as the first bishop to reside in the Archdiocese of Milan in fifty years. He made them a rallying cry, yes, but he also expanded upon them in relentless detail in his many diocesan and provincial synods, the proceedings of which were published as the *Acta ecclesiae Mediolanensis.* Throughout Europe the *Acta* became the blueprint for what a "reformed" diocese should look like, more influential probably than the original Tridentine decrees themselves.[20]

Catholic historians have tended until recently to make almost unqualifiedly positive assessments of this development. In the past two decades, however, such a benign assessment has been challenged even by historians rooted in the Catholic tradition, such as Jean Delumeau in France and John Bossy in England. Bossy objects to the use of the term *reform* in such regards because it is a term derived "from the vocabulary of ecclesiastical discipline" meaning the restoration of some ideal form by the action of superiors.[21] What surely happened, according to Bossy, was a movement from more natural, spontaneous, and fraternal realities to things more rationalized, impersonal, bureaucratic, and punitive.

The term and concept of *social discipline* is increasingly being applied to what we used to call reform. The term was originally used by the German historian Gerhard Oestreich to indicate the processes whereby, in the drastically rearranged landscape of post-Reformation Europe, the growth of centralized and hierarchical institutions of state and church—both Protestant and Catholic—transformed the social order.[22] Although criticized for assuming a simple top-down transmission of social norms and for taking insufficient account of the interactive nature of social change, it nonetheless captures a crucial element of what was happening. Social discipline is a modern concept, but it finds justification in the sources themselves, where *discipline,* not *conversion,* is the key term. It highlights the fact that reform meant the attempt to impose discipline upon bishops, pastors, and the faithful. With Trent and the post-Tridentine bishops, the starting point for ministry was abstract norms, and the goal at which ministry aimed was to make conduct conform to them. The result would be a disciplined clergy and people.

What was entailed can be clarified by a concrete example. Trent in its thirteenth session merely reiterated the requirement first laid down in 1215 at the Fourth Lateran Council that all adult Christians must receive Communion at least once every year at Easter. In the Archdiocese of Milan, Carlo Borromeo implemented in 1574 a rigorous process to assure observance of the decree, including a little slip of paper (the *bolletino*), standardized and in printed form, that the confessor gave to the penitent when the confession was completed.[23] The confessor had to fill out this form for all persons whose confessions he heard, and then the penitents had to show it to the pastor before being allowed to receive Communion. The pastor checked their names against the parish register, so that eventually he had a list of all those who had failed to observe this law. In another measure, pastors were ordered to submit any *bolletini* of obstinate public sinners for episcopal inspection before approving them. The known behavior of such penitents suggested that absolution had been granted all too easily, and the *bolletini* made it possible to identify the lax or negligent confessors.

Measures like these may or may not have been indicated by sixteenth-century circumstances, but they powerfully manifest, almost to caricature, a tradition of ministry that begins with office and canonical discipline. This is the tradition that Trent and post-Tridentine bishops mobilized for the diocesan clergy and that has continued, much modified and enriched by other considerations, down to the present.

There is, however, another tradition of ministry represented by the regular clergy, where the starting point has been not canonical norms but experience. Religious orders differ so much among themselves regarding ministry and priesthood that it seems almost ridiculous to try to cover them all under the rubric of a single tradition. I nonetheless indicated above how many of them were similar in that, by and large, they did not fit the four criteria of the documents of Vatican II to the same degree as the diocesan clergy. Indeed, they often almost contradicted them. They are thus conjoined by a kind of *via negativa*—what they are *not*.

Is there, as well, some positive factor that binds them together to the extent that we might even more coherently speak of a tradition in ministry among them? Although it seems foolhardy to try to generalize about the consecrated life as related to ministry and priesthood, perhaps we can attain some clarity by looking at three classic models—Benedictines, Dominicans, and Franciscans (and later Jesuits).

The Benedictines began their history with no further purpose than to lead the consecrated life in its purity, withdrawn from the world; whatever services they undertake for persons outside the monastery are, at least in theory, conditioned by that purpose. Only much later were large numbers of monks ordained, and ordained with a sometimes tenuous relationship to ministry. For the Benedictines, moreover, the vow of stability gives form to the ministries because, even in conjunction with their great missionary tradition, their ideal remains that whatever ministry is performed be performed within the monastery or its environs.

Dominic was a priest, who gathered other priests to engage in a specific ministry to heretics in southern France, in which a poor life-style was integral to the ministry. In this experience preaching emerged as the primary ministry of the group. Francis, a layman, had a series of deep religious experiences that led him to a ministry of preaching and conversation, which at one point took him far outside Europe to preach to the infidel.

Ignatius experienced a deep religious conversion that led him to Jerusalem and then in Europe to a ministry of preaching, catechizing, conversation, and retreat directing; after engaging in these ministries for some years, he sought ordination to the priesthood. The order he and his companions founded was for ministry "among the Turks or any other infidels, even those who live in the region called the Indies, or among any heretics whatever, or schismatics, or any of the faithful."[24] With such ministry in view, they created for themselves a special vow "concerning missions" that imbued the new order with a radically missionary character so that they be ready at a moment's notice to travel to any part of the world for "the help of souls."[25]

As different as these models are among themselves, they have one thing in common regarding ministry—they originated in some kind of *experience*. The experience was either a recognition of a pastoral *need* or some kind of personal *conversion* or *vision,* or a combination of both. The movement, thus, was from below, not top-downward. Its goal was not discipline but meeting some actuality. Its most immediate inspiration was the story of Jesus and his disciples, not ecclesiastical legislation. These factors lend a certain design to ministry that is different from that represented by the Tridentine tradition.

The design leads to consequences. With the early Jesuits, for instance, the most telling word in their pastoral vocabulary was not *discipline* but *accommodation.* This does not mean that they disdained ecclesiastical norms, for they often showed themselves overzealous in this regard. Nor does it mean that accommodation was their monopoly. Accommodation in fact had found objective expression in medieval casuistry through recognition that concrete circumstances determined the morality of any given act—all priests had access to confessors' manuals in which such accommodation was explained.

But what is interesting about the Jesuits in this regard is how accommodation was elevated to a general mode of procedure in ministry, which led to some amazing implementations of it. In Brazil in the sixteenth century, for instance, they used native women as interpreters in the Sacrament of Penance.[26] That is an example of how a law, namely, the confidentiality of confession, was modified for the good of the penitent, in accommodation to the experience of a special situation.

A more stunning example, fraught with immense consequences for the ministry of the church in the modern era, was the Jesuits' decision to begin operating schools as a formal ministry. They created this ministry for the church in response to a need and an opportunity that they saw, even though it ran contrary to some fundamental guidelines they had initially set for their ministries.[27] This ministry differed in obvious and significant ways from the pattern of sacraments, rites, and preaching in a parish that Trent envisaged for the diocesan priest. It was, moreover, created, not received of old. It took place in a classroom, not a church. It was to a specific group, young boys—including sometimes Protestants and nonbelievers. It operated with a curriculum dominated by the pagan classics, which were treated as instruments of moral instruction for the Christian.

So much for the sixteenth century! The tradition of accommodation persists in the scope of religious orders, as indicated by the homily His Holiness John Paul II delivered to the Jesuits' thirty-third General Congregation in 1983. The pope's message was an updating of ministries for the Jesuits. He urged them, among other things, to "the education of young people, the formation of the clergy, deepening of research in the sacred sciences and in general even of secular culture, especially in the literary and scientific fields, in missionary evangelization...ecumenism, the deeper study of relations with non-Christians, the dialogue of the Church with cultures...[and] the evangelizing action of the Church to promote the justice, connected with world peace, which is an aspiration of all peoples."[28] The list was not meant to be exhaustive.

These ministries, or formalities of ministry, do not quite coincide with the framework for priests provided by the three key documents of Vatican II. Although this homily was addressed to members of only one order, it suggests the broader division of labor that has marked priestly ministry in the Catholic Church for long centuries indeed. Each order or congregation could certainly add to the list from its own perspective on how its traditional ministries are being accommodated to the present situation.

CONCLUSION

In these pages I have drawn a sharp distinction between two traditions of priesthood. I have pressed this distinction to its extreme by creating models or pure types, that is, mental constructs rarely, if ever, verified to the full in historical reality. In describing Carlo Borromeo's legislation on confession, for instance, I have drawn a picture of a hollow shell without spiritual content. This is how most historians today tend to view it, for Borromeo has become in this regard a favorite whipping boy. His massive influence coupled with his well-documented obsession with rules and regulations for every aspect of religious practice almost invites this assessment. Yet we know that San Carlo was a deeply spiritual person who at the time of his religious conversion as a young cardinal made the full thirty days of the *Spiritual Exercises* of St. Ignatius. For the other side, I have chosen to ignore the "observatism" that often dominated thinking and acting in institutions of the consecrated life, so that exactitude in following rules and rubrics became the very definition of "religious perfection." In other words, the two traditions are children of the same parent and bear strong family resemblances to each other.

Nonetheless, I think that the differentiation between them that I have tried to draw corresponds to some utterly fundamental realities of the Roman Catholic Tradition (capital *T*!) in ministry—especially since the thirteenth century, but even earlier. These two traditions have interacted over the course of the centuries and have been mutually influential in numerous ways—both positive and negative. Both of them have given shape to the reality of priesthood in its actual practice, and both can claim legitimacy in the New Testament and in the long history of the church. Both have served people's spiritual (and sometimes material) needs.

Although there has been considerable and healthy overlap, a practical division of labor has in fact prevailed between diocesan and regular clergy through the ages. The "local," or diocesan, clergy have ministered primarily to the faithful according to time-honored rhythms of word and, especially, sacrament in parishes. They are the backbone of the church's ministry to its own. Religious, when they ministered to the faithful, did so in similar ways but particularly in other ways that new circumstances seemed to require. This division of labor has taken the religious even farther afield, away from the faithful, in order to minister in some fashion or other to heretics, schismatics, infidels, pagans, and public sinners.

No other Christian church has two such corps of ministers. Taken together they constitute a special richness in Catholicism. While tensions have always existed between them and sometimes erupted into ugly and scandalous battles, the genius of the Catholic Church up to the present has been its ability to contain them both within itself and not settle for neat resolutions that would reduce one to the other.

NOTES

1. See, for example, Nathan Mitchell, O.S.B., *Mission and Ministry: History and Theology in the Sacrament of Order* (Wilmington: Michael Glazier, 1982), and Kenan B. Osborne, O.F.M., *Priesthood: A History of the Ordained Ministry in the Roman Catholic Church* (New York: Paulist Press, 1988).

2. See Brian E. Daley, S.J., "The Ministry of Disciples: Historical Reflections on the Role of Religious Priests," *Theological Studies* 48 (1987): 605–29, esp. 605.

3. *Decrees of the Ecumenical Councils,* ed. Norman P. Tanner, S.J., 2 vols. (London and Washington: Sheed and Ward, Georgetown University Press, 1990), 1:193. I have departed slightly from the English translation that appears on the facing page.

4. See my *Giles of Viterbo on Church and Reform: A Study in Renaissance Thought* (Leiden: E.J. Brill, 1968), 155–57.

5. For the solution the council adopted, see *Decrees of Councils,* "Super religiosos et eorum privilegia," 1:645–49.

6. See, for example, Benjamin Wood Westervelt, "The Borromean Ideal of Preaching: Episcopal Strategies for Reforming Pastoral Preaching in Post-tridentine Milan, 1564–1631" (dissertation, Harvard University, 1993), 13–59.

7. See Westervelt, "Borromean Ideal," esp. 146–51.

8. See, for example, Elizabeth Rapley, *The Dévotes: Women and Church in Seventeenth-Century France* (Montreal and Kingston: McGill-Queen's University Press, 1990); and Anne Conrad, "Die Kölner Ursulagesellschaft und ihr 'weltgeistlicher Stand'—eine weibliche Lebensform im Katholizismus der Fruhen Neuzeit," in *Die katholische Konfessionalisierung,* ed. Wolfgang Reinhard and Heinz Schilling (Gütersloh: Verlag Aschendorff, 1995), 271–95.

9. *Decrees of the Councils,* 2:742.

10. See *Decrees of the Councils,* 2:742–44.

11. For a general presentation of the issue, see my "Priesthood, Ministry, and Religious Life: Some Historical and Historiographical Considerations," *Theological Studies* 49 (1988): 223–57.

12. *Decrees of the Councils,* 2:1050 (no. 7).

13. See *Christus Dominus* (nos. 33–34), in *Decrees of the Councils,* 2:934.

14. See my *The First Jesuits* (Cambridge: Harvard University Press, 1993), esp. 79–80, 91–104.

15. *Decrees of the Councils,* 2:935 (no. 35).

16. See especially my "Priesthood, Ministry, and Religious Life," as well as "Diocesan and Religious Models of Priestly Formation: Historical Perspectives," in *Priests: Identity and Mission,* ed. Robert Wister (Wilmington: Michael Glazier, 1990), 54–70; "Spiritual Formation for Ministry: Some Roman Catholic Traditions—Their Past and Present," in *Theological Education and Moral Formation,* ed. Richard John Neuhaus (Grand Rapids: William B. Eerdsmans Publishing Company, 1992), 79–111; and *The First Jesuits.*

17. The number of books and articles especially in the past ten years is almost overwhelming. Two in English noteworthy for their level of generalization are: Christopher Black, *Italian Confraternities in the Sixteenth Century* (Cambridge: Cambridge University Press, 1989); and Maureen Flynn, *Sacred Charity: Confraternities and Social Welfare in Spain, 1400–1700* (Ithaca: Cornell University Press, 1989). For an important study of the Jesuits' Sodalities of Our Lady ("Marian Congregations"), see Louis Chatellier, *The Europe of the Devout: The Catholic Reformation and the Formation of a New Society,* trans. Jean Birrell (Cambridge: Cambridge University Press, 1989). The best way to follow research in the field is through *Confraternitas: The Newsletter of the Society for Confraternity Studies,* Toronto, 1990–.

18. See John Bossy, "The Counter Reformation and the People of

Catholic Europe," *Past and Present* no. 47 (May, 1970): 51–70.

19. See John Patrick Donnelly, S.J., "Religious Orders of Men, Especially the Society of Jesus," in *Catholicism in Early Modern History: A Guide to Research,* ed. John. W. O'Malley (St. Louis: Center for Reformation Research, 1988), 147–62.

20. See Giuseppe Alberigo, "The Council of Trent," in *Catholicism* (ed. O'Malley), esp. 220–23.

21. See his *Christianity in the West 1400–1700* (Oxford: Oxford University Press, 1985), 91.

22. See, for example, Stefan Breuer, "Sozialdisziplinierung. Probleme und Problemverlagerungen eines Konzepts bei Max Weber, Gerhard Oestreich und Michel Foucault," in *Soziale Sicherheit und soziale Disziplinierung,* ed. Christoph Sachsses and Florian Tennstedt (Frankfurt a/M: Suhrkamp, 1986), 45–69; and R. Po-Chia Hsia, *Social Discipline in the Reformation: Central Europe 1550–1750* (London: Routledge, 1989).

23. See Wietse Thijs de Boer, "Sinews of Discipline: The Uses of Confession in Counter-Reformation Milan" (dissertation, Erasmus Universiteit Rotterdam, 1994), esp. 180–85.

24. "The Formula of the Institute," in *The Constitutions of the Society of Jesus,* trans. and ed. George E. Ganss, S.J. (St. Louis: The Institute of Jesuit Sources, 1970), 68.

25. See *The First Jesuits,* esp. 298–300; my "The Fourth Vow in its Ignatian Context: A Historical Study," *Studies in the Spirituality of Jesuits* 15, no. 1 (1983); and "To Travel to Any Part of the World: Jerónimo Nadal and the Jesuit Vocation, *Studies in the Spirituality of Jesuits* 16, no. 2, (1984).

26. See *The First Jesuits,* 152–53.

27. See *The First Jesuits,* esp. 100–215.

28. *Documents of the 33rd General Congregation of the Society of Jesus* (St. Louis: The Institute of Jesuit Sources, 1984), 80–82 passim.

2

A Western Monastic Perspective on Ordained Ministry

R. Kevin Seasoltz, O.S.B.

The history of religious institutes shows clearly that they have never had simple relationships with the institutional church, especially on the local level. Because of their numbers and the various privileges accorded them down through the centuries, they not only have posed serious ecclesiological questions about how they fit into the hierarchical structure of the church, but they also have often possessed a kind of jurisdiction parallel to that of the local bishop.

What has been true of religious institutes in general has been especially true of monastic communities. As Emmanuel Lanne has noted, "Monks formed, for a considerable time, local churches within the diocese, and frequently their connections to the local churches were indeed slight, if not at times in blatantly open conflict."[1] Usually nuns did not constitute such a threat because they were kept in a subservient position vis-à-vis male society in general and a male-dominated church in particular. This subservience was guaranteed by a rigorous enforcement of monastic enclosure.[2]

Monastic autonomy has been a vexing question in the life of the church.[3] Historically, the legislation governing the relationship between monasteries and the local churches has generally been a matter of regularly shifting balances, punctuated by periods of conflict and peace. The conflicts have sometimes been eased, sometimes exacerbated by the privileges guaranteeing papal protection or by the affirmation of episcopal rights over all religious institutes in a local diocese.[4] One of the major reasons for the conflicts between monasteries and the institutional church has been the presence and ministry of ordained monks in the communities. In this chapter, I will begin by briefly setting out the roots of monastic life in both prebiblical times and the Scriptures. Then I will trace the development of monasticism and its gradual clericalization, especially in the West, until the eleventh century at which point canons and eventually friars emerged. I will then reflect on the rôle of ordained ministry by monks both inside and outside the community from the restoration of monastic communities in Europe to the foundation of monasteries in the United

States in the nineteenth century. In conclusion, I will discuss some of the issues that face monastic communities and their ordained monks at the present time.

EARLY ROOTS OF MONASTIC LIFE

The origins of Christian religious life are disputed by contemporary scholars, who nonetheless agree that, in its Christian institutionalized form, religious life has existed almost as long as Christianity itself. All the institutes of consecrated life in the church derive, in one way or another, from the first monks and nuns. Thus, the roots of the international and highly centralized Society of Jesus and the simple monastic communities founded in Africa since the Second Vatican Council can be traced to the Egyptian hermits. Contemporary authors, however, point out earlier roots in the traditions of the shamans and the Old Testament prophets.[5]

Shamanism is an ancient spiritual practice dating back to at least 10,000 B.C.E. Although often inherited through a family line, the vocation is considered to be a special calling that sets a person apart for service. The shaman is a mediator between the people and higher powers; however, the role does not consist simply in praying for the people, but in embodying some of the divine powers within oneself for the benefit of others. Although shamanism is often associated with healing, the concern is not only renewed health but also a conversion of life involving improved behavior and attitudes.[6]

The shaman and the priest have often been closely associated in primal culture, but it seems that the priest plays a much more institutionalized role within the formal structures of the community, whereas the shaman, though close to the community at one level, does not take part in many aspects of the community life. Mircea Eliade has suggested that shamanism is better understood in a mystical rather than in an institutionalized context. He describes shamans as chosen ones whose ecstatic experience gives them access to the divine on behalf of the wider community.[7] Hence, parallels with the Old Testament tradition of prophecy are discernible.

Many contemporary writers on religious life consider the Old Testament prophets to be prototypical for the vowed life within the Christian tradition.[8] As biblical scholars have noted, in the Old Testament the prophet and the king are juxtaposed, with the priest closely aligned with the king.[9] The king is perceived to be divinely instituted; therefore the human urge to control through structure is divinely validated. The preservation of the established order is central to the king's role and responsibility.

By contrast, the prophet serves to remind the community of a free and creative God under whom no humanly devised institutions can be perpetually validated. The prophetic movement seeks to develop and nurture the creative dimensions of religious life and to inspire the hope and dreams of the community that the institutional structures are meant to preserve and mediate but that are often stifled when the structures become ends in themselves.[10] The tension between the prophet and the priest in the Old Testament anticipates the future tension between religious life as prophetic and ordained ministry as institutional and, more specifically, between prophetic priesthood within religious communities and the hierarchically structured church.

The role of the prophet is to be countercultural in the sense that it emphasizes alternative values and ways of living, maintains a larger view of reality than the institution itself, and challenges those structures that repress or deny divine-human cocreativity. Institutional structures have a tendency to turn into idols; the prophet's role is to denounce all false idols while pointing continuously to God, who can never be confined, formalized, or limited to any set of institutions.[11]

In the Old Testament, prophetic ministry appears to be contemplative, political, and inclusive. Prophets perceive in depth and struggle to see life as God sees it, while striving to discern the unfolding of the divine plan within the whole of creation.[12]

The political arena is certainly a legitimate sphere in which the prophet should function since it is in that sphere above all that the values that are important to the community are inculturated in institutions. The prophet has a right to speak there, not as an officially deputed representative of the community, but as one commissioned by God to be the voice of the voiceless and a champion of values and rights that are often subverted by the political process.[13] For example, Amos questioned the purpose of power and prosperity among the Israelites; he censured the acts of grave injustice against the poor. Hosea challenged the Temple priests for colluding with political forces rather than championing the rights of the poor and marginalized members of society, rights that religion was meant to promote. Isaiah vehemently denounced the military power that slaughtered thousands of defenseless people in the name of national honor. Micah watched poor people being forced to labor for the benefit of the rich; he vigorously defended the poor. The prophet's witness supports openness, flexibility, and fluidity, including structures that truly serve people's real needs, as well as movements that respect and promote human-divine coresponsibililty.[14]

Although the Old Testament prophets elicit admiration, they also evoke hostility, for to the mainstream culture the prophet is a puzzle, a maverick, and often a pest. Above all, the prophet is a threat to the stability and security of the status quo: the institution tends to remove that challenge rather than engage it because it involves the risk of exposing vulnerability or possible corruption.[15] The prophetic roles are precisely the roles that have been picked up and developed in the Christian era by religious institutes, beginning with monasticism.

In the Old Testament the prophetic tradition is confined to a number of outstanding individuals, such as Jeremiah, Isaiah, Hosea, and Amos. In the New Testament, however, apart from Jesus himself, only a few individuals are affirmed to have prophetic gifts, John the Baptist being the most significant. This does not mean, however, that the Old Testament prophetic tradition disappeared. As biblical scholars note, the Old Testament prophets pointed to Jesus, whose ministry fulfilled the promises of old.[16] But, after the death and resurrection of Jesus, the prophetic vocation largely shifted from individuals to the Christian community as a whole. The Twelve Apostles are important not primarily as individuals but rather as the Twelve, representing communally the twelve tribes of Israel.[17]

BEGINNINGS OF MONASTIC LIFE

The observations that have just been made have important implications for the emerging theology of what came to be known as religious life. They also challenge the claim that the origins of Christian religious life are to be found primarily in the eremitical life, understood as an individualistic experience of God, rather than in individuals basically rooted in the Christian community though usually living at a distance from the important centers of that community. The eremitical life did not necessarily imply isolation. As Graham Gould has pointed out in his recent work, the desert fathers were deeply concerned with the nature of the monastic communities that they formed and with the issues that regularly affected relationships between individuals within their communities.[18] He concludes that the desert fathers viewed community as an essential part of their monastic ideal and rarely regarded individualistic solitude as a way of life to be pursued at the expense of Christian community. Their teaching on the monastic life was concerned not only with topics such as prayer, asceticism, and combat with evil spirits, but also with the place of the monastic life in the wider church and in society, as well as with the nature of monastic community and personal relationships within that community.[19]

The early Christian monastics responded above all to a call to discipleship, not to a call to *diakonia,* to service or ministry within the church. The call to be a disciple of the Lord Jesus, however, was also a call to an ascetical way of life. The latter was consonant with the apocalyptic movement in Judaism, which hoped for the immediate development of the age to come and so contrasted markedly with the present age dominated by evil. Some Jewish communities, such as the Essenes of Qumran, believed that they were the holy remnant of Israel. This conviction led to the development of ascetical practices, which in turn resulted in the building up of closely knit communities. The rules of these communities required members to restrict their consumption of food and drink, live frugally, and control their sexual impulses, often to the point of total sexual abstention.[20]

The desert fathers did in fact renounce life in secular society because they often experienced that society as corrupt, but their withdrawal led to the creation of new monastic communities in Nitria and Scetis that, although they were more loosely organized than the cenobitic communities later established by Pachomius, were definitely not collections of individuals living mutually unrelated lives. Their life-style was a very flexible one, not burdened by complex institutional structures.[21] The *Apophthegmata,* which are the work of many different monks and reflect many different situations, are a clear reflection of choice and flexibility, but in the midst of this variety there is a general consensus on the importance of interpersonal relationships that are the bedrock of community life.[22]

As these monastic groups moved to the frontiers or margins of the church and society, they certainly became centers radiating countercultural values. In that sense they exercised a liminal, prophetic role, generally at a distance from the institutional church. Their primary commitment was to the reign of God in their lives rather than to the institutional structures of the church.[23]

It seems that Jesus himself was not particularly interested in an institutional church. References to church appear only in three texts in Matthew's gospel,[24] and biblical scholars are not in agreement concerning the meaning of those texts. By contrast, it seems that the establishment of the reign of God was the primary preoccupation of Jesus.[25] Although the emphasis began to change by the time of the writing of the Acts of the Apostles and the Pauline letters, it nevertheless seems clear that, for many in the early church, there was the strong conviction that the church is meant to be above all a servant and herald of the reign of God.[26] It is in the communities of Christians that the reign of God should be most deeply incorporated and strongly proclaimed. It was to fulfill this responsibility that the desert fathers and mothers withdrew to the fringes of society and to the margins of the church so that their voices could be voices of those who were voiceless in the institution and their lives could challenge the structures of the church that were becoming increasingly inflexible.[27]

The values of the reign of God transcend the values of all other cultures that have often dominated both secular society and the institutional church; symbolically, those values contradict the symbol of the king or emperor.[28] It is significant that on only one occasion in the synoptic Gospels does Jesus allow himself to be called "king," and that occurs on his final journey to Jerusalem where his symbolic actions speak much louder than his words.[29] As a king, he should have been riding on a horse, the royal beast of domination, warfare, and power; instead he rode on a donkey, the beast of burden used by ordinary people.[30] Royal power was turned on its head and declared to be alien to the economy established by Christ.

The reign of God may be described as establishing a new order of life, marked by right relationships of justice, love, peace, and freedom, characteristics that reflect God's own relationships with the human community. The old ways of domineering control, often characteristic of patriarchal societies, are declared inappropriate. Jesus surely did appreciate and respect his inherited authentic tradition, but he invited people to grow beyond the past traditions of the Old Testament no matter how sacralized those traditions had become. His Christian disciples, then, are meant to be attuned to the stirring of his Holy Spirit, leading the church into the future. Herein lies the prophetic challenge that institutes of consecrated life are meant to espouse today.[31]

For centuries the dominant frame of reference for institutes of consecrated life has been the church as an institution. Individual religious and communities as a whole have been expected above all to be subservient and loyal; they conceived their role as being that of specialists in what was thought to be a state of perfection. They were to provide a model of holiness that the whole church could imitate, one that would guarantee salvation in the next world. In this ecclesiastical culture, the primacy of the reign of God was more or less subverted as it gave way to a church that was often more and more idolized.[32]

If institutes of consecrated life are to reclaim their prophetic role, which often functions much more appropriately on behalf of the reign of God than the institutionalized church, they must once more become liminal or marginal communities. It is useful to recall that many founders of institutes of consecrated life had to confront the institutional church, often to the point of open conflict, in order to be faithful to their prophetic charism and to bring about creative changes in the church. If the primary allegiance of religious is to the reign of God rather than to the institutional church, they must often confront, and contest, and at times denounce, those systems and institutions that militate against the reign of God.

Unfortunately in the past, religious, both as individuals and as communities, have colluded with systems that oppress people; their life-style and value system have often emulated the dominant culture of secular society and have failed to be prophetic in challenging and denouncing oppressively sinful structures. They have lost the subversive vision of the Old Testament prophets and have betrayed their liminal calling to be catalysts for establishing the reign of God.[33]

It should be noted here that no Christian is ever called "priest" in the New Testament. That cultic word was reserved for the Jewish and pagan priests. In fact, the word seems to have been consciously avoided by the New Testament writers when describing ministries in the early Christian community. There are several New Testament passages where the entire community is described as priestly;[34] these texts form the basis for the teaching on the universal priesthood of all Christians, which affirms the radical equality conferred on all in the church through baptism. Ministries were established for service, not for status; they were not distinguished from one another as secular or sacred.[35]

Jesus himself was a layperson, not a priest, in the eyes of Jewish law, for priesthood was transmitted through genealogy rather than through special vocation. He is clearly described as a priest in the Letter to the Hebrews,[36] but that letter actually redefines the meaning of *priesthood.* It asserts that Jesus is the only priest. Hence, Christian ministers in the church who have been called priests are so only by an analogical use of the term, a use that finds no warrant in the New Testament and that would have been understood quite differently in New Testament times.[37] Calling certain ministers in the church "priests" began, it seems, only in the third century because of the retrieval of the Old Testament in the preaching and teaching of the patristic writers, including Gregory of Nazianzus and John Chrysostom.[38]

It should not be at all surprising, then, that there is only passing reference to priesthood in the writings of the desert fathers. When the term is used it often betrays the progressive institutionalization of the teaching role in the fourth century.[39] It seems unlikely that the ordained clergy who are referred to occasionally in the *Apophthegmata* exercised any special authority simply because they were priests. They were originally described as presbyters who fulfilled their ministry in the church as wise men who could be respected by others and serve as the advisory council for the bishop.[40] They gradually were given specific sacramental and pastoral roles by the bishop in areas where people could not attend the Sunday Eucharist in the cathedral. They became, in effect, extensions of the bishops outside the cities. At the same time both bishops and presbyters came to be identified more and more by their sacramental roles; hence they were thought of primarily as priestly figures. The name *presbyter* was dropped, and *priest* came to be used regularly. With this change in terminology, a change also took place in the way people viewed the role of ordained ministers in the church. There was a subtle shift from a functional or ministerial role within the Christian community to a state of life within the institutionalized church. The chief models for priestly life were derived from the Old Testament with its emphasis on rules and regulations governing the rights and responsibilities of priests. Above all, the cultic character of the ordained priesthood was stressed.[41]

It is no wonder, then, that the early monastic rules took a rather dim view of Christian priesthood. It should be stressed at the outset, however, that there was no single monastic tradition. Hence, history can be instructive, but it is not necessarily determinative or normative since each generation of Christian monastics has manifested its own shifts in ecclesial and monastic consciousness with corresponding adjustments in the liturgical forms and governmental structures by which this consciousness is expressed.[42] Certainly there were various monastic movements in the fourth century—some were cenobitic, others were eremetical; some were centered in urban areas, others in the country; some were what we would call more ecclesial, others more marginal. In short, monasticism was a highly diversified institution manifesting itself in a plurality of doctrines, organizational structures, and liturgical practices.[43]

One of the distinguishing marks of early Christian monasticism was the public separation of the monks from the rest of the Christian community. The reasons for this withdrawal are complex. As John O'Malley has noted in the preceding chapter, John Cassian (ca. 360–ca. 435) states the surprising principle that a good monk should beware of bishops and women.[44] In his assertion that the monk should flee from bishops, the ascetic's relationship to the larger church community is being stressed. By the third century, the Christian communities were hierarchically organized under the leadership of a bishop. Offices and roles were increasingly regulated. The ascetic, however, had no assigned place in that order. For the sake of asceticism, then, the monks separated themselves from the established order of the community. They were not protesting against the order of the community; rather, they were concerned with their own salvation, which they felt involved a renunciation of the secular world, including the support of the Christian community. They rejected a career, either in the city or in the Christian community, in order to undertake the regimen of ascetical practices.[45]

Cassian's second requirement, that monks should flee from women, was interpreted quite literally. He urged the strict separation of the sexes within monastic communities. In pre-Christian ascetical communities men and women often shared a common life, but the church found that practice suspect. The solution was to gather together ascetics of the same sex.[46]

The creation of a well-defined cenobitic or communitarian way of monastic life is associated above all with the Egyptian Pachomius (ca. 287–346). Under his guidance eremetical asceticism underwent an important shift in emphasis. All ascetical excesses and bizarre feats sometimes found in earlier hermits were excluded because the ordered community based its life on the norm of the average. In cenobitic monasticism obedience became an essential component; the rule and above all the superior of the community were the authorities that both set monastic requirements and gave encouragement to the monks in their ascetical efforts. Obedience to the monastic superior increasingly withdrew the monks and communities from the control of the local bishops.[47]

Pachomius' monastic ideals contained the seeds of their own collapse, for his monasteries attracted large numbers of novices. Such a development required gifted monastic leaders, but none of Pachomius' immediate successors had his talents. This lack eventually led to the dissolution of his monastic communities. From the end of the fourth century, however, cenobitism flourished in Egypt under Schenoute (333/334–ca. 451). In the early fifth century barbarians attacked the Egyptian monastic colonies, causing the monks to flee to other lands.[48]

Although Palestine and Syria also developed as monastic centers during the fourth century,[49] it was above all Basil the Great (ca. 330–379), bishop of Caesarea, who attempted to integrate the ascetical practices of monasticism within the larger church. With a background in monasticism himself, Basil gave cenobitism in the East, except for Egypt, a very strong impetus. He effectively integrated monasteries into his work for the church as a whole. For example, to city monasteries he assigned various social, charitable, and educational tasks. Along with other bishops in the fourth century, Basil tried to clarify the unregulated relationship between the monasteries and the church at large. The relationship was often tense because many monks got drawn into the theological controversies of their time and took sides in the fierce battles between orthodoxy and heresy.[50] It was the Council of Chalcedon in 451 that officially dealt with the problem by attempting to integrate each monastery into the structure of the diocese in which it was located and conferring on the local bishop the right to found and regulate the monasteries.[51]

Before moving on to the development of monasticism in Italy, something should be said about Irish monasticism, which maintained characteristics quite distinct from monasticism in other parts of the West. Almost all of western Europe was shaped by Roman influence, but the imperial armies never reached Ireland; hence, the church there was minimally affected by Roman law, bureaucracy, art, and architecture.[52]

In the chronicle of Prosper of Aquitaine, there is reference to the sending of Palladius by Pope Celestine I (422–431) to be the first bishop for the Irish Christians. Although there is no certain link between Palladius and Patrick (ca. 390–ca. 460), it is generally agreed that Patrick was sent from Britain to serve as bishop in Ireland probably around 431.[53] He spent the rest of his life there evangelizing, ordaining clergy, developing monasteries, and educating the sons of local chieftains.[54] Patrick accepted the Irish past and built on it a strong legacy. Instead of condemning the practices of the Irish tribes, he worked with them to develop an indigenous form of Christianity.[55]

Although there were men and women in Ireland leading an ascetic life in the fifth century, perhaps even living in communities, after 431 administration of the church was clearly in the hands of bishops who ruled dioceses that were coterminous with the petty kingdoms into which Ireland was divided.[56] Control of the church shifted, however, in the following centuries.

About the middle of the sixth century, a number of monasteries developed into firm establishments superseding the diocesan bishoprics. People entered monasteries for both religious and sociological reasons. They sought the presence of God and the joy that God's presence offers, but they also sought to atone for their sins in order to reach heaven. The Irish were aware of the uncertainties of life and were often oppressed by the ideas of sin and judgment. It has been suggested that monasticism gained many adherents after the terrible plague that swept across Ireland in the middle of the sixth century, taking the lives of many people and leaving behind vivid memories of devastation.[57]

Most of the early Irish Saints were monks. They were looked upon as men having access to the power of God, capable of healing the sick, calming storms, and beating off raiding armies. They usually came from the aristocratic state of society, often related to the local nobility. Thought to have inherited the visionary and prophetic insights of the druids, these monks were also men of great learning and constituted the social elite.[58] They played a significant role in Irish society because they were holy, not because they were ordained priests.

The Eucharist played an important role in the life and spirituality of the early Irish monks. The Stowe Missal is dated around 800, but the eucharistic texts found there were the texts used in Irish monasteries in the sixth and seventh centuries. The framework of that missal is basically the Roman liturgy brought to Ireland in the fifth century by Palladius and other missionaries, but many prayers, intercessions, and readings, readily recognized as of Irish authorship, have been added. The Roman canon, with its emphasis on sacrifice, seems to have contributed in a special way to shaping the character of early Irish eucharistic piety. The high moral standard set by the monks meant that serious sins always entailed deprivation of Holy Communion; hence, the practice of frequent confession as a preparation for Holy Communion was enjoined on both the monks and the rest of the faithful.[59]

Not all of those who lived in the Irish monasteries led an ascetic or celibate life. The land for a monastic foundation was often given by a whole kin group. Some of the family members committed themselves to lead an ascetic life and recited the Divine Office. They formed the inner circle of the monastic communities and included an abbot and sometimes a bishop or priest. Others living within the confines of the monastery farmed the land and were often married.[60]

By the beginning of the eighth century, the Irish church was mainly in the hands of abbots. It was not what today would be called a hierarchical church. It was a monastic church that served the laity by baptizing their children, celebrating mass for them, preaching the gospel to them, and burying their dead. Obviously, at least some of these ministries presumed that the monks were ordained to the priesthood. The monasteries were centers for prayer and asceticism, but they were also important social centers, providing education, hospitality, care of the sick, and patronage for the arts.[61] Many important ministries were exercised by monastic women, some of whom became distinguished abbesses who on occasion governed double monasteries. Irish monasticism was not the highly clericalized institution that it increasingly became on the Continent as the Middle Ages progressed.

THE RULE OF THE MASTER AND THE RULE OF BENEDICT

Of special significance in the history of Western monasticism are the Rule of the Master and the Rule of Benedict, both documents of Italian provenance and dating probably from the first quarter of the sixth century. The two documents support a prophetic or kerygmatic understanding of monasticism and its place in the church and world, as distinct from the hierarchical or institutional character of the church. They value the call to seek God within the framework of the monastic community rather than the call to serve a hierarchically ordered church.[62]

Nevertheless, monasticism in the West gradually became clericalized, with the result that it got involved in various tangled relationships with the hierarchical church. Otto Nussbaum[63] and Angelus Häussling[64] have both illumined our understanding of the various factors that contributed to the change of religious life from a predominantly lay movement of prophetic, kerygmatic witnesses to strongly clerical institutions within the hierarchical church.[65]

Although the Rule of Benedict became normative for monasticism in the West during the Carolingian reform, it was preceded by and was based on the Rule of the Master, a much longer text. The Rule of the Master situates the call to the monastic community within the context of one's baptismal vocation. In fact, it is thought that various passages, especially in the theme section and in the commentary on the Our Father, were derived from a baptismal catechism. Their presence in the Rule attests to a deliberate intention to relate monastic life to the basic Christian life and to see monastic life as an extension of one's baptismal commitment. The monastery is to be a *schola dominici servitii* (a "school for the service of the Lord") with authority structures to support the teaching role of the abbot.[66]

In his prologue, Benedict incorporates much of the material from the early sections of the Master's Rule. His objective is to situate the call to monastic life within the parameters of the baptismal vocation. He stresses the kerygmatic function of the community in naming it a *schola,* a school. The major components of the curriculum in the school according to both Rules are the celebration of the Divine Office, *lectio divina,* asceticism, personal prayer, and work. It is noteworthy that in the Rule of the Master only six chapters (21, 22, 45, 76, 80 and 93) deal with eucharistic matters, whereas much of the text devoted to common worship treats of the Liturgy of the Hours. Benedict devoted twelve chapters to the Divine Office (8–19), but he does not even use the term *eucharistia.* He uses the term *missa* in chapters 17, 35, 38, and 60, but it is usually translated to mean "dismissal." His specific eucharistic references deal with Communion services, similar to those carefully described in the Rule of the Master.[67]

No extensive evidence exists concerning the frequency of eucharistic celebration in the early centuries of the church. As Daniel Callam has shown, the origin of a daily celebration of the Eucharist seems to have been the custom in the early church of receiving Communion privately at home.[68] Callam maintains that in monastic communities devotion to the Eucharist took two forms, corresponding to the two forms of monasticism in the West, clerical and lay. The eucharistic life of unordained ascetics would have been dependent on the local church; there would have been a reception of the Eucharist in the monastery when there was no celebration in the local church or when a priest did not celebrate within the monastery. But when there was a local bishop closely related to the monastery, such as Ambrose, Eusebius of Vercelli, Martin of Tours, Chromatius of Aquileia, Paulinus of Nola, and Augustine, there would most likely have been a full celebration of mass, perhaps even daily. These monk-bishops would have most likely sought to share their keen devotion to the Eucharist with the other monks, including those who happened to be ordained.[69]

Since neither the Rule of the Master nor the Rule of Benedict have much to say about the celebration of the Eucharist, some surmise that perhaps the eucharistic celebration was so well known by the monks that there was no need to legislate concerning its practice. But that argument fails in the face of the fact that many details in both rules deal with very mundane and routine aspects of life.

Adalbert de Vogüé has suggested that in the early period of Christian monasticism ascetics, both men and women, probably related to the Eucharist in one of three ways: (1) They could have taken part in the weekly celebration of the Eucharist by the local Christian community. This practice was probably the one adopted by the early Pachomian monastic communities and also by the nuns gathered around Paula at Bethlehem. (2) The monastic communities could have imported ordained ministers to celebrate the Eucharist within the confines of the monastery. (3) The monastic communities could have taken part in a Eucharist celebrated by one of their own members who had been ordained a priest.[70]

The three possibilities set forth by de Vogüé provide a convenient context for analyzing not only the material on the Eucharist but also the material on the ordained ministry found in the Rule of the Master (RM) and the Rule of Benedict (RB). In chapter 62, the Rule of Benedict states, "If any abbot wish to have a priest or deacon ordained for his monastery, let him select one of his subjects who is worthy to exercise the priestly office." In chapter 60, however, there seems to be a reluctance to admit to the monastic community those who have already been ordained: "If anyone of the priestly order ask to be received into the monastery, permission shall not be granted too readily." It is very clear in the Rule that no deferential treatment should be meted out to the priest because he is a priest; he is to be treated simply as a monk, and his rank in the community is to be determined by the date of his entrance into the monastery, unless the abbot should decide otherwise.[71]

Benedict's teaching stands in marked contrast to what is contained in the Rule of the Master. There, in chapter 83, we read: "Priests are to be considered outsiders in the monastery, especially those who retain and exercise their presidency and preferment in churches. If their choice is to live in monasteries for the love of God and for the sake of discipline and the pattern of a holy life, even so it is only in name that they are called fathers of the monastery, and nothing is to be permitted them in the monasteries other than praying the collects, saying the conclusion, and giving the blessing." In the Rule of the Master, the abbot himself is identified as a layman;[72] nothing is said about the decision to have one of his monks ordained a priest.

Although the Master seems to be opposed to the presence of priests in the monastery, he did make provision for his monks to receive Communion under both kinds every day. This Communion rite was not the celebration of the Eucharist; it was presided over by the abbot, a layman not a priest, and it took place in the oratory before the daily meal.[73] De Vogüé maintains that the Master's monks probably went to the parish church for the Sunday celebration of the Eucharist presided over by the diocesan clergy.[74] There are only two specific occasions noted in the Master's Rule when the Eucharist was celebrated in the monastic oratory: on the occasion of the blessing of a new abbot and on the patronal feast of the saint to whom the oratory was dedicated.[75]

In the so-called "liturgical code" of the Rule of Benedict (chaps. 8–20), there is no note taken of the celebration of the Eucharist. We have little certain knowledge of eucharistic practice in the Rule of Benedict.[76] De Vogüé, for example, concludes that "at most it is possible that a conventual mass in St. Benedict's monastery was celebrated on Sundays and feast days. But perhaps mass was celebrated less often, even without fixed regularity."[77]

There may have been a daily Communion service in Benedict's monastery, but unlike the Master, Benedict provides us with no description of the rite. Although Benedict was most probably familiar with the practice of monks attending the Sunday Eucharist, there is no clear evidence that it was celebrated in the monastery or that the monks went to the local parish. In chapter 35, Benedict does mention the solemn days when the server at table should fast *usque ad missas;* likewise, in chapter 38, he notes that the weekly table reader should ask for prayers *post missas et communionem.* It is possible that both of these texts refer to the celebration of the Eucharist, but they do not yield any clear evidence of eucharistic practice. Possibly Benedict was not very specific in his comments about the Eucharist because he did in fact make provision for the ordination of one of his monks as a priest; hence the community would not have been so dependent on priests from outside the monastery. It is quite possible, then, that given the abbot's freedom to have or not to have one of his monks ordained, there was diversity of practice in early Benedictine communities concerning the reception and celebration of the Eucharist.[78]

Häussling emphasizes that according to both the Rule of the Master and the Rule of Benedict the Eucharist and the Divine Office were not considered bound together as constituting the liturgy of the community. The Eucharist, in a sense, was imported into the cloister from outside, while the monastic office developed as the regular communal prayer of a praying community; it reflected the liturgical autonomy of the monastic church.[79]

The Master reveals something about his implicit ecclesiology when he writes about the Eucharist. As de Vogüé has noted, "*Ecclesia,* habitually contrasted with *monasterium,* meant to the Master the secular church in the twofold sense of society and edifice."[80] In other words, *ecclesia* is looked upon as beyond and as more extensive than the monastery. The monks are involved in the Sunday celebration of the church's Eucharist, and, as was customary for lay Christians, they would have taken the Eucharist home with them after Sunday mass in order that there might be Communion during the week. The local bishop would have come to the monastery in order to impart a blessing on the abbot, and a priest from outside the community would have celebrated the Eucharist on the abbey's patronal feast.[81] In Benedict's Rule there are only two references to *ecclesia,* one a scriptural quote, the other a reference to the Roman practice of celebrating the Divine Office.[82] Benedict is reticent about his understanding of how the monastery relates to the *ecclesia.* The word *episcopus* occurs only twice, in reference to the bishop intervening in the case of a recalcitrant monk who is a priest and to the bishop as one who might prevent the election of an unworthy abbot.[83]

Another significant ecclesiological theme in these rules is their understanding of the role of the abbot in the community. Because the monastery is a *schola,* the abbot is cast in the prophetic role of teacher, selected to instruct his brothers in the ways of the Lord.[84] The monasteries were conceived of as sapiential communities of ordinary Christians searching for God by their commitment to a rule and docility to a teaching abbot. They were essentially lay communities within the larger *ecclesia,* but they were not modeled after an ideal church, either in Rome or Jerusalem.[85]

Recent studies on the Rule of Benedict have emphasized the spiritual nature of the text.[86] In light of these commentaries, the monastic life is characterized as a manifestation of the charismatic nature of the church. Like all charisms, it develops and thrives when its spiritual vitality is fostered by wise organization, but it degenerates and atrophies when reform and control are arbitrarily imposed from either within or outside the monastery itself.[87]

The materials in Benedict's Rule can be divided into two categories: there is the doctrinal or spiritual teaching, and there are detailed prescriptions for running the monastery. On the one hand, the doctrinal material has a perennial value and holds a privileged and normative position in monastic theology and practice for all monks and nuns who make their profession according to Benedict's Rule. It expresses Benedict's ideal, elaborates the theology underlying the ideal, and roots the ideal in revelation.

On the other hand, the practical provisions in the Rule are of the same nature and preoccupied with the same particulars as monastic constitutions and customaries. Just as these are frequently modified in the course of history, so too Benedict's more specific injunctions can be changed. Recognizing his inability to make provision for every contingency, he built into the Rule express authorization for certain modifications in instances where these would better serve his general intention. Furthermore, a discriminatory power over the whole gamut of monastic observances seems to be vested in the abbot of each monastery when the Rule directs him to "temper all things that the strong may still have something to strive after and the weak may not draw back in alarm."[88]

Benedict's concern was to refrain from stifling spiritual freedom by detailed legislation. He sought, not to provide for every possible contingency, but rather to educate the abbot and his monks and to form their consciences so they would be able to understand the demands of each situation and respond to the Word of God as it revealed itself in and through the actual life of the community. "It is in this emphasis on inner principles rather than in any enforcement of a definite organization that we find the secret of the Rule's power."[89]

It follows from the very nature of Benedict's Rule, then, that each monastery should have a certain autonomy. It should be self-sufficient and enjoy a measure of exemption from governmental controls other than those provided for in the Rule itself. However, from the time of Cluny and its many foundations made in the tenth and eleventh centuries, monasticism became increasingly clericalized and entangled in economic, political, and ecclesiastical spheres. It became markedly institutionalized because it needed more structures to regulate the inner life of its very large communities; it needed more structures to regulate the relationships among the various monasteries that from the time of Cluny were frequently brought together in what we now call congregations; likewise, it needed more structures to regulate the relationships between the clerical monks and the local bishops.[90] The problems raised by extensive institutionalization have plagued monasticism down to the present day. In many instances they have stifled the monastic charism and have distracted communities from the spiritual values that are primary in Benedict's Rule.

It should be noted here that our information concerning early monastic communities of women and their relation to ordained ministers and the Eucharist is scant. The *Lausiac History* of Palladius observes that in some

Pachomian monasteries of women, priests and deacons came to the monastery on Sundays for the celebration of the Eucharist.[91] In sixth-century Gaul, communities of women living according to Caesarius of Arles' Rule for Nuns must have observed a similar practice. The Rule stresses that no man may enter any part of the enclosure "except the bishop, the provisor and priest, the deacon and subdeacon, and one or two rectors whose age and life commend them, and who are needed to offer mass sometimes."[92] In place of the celebration of the Eucharist on Sundays, some communities of women may have just received Communion on Sundays. One might come to that conclusion in light of the Rule of Aurelian of Arles. According to that document, generally thought to be contemporary with the Rule of Benedict, mass was celebrated when the abbess thought it appropriate.[93]

Sacramental theology in the West has undergone extensive development since the time of the Master, Benedict, Caesarius, and Aurelian. This theological development has in turn influenced sacramental practice; shifts in practice have also influenced the theology. There is little doubt that early monasticism, its spirituality, and its practices had a major influence on subsequent Christianity in the West. As Callam observes, "The gradual adoption, often under duress, of monastic observances by the clergy and *mutatis mutandis* the laity of the Latin Church represents the triumph of a monastic spirituality which embodied and developed what were…traditional practices of Christianity: fasting, retirement, vigils and other forms of prayer, celibacy, and daily Communion. In manifold, ever developing, sometimes bizarre forms, this spirituality retained its vigor in the Latin church until our own day."[94]

CLERICALIZATION OF MONASTICISM

Although the monks of the first seven centuries generally did not distinguish themselves from the ordinary lay Christians in their eucharistic piety and practice or in their understanding of ordained ministry, the situation changed remarkably in the next few centuries. By the eleventh century, many monks were ordained priests, and daily mass was considered normal in the monasteries. In fact, many masses were usually celebrated each day. In addition to the masses celebrated by individual priests in what we would probably denote a "private" fashion, there was the *missa matutinalis,* the *missa major,* and sometimes a *missa in suffragio.* Gregory III, Alcuin, Benedict of Aniane, Adalhard of Corbie, and Angilbert of Centula would have all been familiar with the multiplication of daily masses in the monasteries of the eighth and ninth centuries. Certainly by the time of the Carolingian and Cluniac reforms, the Eucharist played a key role in the spiritual orientation of Benedictine communities.[95] The *Regularis Concordia,* a tenth-century English document formulated under St.

Dunstan, speaks of two community masses celebrated daily, one after terce and the other after sext.[96]

It is not possible to state how many monks were in fact ordained priests in any particular monastery during Benedict's time. From his reading of the diary of Egeria, a document written by a pilgrim when she visited the East between 381 and 384,[97] Nussbaum allows that monasteries attached to pilgrimage sites probably had sufficient priests to attend to the pastoral needs of the people, but his overall conclusion is that there were probably very few priests in most monasteries, even the larger ones.[98] By the tenth century, however, that situation had changed remarkably. Statistics from that century indicate that in some monasteries more than half of the monks were ordained.[99]

The clericalization of monasticism was due to a number of complex developments both within and outside the monasteries. Nussbaum and Häussling rely on similar sources but emphasize different aspects of the development, especially in their interpretation of the role the Eucharist played in the process. Nussbaum emphasizes the need for the monks to provide the Eucharist as part of their parochial responsibility, their desire to bring the Eucharist to missionary lands, and above all their growing commitment to the Eucharist as the center of their spiritual lives, resulting in the celebration of mass by all the ordained monks, even on a daily basis.

Subjective eucharistic piety would have been a primary cause for increased devotion to the Eucharist. Another major factor encouraging the multiplication of masses was a desire to offer the mass for the dead, something that was consonant with the medieval system of penitential tariffs. The custom of offering mass stipends led to the abuse whereby some priests would celebrate as many as a dozen masses daily without any community being present.[100]

Häussling focuses on the development of the conventual mass and on the social and cultural factors that affected the increasing importance of the Eucharist in the daily horarium of monastic communities. He stresses the effort by monasteries to replicate the solemn liturgy as it was celebrated in Rome. The local church gathered in an abbey was thought to parallel the local church of the diocese, especially the Diocese of Rome. Just as there were various daily celebrations in Rome at the numerous titular churches and sanctuaries, so it was thought desirable to have many daily eucharistic celebrations in each monastery in order that the liturgy might be as solemn as possible. Such a liturgy obviously called for a great number of priests; therefore many monks were in fact ordained.[101] It should be observed also that the practice of daily Communion by the nonordained in the community seems to have declined by the tenth century, since the *Regularis Concordia* makes a point of encouraging the monks to receive Communion daily.[102] (They would have refrained from communicating because of their personal sense of sinfulness and consequent feeling of unworthiness.)

These developments naturally had an effect on the architecture of the monastic churches. Certainly altars had to be built for the priests to celebrate all these masses. Nussbaum notes that an early-ninth-century plan for the abbey church of St. Gall in Switzerland provided for nineteen altars. He concludes that the multiplication of altars was the result of the clericalization of monasticism and the introduction of private masses,[103] whereas Häussling maintains that the introduction of side altars was rooted in the development of the stational and titular churches in Rome and the monastic effort to emulate what went on there.[104]

Eucharistic developments undoubtedly had a serious effect on ecclesiology. Following the Carolingian reform, the monasteries increasingly incorporated imperial court rituals, whereby the *missa major* involved elaborate chants, deacons and subdeacons and various other liturgical ministers, as well as the use of bells, incense, and lights.[105] Distinctions within the monasteries became increasingly important, a factor reflected in the various titles and ranks assigned to monks, especially those ordained. In 826 a Roman document insisted that ordination to the priesthood was an essential quality for the one elected abbot of a community.[106]

Because the priests were occupied with liturgical matters, unlettered laymen were introduced into the monastery to take care of the manual labor. As time went on they were neither given solemn vows in the community nor were they eligible for chapter rights. The understanding of a monastery shifted from a *schola dominici servitii,* in which all members were basically equal because of Christian baptism and where all strove to search for God, to a hierarchically structured community in which some members were obviously more important than others. The result was a marked division in communities and a shift from a vocation to pursue holiness within the monastery to a call to serve the larger hierarchically structured church.

The pomp in eucharistic celebration highlighted the descent of the Body and Blood of Christ upon the altar; hence the broader eucharistic themes of thanksgiving and blessing were neglected. At a time when relics were widely venerated, the Eucharist became the most precious of all relics resting on the altar.[107] With multiple consecrations taking place, often at the same time in the same church, the Augustinian understanding of the Eucharist symbolically related to the gathered assembly as the Body of Christ diminished, and the focus of the eucharistic celebration on the monastic community as a whole was gradually lost.[108] Widespread abstention from Communion on grounds of unworthiness and reverence prompted people to seek devotional compensation by adoration of the divinity of Christ in the eucharistic species.[109]

Despite the Roman rite's emphasis on the communal character of the liturgy (with its regular use of plural pronouns), concerns for eliminating one's personal sinfulness and the desire to liberate the souls in purgatory from the

temporal punishment due to their sins promoted a strong semi-Pelagian attitude. Emphasis on good works, above all the good work of saying mass, rested
quite comfortably with the teaching in the Celtic penitentials, above all in the
monasteries of southern Gaul that were influenced by the teaching of John
Cassian.[110] The focus shifted from God's initiative in Christ saving the community to an individualistic effort to merit God's grace. Because of this
emphasis on the individual, the experience of the Eucharist became a private
affair for both the ordained and the lay members of monastic communities.
The church became the place where the treasure of grace and salvation
resided, with the priests mediating those graces to the laypeople.

Symbolically, the church was no longer the larger ecclesiastical institution beyond the monastery; the church was the monastery itself where many
masses were celebrated each day.[111] Hence, the monastic vocation got separated from its baptismal roots and was increasingly based in an individualistic
piety. The ideal monk, and later the only one who could claim the name of
monk in the full sense of that word, was the ordained monk who could say
mass and intercede for others. Instead of being students in a *schola dominici
servitii,* ordained monks became surrogates praying before God on behalf of
other Christians, who were frequently absent from the liturgy itself.[112]

Along with the increased clericalization of monasticism went a shift in
the relationship between monasteries and the hierarchical church. In the
Middle Ages, monasteries were often very vulnerable to influence by local
ecclesiastical and secular authorities. Sometimes bishops and princes exercised so much power over monasteries that monks had little control over their
personal or communal lives. This was the situation when the abbey of Cluny
was founded in France in the early years of the tenth century with a commitment to return to basic Benedictine principles. But what distinguished Cluny
above all was that it was subject, not to local ecclesiastical or secular authorities, but only to the pope himself.[113] There we have a clear example of the
canonical institute called exemption. When the papacy was strong, this had
significant implications for the life of the monasteries. Because of its impressive monastic life and a series of effective long-lived abbots, Cluny not only
made many foundations but also associated other existing monasteries with
itself, with the result that the abbot of Cluny became the superior of all dependent Cluniac monasteries. All monks made profession of vows to the abbot of
Cluny and committed themselves to follow the customs of Cluny. In this way,
something very important in the Benedictine tradition, namely, local autonomy, was sacrificed.[114]

In 1098 Robert of Molesmes and several other Benedictine monks laid
the foundations for the Cistercian order. They sought to establish a form of
Benedictinism stricter and more primitive than any existing at the time. They
emphasized the ascetical elements of the Rule of Benedict, insisted on silence,

eliminated liturgical splendor, and downplayed communal interrelations. The clerics in the Cistercian communities executed a heavy burden of liturgical offices, while the lay brothers managed the farm and observed a somewhat less severe rule. Each Cistercian house managed its own affairs in accord with the decrees of an annual general chapter and was regularly visited by the abbot of the founding abbey.[115] After the Fourth Lateran Council in 1215, their schemes of regular general chapters and visitations were made obligatory for other monastic orders. That same council ordered all the monasteries to organize themselves into congregations. The Holy See thus sought to order and centralize monastic government. Apart from England, however, the decree was not implemented for complex reasons, but perhaps above all because local autonomy is one of the most cherished characteristics of Benedictine monasticism.[116]

In the eleventh century, there developed another issue germane to our subject. The relationship between the ordained priesthood and jurisdiction was discussed by both canonists and theologians alike. At first the two concepts were not clearly distinguished, implying that the two were essentially interrelated. Eventually, however, a precise distinction was made. On the one hand, priesthood came to be thought of primarily as involving a power, a *potestas,* a development that tended to depart from the New Testament understanding of ministry as service. This power was thought to involve a sharing in the very power of Jesus Christ to bring salvation to sinful people. Naturally, it was thought to be exercised primarily in the celebration of the Eucharist. On the other hand, jurisdiction came to be thought of as the power of governance, the power connected with ecclesiastical offices enabling one to perform specific legal acts of a legislative, executive, or juridical nature. Jurisdiction was looked upon as involving official church authorization in certain places or at certain times to use the power invested in one through ordination. In that sense it was thought to be independent from the power of ordination, but, in fact, it presupposed ordination to the priesthood.

Although the exercise of jurisdiction depended on ordination, one could be ordained without being given jurisdiction in certain areas. Just as ordination was conferred by the hierarchical church, so was jurisdiction given by the hierarchical church. In a monastic context, this development clearly separated the sacrament of order from its rootedness in the monastic community itself and made the exercise of all jurisdiction in the monastery dependent on the hierarchical authority of the church outside the monastery.[117] It also made the ordination of monks more significant in the monastic community because only ordained monks could exercise any form of jurisdiction.

What becomes clear in an investigation of the Middle Ages is that monastic vocation, Eucharist, clericalization, and ecclesiology are all interwoven. In so many ways, monastic communities, as the forerunners of today's institutes of consecrated life, ceased to be prophetic, marginal, charismatic communities. They became institutions, often rich and powerful, from social and economic points of view, within the larger institution of the church. These characteristics often prevail in monasteries at the present time.

SUPPRESSION AND RESTORATION OF MONASTICISM

The Council of Trent repeated the Fourth Lateran Council's demand for centralization among Benedictines. With the Roman curia more effectively organized than it was in the late Middle Ages and with communication improved, Rome was able to enforce its decision, so that gradually almost all the Benedictine abbeys grouped themselves into congregations.[118] Toward the end of the eighteenth century and the early years of the nineteenth century, Napoleon's armies swept across Europe. They regarded monasteries simply as part of the medieval clutter that must be swept away, enmeshed as they were with the ancien régime and its feudal and hierarchical structure. Monastic vows seemed a rejection of the principle of liberty, hierarchical structures an obstacle to equality, and commitment to a transcendent God as opposed to fraternity.[119] This antimonastic sentiment surfaced in other parts of Europe. Henry VIII had already closed all the abbeys in England by 1539 in order to get their wealth, while on the Continent, most of the monasteries were ransacked by the end of the first decade of the nineteenth century.

Following the defeat of Napoleon at Waterloo on 18 June 1815, Benedictine monasteries were gradually rejuvenated, partly due to the strong support of two popes who had originally been monks themselves. Pope Pius VII (1800–1823), who had been a Benedictine monk of Cesena, restored the Benedictine abbeys in the Papal States, two of which, S. Paulo in Rome and Subiaco, became major centers of the Benedictine revival throughout Europe. In his concordats with the newly established Catholic powers, the pope required that the former abbeys be reconstituted.[120]

Pope Gregory XVI (1831–1846), who had been a Camaldolese monk for about fifty years, also supported the Benedictine revival because he discovered that Benedictines could be counted on to support the papacy. In fact, the revival movements, such as those spearheaded by Prosper Guéranger at Solesmes and Maurus and Placid Wolter at Beuron, were generally ultramontaine; they favored Roman policies over those of the local church.[121]

It is interesting to observe in the light of this history that when Benedictine monasteries of men were revived throughout Europe in the nineteenth century, the leaders and the recruits were often diocesan priests, who naturally brought with them the understanding of the priesthood and Eucharist that had developed since the Council of Trent. Prosper Guéranger, the founder of Solesmes, had been a priest-secretary to an aged archbishop; Maurus and Placid Wolter, the founders of the Beuronese Congregation, were also diocesan priests. In Bavaria, where there was a superfluity of diocesan priests, the bishop of Regensburg encouraged them to join the new monastic houses. In France, Jean-Baptiste Muard, a diocesan priest with saintly and apostolic ideals, founded the monastery of Pierre-qui-Vire where he hoped to combine penitential practices with missionary initiatives.[122] This, naturally, gave a strong clerical character to Benedictine houses of men.

Many of the monasteries were deeply involved in pastoral work, providing mass and the other sacraments for the faithful. The French and Beuronese Congregations, however, deliberately sought to differentiate themselves from the Swiss, Bavarian, English, and Austrian Congregations by maintaining a more rigorous monastic observance and stricter adherence to enclosure. Nevertheless, both of these congregations took on special pastoral work such as giving retreats and parish missions.[123] They were also primarily clerical congregations since at that time both of these ministries required ordination to the priesthood. Furthermore, admission to solemn vows and chapter rights presupposed ordination to the priesthood.

Clericalism also characterized the restored monasteries of England. One of the primary goals of the seventeenth-century monks who refounded the English Congregation was the conversion of England. To this end, monk-priests were sent to England from the Continent, where they had lived in exile after Henry VIII's suppression of their monasteries; they were to celebrate mass and to instruct the English people in the Catholic faith. All of the monks took an oath acknowledging their willingness to serve on the English mission. Those who died as martyrs were honored because of their priestly work. In this they were looked upon as descendants of St. Augustine of Canterbury and his missionary monks, who first brought the Christian faith to the Anglo-Saxon countries.

When the Benedictine communities moved back to England in the last century, they opened schools that were generally conducted by the very young monks who were also preparing for ordination to the priesthood. When those monks were called to serve on the mission, they were withdrawn from the jurisdiction of their local superiors and subjected to the congregational authorities responsible for administering the missions. In other words, the autonomy of each monastery gave way to the same kind of centralized authority that prevailed in the more apostolic religious institutes such as the Jesuits, Dominicans, and Franciscans. It was not until the early part of this century that the autonomy of each English monastery was restored. The strong clerical character of the English congregation, which has prevailed to the present time, resulted in deep involvement of the monks in the life of the parochial church in England.[124]

The German and Swiss monks who came to the United States in the last century were also keen missionaries. Boniface Wimmer sought to minister to German Catholic immigrants by founding rural Benedictine monasteries that could set up extensive mission stations and also schools for the training of future priests. Wimmer himself had to struggle for an activist missionary interpretation of Benedictine monasticism against the frequent objections of confreres who sought a stricter observance and greater fidelity to enclosure but who never seemed to question the predominantly clerical character of the monasteries. Frontier bishops across the United States petitioned Wimmer to open houses in their dioceses in order to bring the mass and the sacraments to the numerous nineteenth-century immigrants who arrived in the United States. There is no doubt that Wimmer left his mark on American Benedictinism. His foundations were established on a large scale; they were outward-looking and quite diversified in their operations. Nevertheless, much of their work presupposed that many of the monks were ordained to the priesthood.[125]

The Swiss foundations in Indiana and Missouri were less flamboyant. Although their monastic observance was generally stricter than that in Wimmer's houses, they too got deeply involved in parochial work and also in the training of diocesan priests.[126]

As the new monasteries developed in the nineteenth century, they were assured of papal support; hence they had regular recourse to Rome as their normal mode of procedure in all their constitutional developments—and this long before the definition of papal infallibility in 1870 ushered in an era during which deferment to Rome would be a universal practice on the part of institutes of religious life. In the catalogue of Benedictines, the pope was introduced as the "Abbot of abbots." Pope Leo XIII took advantage of the cooperation between the Holy See and Benedictine congregations to mandate the establishment of a central Benedictine college in Rome. Sant' Anselmo was founded in the 1890s on papal property, perched upon the Aventine Hill. He also established the office of the abbot primate, elected by the Benedictine abbots of the world, whose authority is primarily a moral one, offering support to Benedictines around the world and relating Benedictine monasteries to the various Roman dicasteries. The establishment of that office indicated Rome's desire to centralize the Benedictines, who have regularly insisted on their local autonomy. Pope Pius XI once complained that the Benedictines are really an *ordo sine ordine,* an order without any order. But Benedictines are not an order at all. They are simply the sum of monasteries scattered across the world that happen to follow the Rule of Benedict. In more recent times, Pope Paul VI described the Benedictines as a "confederation" and succeeded in getting several smaller monastic groups, such as the Camaldolese, to join the confederation.[127]

Several clear conclusions may be deduced from this historical survey. Monastic communities following the Rule of Benedict became highly clericalized not only in the Middle Ages but also in the nineteenth-century restoration. Ecclesiastical law demanded that the abbot be an ordained priest, a requirement certainly not set out in the Rule. Likewise, the basic equality of all the monks, presumed and stressed in the Rule, was eroded and gave way to a two-tiered structure in which the clerical monks were really the only true Benedictines in the full sense because they alone took solemn vows and had chapter rights. The lay brothers, though often living a very devout religious life, were looked upon as the primary manual work force in the community. They took simple vows, did not participate in chapter, and usually recited rosaries, devotional prayers, and perhaps a vernacular office rather than the full monastic *opus Dei.* They were usually separated from the clerics in their living spaces and often wore a distinctive habit. In order to have an authentic Benedictine vocation, a man really had to have two vocations—one to the monastic life and the other to the priesthood.

These foregoing observations raise two significant questions: What is the place of prophetic, charismatic, marginal monastic communities in the church today? and How should ordained ministry function within such communities?

SOME CONTEMPORARY MONASTIC ISSUES

Since the Second Vatican Council, successful efforts have been made in many monasteries to declericalize the community and to emphasize, both in theory and practice, the essential equality of all monks rooted in their baptismal commitment and profession of monastic vows. Less successful have been any efforts to de-episcopalize the abbatial office, which in practice means that the office of major superior in the community is still closely aligned with the hierarchical church. In the concluding section of this chapter, a number of contemporary issues will be discussed that call for further discussion and appropriate adjustments in the structure and life of monastic communities if the monasteries are once again to be vibrant expressions of the charismatic, prophetic, and contemplative dimensions of the church rather than institutions that simply parallel the hierarchical church on a local level.

In its discussion of ordained ministry, the Second Vatican Council placed its emphasis on the bishop as the principal pastor of the local church and related the presbyter to the bishop as his assistant.[128] Instead of being an *alter Christus,* the presbyter was considered an *alter episcopus* in the sense that he participates in the bishop's ministry in the parish and depends on the bishop in the exercise of that ministry.[129] This close relationship between the presbyter and the local bishop was prominent in the patristic period but has not been at all common since the Middle Ages. Instead, the presbyter has been thought of as acting *in persona Christi*—an association that often has resulted in an excessively individualistic sense of identity on the part of the presbyter.[130] Monks who are ordained to the priesthood, however, do not in fact think of themselves as primarily related to the local bishop but rather as primarily related to their abbot and monastic community. Pope Paul VI seemed to sense the tension that the conciliar teaching posed for monastic priests in an address he gave to major religious superiors in 1969.[131] He noted that monasticism was not originally oriented toward pastoral care outside the monastery, but he insisted that monastic priesthood was not an aberration. He asserted that there is a basic harmony between being a monk and a priest, since both monastic profession and presbyteral ordination configure a man in a special way to Christ as priest and victim. He viewed priesthood not in a functional way but in an ontological or spiritual way. In keeping with the Benedictine tradition, he urged monastic priests to pursue a life of humility and obedience in imitation of Christ the victim.[132] Certainly Paul VI's stress on the monastic presbyter's relationship with Christ as victim is consonant with Benedict's own understanding of the priest as a community servant imitating Christ the servant.

The Second Vatican Council's emphasis on the presbyter as closely associated with the local bishop is reflected in the 1990 revised edition of the ordination rites,[133] which requires that members of institutes of consecrated life promise respect and obedience not only to their legitimate religious superiors but also to the diocesan bishop in order to foster the unity of all the clerics in each local church. On the practical level this requirement cannot help but create tensions between local bishops and monastic superiors, especially when monastic presbyters are involved in ministries apart from the monastery. When the local bishop and monastic superior do not agree about a pastoral appointment or about a monk-priest's ministry, whom should the monk-priest obey? What does obedience to the local bishop really mean? The directive seems to call into question the legitimate autonomy of the Benedictine monastery and the primary responsibility of the abbot for all his monks, including the ordained.

The gospel, to which Benedictines make their first commitment, is not in the first instance a legal code, nor is the Rule of Benedict. It follows from the very nature and content of the Rule that each monastery should have a certain autonomy. This autonomy does not imply isolation from the rest of the church, but rather, presumes that the monastery, as a legitimately constituted expression of the church's spiritual life and sanctity, enjoys the right kind of freedom and fulfills the right kind of responsibility so that it might be true to its distinctive mission among God's people in the world.[134]

Benedictine autonomy is determined above all by the distinctive role of the monastic superior, who is presumed to have an enduring relationship with the individual monks in the community. Since the superior, as a special sacrament of Christ and as a source and symbol of unity in the community, is responsible for the spiritual formation of the community, its works, and its temporalities, that role is usually assumed for a term of office considerably longer than one would find in other institutes of consecrated life.

Because of the superior's unique role in the monastery, the Benedictine vow of obedience is qualitatively different from that taken by others in institutes of consecrated life. In nonmonastic communities, superiors are changed frequently, and the individual members of the community are often moved from one local community to another, so that the individual's relationship to particular community members usually does not extend over a long period of time. By contrast, Benedictine obedience is meant to be deeply personal.

It implies obedience first of all to the gospel and the Rule, and then to the superiors and the other members of the community, insofar as they mediate the Word of God into the life of the community and its members. The superior's authority and the individual's vow of obedience are complementary and correlative, since they both exist for the monastic growth of the individual members and the community as a whole. For that reason, the Rule provides for extensive cooperation between the superior and the community members, especially concerning the works and temporalities of the community. Whenever any matter of importance is to be decided, the superior is to seek counsel from all members of the community, whose advice is to be taken seriously because of their lifelong commitment to and responsibility for that particular community.[135]

Benedict's Rule manifests a firm faith in human nature. It challenges the community to be responsible for its own development and destiny and precludes undue interference from outside the community. This sense of responsibility is coherent with the vow of stability that Benedictines profess. Personal freedom of conscience must always be held in tension with one's commitment to both the abbot and the rest of the community. Laissez-faire individualism is out of place in a Benedictine community, for the members undertake a special loyalty to the community in a spirit of charity that is not an abstract ideal but one that requires a daily acceptance and support of the community.[136]

The essence of the monastic life is the search for God under a rule and an abbot in a cenobitic context. One becomes a monk through profession, not through ordination. Nevertheless, the monastic priesthood is certainly legitimate, provided the cautions about the monastic priest so emphasized in the Rule of Benedict are brought to bear on the ministry of the monk-priest. In determining the number of monks to be ordained, an abbot should keep in mind the real needs of the monastery and its works, which often include runnning a school, seminary, retreat house, and certain parishes closely associated with the abbey. It is important to stress that Benedictine parishes should not simply duplicate diocesan parishes but should clearly manifest the spirit of monastic life.

Monasticism is meant to bear witness to the charismatic, prophetic dimensions of the church's life; in a sense it is meant to function on the margins of the diocese. Hence, monks are not meant to substitute for diocesan priests in parishes on a regular basis, nor are they to assume independent chaplaincies that have little or nothing to do with life at the abbey. For monks to supply for diocesan priests on a long-term basis simply because there is a shortage of secular clergy is not really consonant with the monastic vocation, which is essentially cenobitic.

Most in keeping with the cenobitic character of monastic life would be a team approach to pastoral service in which Benedictines, clerics, and laypersons could work together and complement one another in bringing the Benedictine charism to bear on the life of the diocese. If Benedictines assume responsibility for parishes, the parishes should have a distinctive Benedictine character, not only because of the Benedictine personnel involved, but also because their pastoral work should be rooted in and conditioned by a commitment to the major themes and values in the Rule. This pastoral work should include well-planned and -celebrated liturgies; regular celebration of the Liturgy of the Hours; effective proclamation and sharing of God's Word expressed in preaching but grounded in a life of *lectio divina* and personal prayer; the availability of spiritual guidance; special concern for the young, the sick, the poor, and the aged in the parish; and a general ministry of Benedictine hospitality toward all.[137]

The Benedictine tradition has been recognized for its careful attention to liturgy, but the celebration of liturgy is related to the rest of monastic life. Contemporary liturgical reform often results in a cultic self-consciousness that fails to ground liturgy in the rest of Christian life and mission. Monastic communities could offer an alternative way of viewing liturgy in which liturgy and life are in fact effectively integrated.[138] The charge is sometimes made that contemporary liturgy is much too centered on the presider, who often *performs* or stars rather than seeks to be self-effacing as a servant of the community. A proper understanding of ordination in a monastery, with its stress on humility, service, and obedience, should help put an end to clericalism and anticlericalism alike within the community. Within the monastery special status or favors attached to ordination should be carefully eliminated.[139]

Since the Second Vatican Council, many traditionally Benedictine parishes in the United States have been returned to diocesan responsibility, especially those parishes with only one priest in residence. This has been due to the decline in the number of Benedictines available for such parochial work and to the preference of many younger monks who are priests to live a cenobitic life in the monastery rather than an isolated life in a parish. This transitional period offers Benedictine communities the opportunity to take a hard look at the parishes and other institutions they decide to retain and to give them a distinctively Benedictine character. Benedictines who serve in parishes, seminaries, retreat houses, or other institutions should do so precisely as cenobitic monks whose incarnational life of *lectio divina,* Liturgy of the Hours, personal prayer, and community can reflect basic Christian values to the larger church, values which are often not effectively sacramentalized in the wider institutional, hierarchically structured church.[140]

An area of some tension within monastic communities is the restriction of the right to preach a homily to ordained deacons, presbyters, and bishops. In a Benedictine community it is the superior who has the right and responsibility affirmed by the Rule to break open the Word of God for the community and to assure that the community is formed according to God's Word. Traditionally the superior gave the community regular conferences on monastic spirituality or deputed others to do so. With the emphasis on the homily in both conciliar and postconciliar liturgical documents as well as in the new Code of Canon Law (canon 767), the celebration of the Eucharist has become a regular occasion during which the Word of God is effectively shared and broken for Benedictines, usually on a daily basis. In communities where there are very few priests, the homily is sometimes given by monks who are not ordained but who are deputed to do so by the abbot. The practice has generally been very well received and has proved to be a wholesome way of enriching the spiritual lives of community members. It should be emphasized that a democratic approach to this issue has not been taken by Benedictine communities. Not every monk preaches; only those authorized by the superiors can. Hence, there is what might be called a licensing process whereby the superiors designate and delegate those who are to preach. The practice is really in keeping with the responsibility of professed Benedictines to use their gifts and training responsibly for the good of the community under the direction of the superior.[141]

Another area that has been reviewed in light of the new Code of Canon Law is the requirement that Benedictines who are ordained to either the permanent or transitional diaconate must have received the ministries of lector and acolyte and have exercised them for a suitable period of time (canon 1035). It should be observed here that by their monastic profession, Benedictines are committed to serve the community in their liturgical celebrations under the superior's direction. This service normally includes exercising the role of reader and minister at the altar. It is inappropriate to institutionalize these or similar ministries in Benedictine monasteries by formally installing monks according to approved liturgical rites, even when they are to be ordained deacons. Apart from the fact that the legislation is biased against women in that it precludes their installation in such ministries, application of the procedures in monasteries would imply inadequate understanding of the meaning of monastic profession and the implicit responsibilities assumed at that time. A formal installation would be little more than empty ritualism.[142]

A final liturgical subject that calls for commentary is that of pontifical insignia worn by abbots. Not only has monasticism been clericalized throughout history, but also the abbatial office has been episcopalized. Canon 625 of the 1917 Code of Canon Law affirmed that ruling abbots who were liturgically blessed could use pontifical insignia, except the violet skullcap. The new Code does not mention these privileges; hence the practice is governed by the *motu proprio Pontificalia Insignia* issued by Pope Paul VI on 21 June 1968, the instruction of the Sacred Congregation of Rites *Pontificalis Ritus,* issued on the same day, and the Rite of Blessing of an Abbot and Abbess issued by the Sacred Congregation for Divine Worship on 9 November 1970.[143]

In the new rite both the ring and the miter are optional; hence they need not be taken by the abbot. In light of the simplification of *pontificalia* called for by both Paul VI and the Sacred Congregation of Rites but above all in light of the simplicity, the humility, and the shunning of triumphalism and power that are to be found in a Benedictine abbot according to the Rule, it would seem most appropriate that abbots assume only those symbols that are truly fitting to the abbatial office, namely, the pectoral cross and the pastoral staff. As a symbol of his commitment to the community, the abbot may choose to wear a simple ring without a gem. The miter, which is certainly an episcopal symbol and is regularly interpreted as such by most people today, is not an authentic abbatial symbol, nor is the throne. As Paul VI pointed out in his *motu proprio,* the Second Vatican Council brought out sharply the distinction between bishops and priests of secondary rank. He asserted that "we should take into consideration the mentality and conditions of our own era, which attaches great importance to the authenticity of signs and to the real need that liturgical rites be marked by a noble simplicity. Accordingly it is very necessary to restore authenticity to the use of pontifical insignia as expressions of the rank and the charge of those who shepherd the people of God."[144] Unless they have been ordained bishops, abbots are priests of secondary rank and should appear to be what they are. When an abbot pontificates wearing a miter as the principal celebrant of a Eucharist while concelebrating with his priest-monks, the image that he communicates is that of a bishop celebrating with his presbyterium.[145]

Paul VI's *motu proprio* is clear that abbots should not wear or use *pontificalia* outside of their monasteries and churches. In practice, however, that directive is frequently not followed, for abbots often wear the miter at important diocesan celebrations and, on such occasions as episcopal ordinations, take their places with the assembled bishops rather than with the other religious superiors and clergy of the second rank where they belong.[146]

Furthermore, in various dioceses the bizarre practice has developed whereby abbots are delegated by the local bishop to celebrate the sacrament of confirmation in diocesan parishes, expecially when the bishop is incapacitated. Presumably bishops delegate abbots because they think the abbots can look like bishops and so give the impression that a bishop is actually ministering the sacrament. The practice is pastorally and liturgically repugnant. The rite of confirmation is clear that the minister of the sacrament is ordinarily the bishop so that there will be a more evident relationship to the first Pentecostal pouring forth of the Holy Spirit on the apostles, whose successors are the bishops. When the bishop cannot confirm, the extraordinary minister should be drawn from the diocesan presbyterium; he should have a particular diocesan function or office such as that of vicar general, episcopal vicar, or pastor of the place where the sacrament is to be celebrated. The canons of the new Code on the minister of confirmation (canons 882–888) should be interpreted in light of the theology and liturgy of the sacrament set out in the revised rite of the sacrament. When abbots are invited by bishops to take their place in celebrating the sacrament, they should not only decline the invitation but also explain their reasons for declining.[147]

The Rule of Benedict certainly relativizes clerical status; it is critical of clerical privilege and sensitive to the dangers of clerical ambition within the community. It stresses self-effacing service, communal equality, humility, obedience, and the primary obligation to seek God. In the monastery, however, ordained ministry and charismatic discipleship can nourish and challenge each other. If the monk-priest's ministry is permeated by a firm commitment to the community and abbot, to the values of the gospel and the Rule, then his service can be a life-giving source not only to the monastery but also to the wider church and the world.[148]

NOTES

1. Emmanuel Lanne, "L'Eglise local et d'Eglise universelle," *Irénikon* 43 (1970): 503. See also J. Dubois, "Esenzione Monastica," *Dizionario degli Istituti di Perfezione* (Rome: Edizione Paoline, 1973) 3:1295–1306.

2. Emile Jombart and Marcel Viller, "Cloture," *Dictionnaire de Spiritualité* (Paris: Beauchesne 1953), 979–1007, esp. 987–1002.

3. R. Kevin Seasoltz, "Monastic Autonomy and Exemption: Charism and Institution," *The Jurist* 34 (1974): 316–55; and Velasio de Paolis, "Exemptio an Autonomia Institutorum Vitae Consecratae?" *Periodica* 71 (1982): 147.

4. Robert Ombres, "Justa Autonomia Vitae: Religious in the Local Church," *The Clergy Review* 69 (September 1984): 310.

5. Vincent Desprez, "The Roots of Christian Monasticism: The Jewish Bible and Ancient Religions," *The American Benedictine Review* 41 (1990): 348-56; Diarmuid O'Murchu, *Reforming Religious Life: An Expanded Vision for the Future* (Slough, England: St. Paul's, 1995), 30-43; and idem, *Religious Life: A Prophetic Vision: Hope and Promise for Tomorrow* (Notre Dame, Ind.: Ave Maria Press, 1991), 14–41.

6. Mircea Eliade, *Shamanism: Archaic Techniques of Ecstasy* (New

York: Pantheon Books, 1964), 508–9; Sr. Donald Corcoran, "Contemporary Forms of Spirituality and Monastic Life," in *The Continuing Quest for God: Monastic Spirituality in Tradition and Transition*, ed. William Skudlarek (Collegeville, Minn.: The Liturgical Press, 1982), 248; and O'Murchu, 31–33.

7. Eliade, 6.

8. O'Murchu, 33–38; Evelyn Woodward, *Poets, Prophets and Pragmatists: A New Challenge to Religious Life* (Notre Dame, Ind.: Ave Maria Press, 1987); and R. Arbesmann, "Fasting and Prophecy in Pagan and Christian Antiquity," *Traditio* 7 (1949): 1–71.

9. Walter Brueggemann, *The Prophetic Imagination* (Philadelphia: Fortress Press, 1986); idem, *The Hopeful Imagination* (Philadelphia: Fortress Press, 1986); and Joseph Blenkinsopp, *Sage, Priest, Prophet: Religious and Intellectual Leadership in Ancient Israel* (Louisville: Westminster Knox Press, 1995).

10. O'Murchu, 34. See also Blenkinsopp, 115–65.

11. *Ibid.*

12. Joan Chittister, *Womanstrength* (Kansas City: Sheed and Ward, 1990), 52.

13. O'Murchu, 35.

14. T. R. Hobbs, "The Search for Prophetic Consciousness," *Biblical Theology Bulletin* 15 (1985): 136–41; and O'Murchu, 35.

15. See Anne Wilson Shaef, *When Society Becomes an Addict* (San Francisco: Harper and Row, 1987).

16. O'Murchu, 37–38.

17 Leonardo Boff, *Ecclesiogenesis* (Louisville: Westminister Knox Press, 1986), 51.

18. Graham Gould, *The Desert Fathers on Monastic Community* (Oxford: Clarendon Press, 1993), 1–17, 183–87.

19. Gould, 183.

20. Karl Suso Frank, *With Greater Liberty*, trans. Joseph T. Lienhard (Kalamazoo: Cistercian Publications, 1993), 17–18.

21. *Ibid.*, 19–35.

22. *Apophthegmata Patrum: The Sayings of the Desert Fathers*, The Alphabetical Collection, trans. Benedicta Ward (Kalamazoo: Cistercian Publications, 1975); and *The Wisdom of the Desert Fathers: Apophthegmata Patrum*, trans. Benedicta Ward (Oxford: Fairacres Press, 1975).

23. O'Murchu, 44–61, 67–74.

24. *Ibid.*, 68.

25. *Ibid.*

26. *Ibid.*

27. Frank, *With Greater Liberty*, 31.

28. O'Murchu, 68.

29. *Ibid.*

30. *Ibid.*

31. See Judith Merkel, *Committed by Choice: Religious Life Today* (Collegeville, Minn.: The Liturgical Press, 1992); Sandra M. Schneiders, *New Wineskins: Re-imagining Religious Life Today* (New York: Paulist Press, 1986); Barbara Fiand, *Living the Vision* (New York: Crossroad, 1990); and Duncan Fisher, "Liminality: The Vocation of the Church," *Cistercian Studies* 24 (1989): 181–205; 25 (1990) 188–218.

32. O'Murchu, 70–71.

33. *Ibid.*, 71–76.

34. Rv 1:6; Rv 5:10; Rv 20:6; 1 Pt 2:5; 1 Pt 2:9.

35. See David N. Power, *The Christian Priest: Elder and Prophet* (London: Sheed and Ward, 1973); Kenan B. Osborne, *Priesthood: A History of the Ordained Ministry in the Roman Catholic Church* (New York: Paulist Press, 1988); Paul Bernier, *Ministry in the Church: A Historical and Pastoral Approach* (Mystic, Conn.: Twenty-Third Publications, 1992); and Nathan Mitchell, *Mission and Ministry: History and Theology in the Sacrament of Order* (Wilmington: Michael Glazier, 1986), 72–199.

36. Jean Galot, *Theology of the Priesthood* (San Francisco: Ignatius Press, 1985), 55–69.

37. Osborne, 3–29.

38. *Ibid.*, 148–55.

39. Gould, 158.

40. Osborne, 44–53; O. Berlea, "Dai presbiteri ai sacerdoti," in *Il Prete per gli Uomini d'Oggi,* ed. G. Concetti (Rome: An. Veritas Ediatrice, 1975), 159–92; and A. Lemainre, "I presbiteri alle origini della chiesa," in *Il Prete*, 81–82.

41. Bernier, 82–103.

42. See Réne Bonpain, "Les Adaptions de la Règle de Saint Benoît ou le Double Relativité de l'Observance," *Collectanea Cisterciensia* 31 (1969): 247–64.

43. See Rudolf Lorenz, "Die Anfänge des abendländischen Monchtums im 4. Jahrhundert," Zeitschrift für Kirchengeschichte 77 (1966): 1–61; and Armand Veillieux, "La Liturgie dans le Cenobitisme Pachômien au Quatrième Siècle," *Studia Anselmiana* 57 (Rome: Herder, 1968).

44. *De institutis coenobiorum* 11:18; *Institutes*, ed. Jean Claude Guy, *SC* 109 (Paris: Cerf, 1965).

45. Frank, *With Greater Liberty*, 32–33.

46. *Ibid.*, 33–34.

47. *Ibid.*, 42.

48. *Ibid.*, 44.

49. *Ibid.*, 464–48. See also R. M. Price, *A History of the Monks of Syria* (Kalamazoo: Cistercian Publications, 1985).

50. *Ibid.*, 50–51. See also Karl Suso Frank, *Basilius von Caesarea: Die Monchsregeln* (Saint Ottilien: Eos, 1981).

51. Leo Ueding, "Die Kanones von Chalkedon in ihrer Bedeutung für Mönchtums und Klerus," *Das Konzil von Chalkedon*, ed. Alois Grillmeier and Heinrich Bacht (Würzburg: Echter, 1954), 2:569–676.

52. Michael Curran, "Early Irish Monasticism," in *Irish Spirituality*, ed. Michael Maher (Dublin: Veritas, 1981), 10–21; and Kathleen Hughes and Ann Hamlin, *Celtic Monasticism* (New York: Seabury Press, 1981), vii.

53. See Kathleen Hughes, *The Church in Early Irish Society* (Ithaca: Cornell University Press, 1966).

54. See L. Gougaud, *Christianity in Celtic Lands* (London: Sheed and Ward, 1931); and J. Ryan, *Irish Monasticism* (Ithaca: Cornell University Press, 1972).

55. Curran, 10.

56. *Ibid.*, 10–11.

57. Hughes and Hamlin, 7.

58. Curran, 11.

59. *Ibid.*, 19.

60. *Ibid.*, 11.

61. *Ibid.*

62. Todd Ridder, "The Clericalization of Monasticism," *Review for Religious* 49 (1990): 228.

63. Otto Nussbaum, *Kloster, Priestermönch und Privatmesse* (Bonn: Peter Hansteln Verlag, 1961).

64. Angelus Häussling, *Mönchskonvent und Eucharistiefeier* (Münster: Aschendorffsche Verlagsbuchhandlung, 1973).

65. Ridder, 228.

66. Adalbert de Vogüé, introduction to *The Rule of the Master*, trans. Luke Eberle (Kalamazoo: Cistercian Publications, 1977), 56; and Ridder, 229.

67. Häussling, 19–21; and Basil Steidle, "'Missae' in der Regel St. Benedikts " *Benediktinische Monatsschrift* 28 (1952): 456–61.

68. Daniel Callam, "The Frequency of Mass in the Latin Church ca. 400," *Theological Studies* 45 (1948): 613–50.

69. *Ibid.*, 650; and Kevin Irwin, "On Monastic Priesthood," *American Benedictine Review* 41 (September 1990): 229–30.

70. Adalbert de Vogüé, *La Communauté et l'abbé dans la Regle de saint Benoît* (Paris: Desclee de Brouwer, 1961), 327–47; idem, *Le Règle de saint Benoît* (Paris: Cerf, 1972), 1:104–13; idem, "Le Pretre et la Communauté monastique dans l'Antiquité," *La Maison-Dieu* 115 (1973): 62–65; and R.

Kevin Seasoltz, "Monastery and Eucharist," in *Living Bread, Saving Cup*, ed. R. Kevin Seasoltz (Collegeville, Minn.: The Liturgical Press, 1987), 262.

71. *The Rule of the Master*, chap. 83; and Seasoltz, 262.

72. *Ibid.*

73. RM, chap. 21.

74. *Ibid.*, chap. 93.

75. *Ibid.*, chap. 45.

76. See Häussling, 19–21; and Steidle, 456–61.

77. "Problems of the Monastic Conventual Mass," *Downside Review* 87 (1969): 328.

78. Seasoltz, "Monastery and Eucharist," 264.

79. Häussling, 31; and Ridder, 231.

80. De Vogüé, introduction to RM, 32.

81. RM, chap. 93; RM chap. 45.

82. RB, Prologue, v. 1; chap. 13:10; and Ridder, 231.

83. RB, 62:10, 64:4; and Ridder, 231.

84. RM, chaps. 2, 3, 92, 93; RB 64:2; and Ridder, 231–32.

85. De Vogüé, introduction to RM, 57–62; and Ridder, 242.

86. Valerian J. Odermann, "Interpreting the Rule of Benedict: Entering a World of Wisdom," *American Benedictine Review* 35 (March 1984): 31–35; R. Kevin Seasoltz, "Benedictine Monasticism and the New Code: Some Reflections on Autonomy, Work, and Worship," *American Benedictine Review* 37 (March 1986): 5.

87. Seasoltz, "Benedictine Monasticism," 5.

88. RB, 64:19.

89. H. B. Workman, *The Evolution of the Monastic Ideal* (London: Charles N. Kelly, 1913), 148. See also Daniel Rees and others, *Consider Your Call: A Theology of Monastic Life Today* (Kalamazoo: Cistercian Publications, 1980), 49–51.

90. Seasoltz, "Monastic Autonomy," 318–19.

91. *Palladius: The Lausiac History*, trans. Robert T. Meyer (Westminster, Md.: The Newman Press, 1965), 95.

92. *The Rule for Nuns of St. Caesarius of Arles: A Translation with Critical Introduction,* trans. Mother Maria Caritas McCarthy (Washington, D.C.: The Catholic University of America Press, 1960), 182–83.

93. *Regula ad Virgines*, PL 68:406B: "Missae vero quando sanctaeabbatissae visum fuerit tune gent."

94. Callam, "The Frequency of Mass," 650.

95. Häussling, 32–72; and Seasoltz, "Monastery and Eucharist," 265–66.

96. *Regularis Concordia: The Monastic Agreement of the Monks and Nuns of the English Nation*, trans. Thomas Symons (New York: Oxford

University Press, 1953), 16, 21. See also *Tenth-Century Studies: Essays in Commemoration of the Millennium of the Council of Winchester and Regularis Concordia*, ed. David Parsons (London: Phillimore and Co., 1975), esp. the essays by D. H. Farmer, "The Progress of Monastic Revival," 10-19; and Thomas Symons, "'Regularis Concordia': History and Derivation," 37–59.

97. *Egeria's Travels to the Holy Land*, trans; John Wilkinson (Jerusalem: Ariel Publishing House, 1981).

98. Nussbaum, 66–69.

99. *Ibid.*, 102.

100. See M. Francis Mannion, "Stipends and Eucharistic Praxis," in *Living Bread, Saving Cup*, 324–46.

101. Häussling, 298–347.

102. *Regularis Concordia*, 19.

103. Nussbaum, 193–94; and Ridder, 236.

104. Häussling, 181–82.

105. Nussbaum, 129; and Ridder, 234.

106. *Ibid.*, 89–90; and Ridder, 238.

107. G. J. C. Snoek, *Medieval Piety from Relics to the Eucharist: A Process of Mutual Interaction* (Leiden: E. J. Brill, 1995), esp. 227–307.

108. Ridder, 239.

109. See Daniel J. Sheerin, *The Eucharist* (Collegeville, Minn.: The Liturgical Press/Michael Glazier, 1986), 93–102; and Josef Jungmann, *The Mass of the Roman Rite* (New York: Benziger Brothers, 1955), 2:205–12.

110. Nussbaum, 154, 157; and Ridder, 235.

111. Ridder, 235.

112. *Ibid.*

113. Seasoltz, "Benedictine Monasticism," 6.

114. See Joseph Warrilow, "Cluny: Silentia Claustri," in *Benedict's Disciples*, ed. D. H. Farmer (Leominster: Fowler Wright Books, 1980), 118–38; and H. E. Cowdrey, *The Cluniacs and the Gregorian Reform* (Oxford: Oxford University Press, 1970).

115. Cuthbert Butler, *Benedictine Monachism* (London: Longmans, Green and Co., 1919), 240.

116. *Ibid.*, 240–41.

117. See A. Stickler, "De potestatis sacrae nature et origine," *Periodica* 71 (1982): 65–91.

118. Seasoltz, "Monastic Autonomy," 336–38.

119. Daniel Rees, "The Benedictine Revival in the Nineteenth Century," in *Benedict's Disciples*, 282–307.

120. Irwin, 238.

121. *Ibid.*

122. Rees, "The Benedictine Revival," 281; and Irwin, 238–39.

123. Rees, 295.

124. Rees, *Consider Your Call*, 339–41.

125. Rees, "The Benedictine Revival," 287–89. See also Jerome Oetgen, *An American Abbot: Boniface Wimmer* (Latrobe, Pa.: Archabbey Press, 1976).

126. Rees, "The Benedictine Revival," 289; and Irwin, 239–40.

127. Terrance Kardong, *The Benedictines* (Collegeville, Minn.: The Liturgical Press/Michael Glazier 1988), 157.

128. See J. Lecuyer, "Decree on the Ministry and Life of Priests: History of the Decree," *Commentary on the Documents of Vatican II* (New York: Herder and Herder, 1969), 4:183–209.

129. M. Edmund Hussey, "Needed: A Theology of Priesthood," *Origins* 17 (February 4, 1988), 577–83; and Irwin, 241.

130. Hussey, 579; and Irwin, 246.

131. Pope Paul VI, "Ai Superiori Maggiori degli Ordini e Congregationi Religiose," in *Insegamenti di Paolo VI* (Vatican City: Tipographia Poliglotta Vaticana, 1966), 4:571–76.

132. Irwin, 244–245.

133. *Pontificale Romanum ex decreto Sacrosancti Oecumenici Concilii Vaticani II instauratum auctoritate Pauli Pp. VI cure recognitum De Ordinatione Episcopi Presbyterorum et Diaconorum, Editio typica Altera* 1990 (Urbs Vaticana: Typis Polyglottis Vaticanis, 1990).

134. Seasoltz, "Benedictine Monasticism," 6.

135. Seasoltz, "Monastic Autonomy," 334–35.

136. *Ibid.*, 335–36.

137. *Ibid.*, "Benedictine Monasticism," 25.

138. Irwin, 259–60.

139. *Ibid.*, 260.

140. Seasoltz, "Benedictine Monasticism," 19–21.

141. *Ibid.*, 27–29.

142. *Ibid.*, 29–30.

143. *Ibid.*, 30–31.

144. *AAS* 60 (1968):475.

145. Seasoltz, "Benedictine Monasticism," 31.

146. *Ibid.*, 32.

147. *Ibid.*

148. Brian E. Daley, "The Ministry of Disciples: Historical Reflections," *Theological Studies* 48 (1987): 628; and Irwin, 262.

3

Theologies of Religious Life and Priesthood

David N. Power, O.M.I.

The Second Vatican Council put a new face on the discussion of the states of life in the church by finding parallel ways to treat the calls of baptism, ordained ministry, and religious life. It treated them all as participations both in the threefold work of Christ as priest, prophet, and king, and in the ministry and mission of the church. It also gave a more ontological basis to this comparison by using the idea of consecration and by describing each of the three vocations as a share in the consecration of Christ in the incarnation and in his baptism. Since the council there has been considerable theological discussion about the specific character of both consecration and ministry, as well as about their relation to one another.

Thirty years after Vatican II, it can be asked whether these categories are valid and if some new approach is needed to develop more realistic theological understandings. Has the retrieval of charisms by religious bodies affected the practice and understanding of ministry in general and of ordained ministry in particular? Against that background, this chapter asks how past and present theologies of religious life and priesthood intersect, especially as these touch on the life of orders and congregations with priests in their membership as they work to retrieve their founding charism.

This chapter first reviews major points from the recent teaching of the magisterium on priesthood, on religious life, and on the practical reality of being both a religious and an ordained priest. Second, it looks at past contributions on the relation between priesthood and religious life, since these continue to affect current practice and discussion. Third, the issue is examined in light of developments in contemporary theology. Finally, because every theological development gives rise to questions about practice, this chapter will explore what the adoption of a praxis orientation might mean for the future.[1]

CURRENT MAGISTERIAL TEACHING

Religious Priests

In the Western church, the spiritual norms and expectations of religious life have been imposed upon priestly life. Beginning with Vatican II, however, a kind of reversal has taken place whereby religious institutes look to priestly ideals to express the renewal of religious life. In the immediate aftermath of the Second Vatican Council, for example, some institutes looked to the document on the ministry and life of priests, *Presbyterorum Ordinis,* in reviewing their constitutions and rules. There they found material that proved helpful in expressing the meaning of mission, of the evangelical counsels, and of the common life, especially as these related to apostolic ministry.

On the other hand, the trend to make communal life and the following of the evangelical counsels the model for diocesan clergy seems to have gained momentum. It is even stronger in a recent instruction of the Congregation for the Clergy than it was at the council.[2] This document simply said that priests who are members of religious bodies must participate in the life of local churches through the service of their particular charism.[3] At the same time, it states that all priests, not only those belonging to missionary institutes, have a missionary vocation that embraces the concerns of evangelization and of the whole world.[4]

This seems to make the distinction between diocesan clergy and religious clergy even more obscure. Both *Mutuae Relationes,* the instruction on the relation between bishops and religious, and the *Instrumentum Laboris,* which prepared the ground for the special Synod on Consecrated Life of 1994, treat this issue specifically. In doing so, both documents distinguish between the charisms of the diaconate, presbyterate, and episcopate[5] and the special charisms of members of religious bodies as these affect priestly and apostolic ministry. Quoting the letter *Pastores Dabo Vobis* of Pope John Paul II, the *Instrumentum Laboris* states that priests

> who belong to religious orders and congregations represent a spiritual enrichment for the entire diocesan presbyterate to which they contribute special charisms and special ministries.[6]

Using the notion of consecration, which it applies to baptism, ordination, and religious commitment, the document goes on to say:

> The harmonious blend of the two aspects of the one personal vocation, that is, the sacramental and charismatic grace of the consecrated life, can bear abundant fruits in holiness and in the apostolate to the degree to which religious priests have a clear understanding of the nature of their ecclesial ministry, draw inspiration and

strength for their spiritual life from the fonts of their own institute, live according to their own style of life, and are available for an apostolic outreach in the universal and particular Church.[7]

This attributes a role to religious priests in both the particular and the universal church.[8] At this point, the text offers some specific consideration for those who have a special link with the Petrine ministry through the privilege of exemption.[9] It also portrays the life of all ordained religious, both priests and deacons (including hermits and contemplative monks), as related to "apostolic outreach" in one way or another.

Religious Life

The Second Vatican Council lessened the rift that seemed to exist between religious life and the life of the baptized by treating religious life within the context of the universal call to perfection. It presented consecrated life as one way of life alongside others. The council used the theological notion of consecration to connect the call to holiness in the life of laypersons, priests or religious, since they are all ways of living out the fundamental consecration of baptism. All specific vocations in the church are related to the consecration of Christ to the Father and to the salvation of the world in his incarnation, his baptism at the Jordan, and in his Pasch.

The council also emphasized the importance of community life. In the discussion of the three traditional vows it changed the usual order and listed chastity before poverty. This was, in part, apologetic—a response to problematic issues of chastity in the lives of the faithful, of priests, and of religious. The council also put forward a theological reason for this reordering: chastity represented the loving choice of Christ above all other loves, and the readiness to consecrate oneself to the work of Christ with a love that is unrestricted. In connection with such a viewpoint, the conciliar documents underline religious life's eschatological character as a sign of God's kingdom. The council also stressed the need for each institute to attend to its own particular charism.

The *Instrumentum Laboris* for the special Synod on Consecrated Life of 1994 pursued these same lines of thought, developing them in some new directions. It gave special attention to the eschatological witness of religious life, especially in view of what Pope John Paul II has dubbed the new evangelization that must prepare the second millennium. All types of religious life, whether contemplative, apostolic, or apostolic and missionary, are at the special service of the universal church. The document attributed an apostolic quality to each and every form of evangelical life, including the contemplative and the monastic.

The Message of the Special Synod

The final message of the Synod on Consecrated Life took consecration as the fundamental category for defining evangelical communities.[10] In doing so, it continued the approach of the Second Vatican Council, which used consecration as the common foundation for the theologies of baptism, ordination, and religious life. It returns however, to language that sees the religious life as more perfect, by seeing in it a "deeper" experience of the Redeemer's mysteries, a "closer" likeness to him, and a "more intimate" communion with him. Among charisms and callings, the religious life is indispensable to the church in order to give expression to its eschatological character, that is, to its service to the kingdom of God.

The call to mission is necessarily associated with consecration: "the consecrated person receives consecration for mission in the Church according to the specific nature of each institute."[11] The consecrated life is also marked by a prophetic character. By this the document refers to a witness to evangelical values, which are embodied in the vows of chastity, poverty, and obedience. In this way of life, the synod finds a response to the excesses of the world and a particularly apt way to serve the inculturation of gospel values among different peoples. The witness of the evangelical life helps people both to recognize seeds of the Word in their own way of life and to incorporate into it the gospel values of Christ and of the kingdom of God.

In addition to this general concern with the prophetic quality of religious life, the document also demonstrates a concern about poverty, a topic which surfaced during the synodal deliberations.[12] In a special section on the subject, poverty is linked with the church's preferential option for the poor. This option, of which religious should give particular evidence, is in itself a "fundamental and radical option for the poor Christ." As such, it means that religious bind themselves to all those dispossessed and those who suffer. Besides being a denunciation of deprivation and injustice, living this evangelical poverty proclaims "the inexhaustible wealth of Christ."

In this paragraph on poverty, the synodal message attempts to reconcile several factors. First of all, it recognizes the place that the call to follow the poor Christ has had in the history of religious life. This is something quite distinct from whatever was juridically or even theologically included under the specific vow of poverty. Second, to meet the prophetic call of these times, the synodal message links evangelical poverty with the preferential option for the poor that was first enunciated by Pope John XXIII and since has been pursued by a number of episcopacies around the world and by religious communities. Third, so as to avoid equating evangelical poverty with the struggle for justice, the document sees in it a proclamation of the riches of Christ. This involves the personal and corporate detachment of religious, which enables them, "from the depth of their being," to give themselves to the mission of spreading

God's kingdom. It should be noted that, though they are not denied, the traditional relations between evangelical poverty and the common life, or between poverty and contemplation, are passed over in this discourse.

In the process of renewal, religious communities have often put an emphasis on community life, under the title of *apostolic community*. It is interesting, therefore, that the synodal message gives little attention to this aspect of their life. It does, however, give explicit importance to discerning and renewing the special charism of each institute and to following this with attention to both the needs of the particular church and to the service of the universal church.

The message does not address the issue of the relation between priesthood and religious life, although it notes the varied forms of religious societies down through the ages and in the present time. Beginning with the witness value of consecrated life in itself, it attributes a missionary and apostolic character to each and every form of communal consecrated life.[13] Of religious communities, the message also notes that their prophetic quality provides a credible foundation for the inculturation of the gospel among peoples.[14] What it says of evangelical poverty and its connection with mission has already been noted.[15]

The Propositions

At the end of the synod, the assembly submitted fifty-five propositions to the pope for his consideration for inclusion in an official document.[16] They are not of equal importance, but one may discern certain trends and concerns, as well as theological orientations. Consecration (proposition no. 3) is accepted as the basic category for describing religious life, as was the case from the very convocation of the synod. The consecration through religious profession is compared to that of baptism and said to be rooted in it. It is, however, described as a special sacred bond calling for a more radical following of Christ. As with the Second Vatican Council, chastity is given primacy in the union of religious with Christ, but the evangelical counsels together are considered essential to the consecrated life. Furthermore, in presenting the nature of consecrated life, the propositions in various ways call for an elaboration of its anthropological, ecclesiological, christological, and pneumatological dimensions.

In considering what religious life offers to the church, the propositions call for a special participation of its members in the church's mission (no. 35). This means playing a role in both the "first evangelization," needed to spread the gospel further afield, and in the "second evangelization," called for by John Paul II to reawaken traditionally Christian countries to the urgency of the gospel. This highlights the prophetic quality of living the religious life (no. 39), as it calls both the church and society into question in the name of the gospel without sundering the communion of the church under the government of its bishops. The challenge needs to be taken on in a spirit of openness, fostering collaboration among all the sectors of the church, as well as with all peoples who work toward the good of society. This openness paves the way to an ecumenical (no. 45), and even interreligious, approach to the mission of the church (no. 46). In addition, it makes of religious life a precious instrument in the inculturation of the gospel, reaching to the very roots of peoples and their cultures (no. 40).

While these many characteristics and concerns are to be present in all forms of religious consecration, several propositions offer a kind of typology of the different ways in which religious life takes shape today. Thus, they list monastic life (no. 5), institutes dedicated totally to contemplative life (no. 6), apostolic religious life (no. 7), religious institutes of brothers and sisters that do not have ordained members (no. 8), mixed institutes combining ordained and nonordained in their ranks (no. 10), secular institutes (no. 11), societies of apostolic life (no. 14), consecrated women (no. 9), the order of virgins (no. 12), and newly emerging forms of consecrated life (no. 13).

Other propositions take up such sundry matters as the religious habit, the use of social means of communication, formation, the spiritual life, or the writing of rules. The previously mentioned proposals, however, seem to constitute the theological and missionary emphasis of the synodal concerns, which were then submitted to the pope for his consideration.

The Apostolic Exhortation Vita Consecrata

On March 25, 1996, Pope John Paul II issued the postsynodal apostolic exhortation *Vita Consecrata*.[17] It is not surprising to find that the exhortation embraces the orientations and themes of the *lineamenta* and the synodal propositions. The three aspects of consecrated life that constitute the framework within which it is to be viewed are consecration, communion and mission, all three related by the pope to the mystery of Christ and the Trinity. To take into account new forms of consecrated life, the exhortation generally avoids the word *religious* in favor of *consecrated men and women.*

Distinguishing among the call of laity, priests, and the consecrated, the exhortation repeats the council's image of a special consecration and particular contribution to the life of the church. To the baptized belong activity in the world, to the clergy, ministry, and to consecrated men and women, "special conformity to Christ chaste, poor and obedient."[18]

The renewal of consecrated life in general and of institutes in particular are referred to in terms of the founding charisms and insertion into cultures for purposes of adaptation and evangelization.[19] In this context, the pope takes note of the prophetic witness of the consecrated life, rooted in the following of Christ through the evangelical counsels and related to mission.[20]

A number of things in the exhortation relate especially to priests who follow one form or another of the consecrated life. A general principle is enunciated:

As for priests who profess the evangelical counsels, experience itself shows that the sacrament of holy orders finds a particular fruitfulness in this consecration, inasmuch as it requires and fosters a close union with the Lord.[21]

Even those who follow the contemplative way of life have a part in the life of the church and its mission. This is especially so in their celebration of the Eucharist, in which they "carry out an act of the Church and for the Church," in communion with Christ "who offers himself to the Father for the salvation of the world."[22] The pope emphasizes the contribution that consecrated life makes to the local or particular church. This is a point of special relevance for priests who are members of worldwide communities, both because of their special founding charism and because of the communion that they foster with the universal church. It is in communion with the local bishop, however, that they have to live this special vocation.[23] In all of this, the exhortation is attentive to the special characteristics of consecrated life in these times, to the importance of the local church and the ways in which communities of consecrated life enrich it, to the relation between consecrated life and the church's mission in this day, and to the roots of this life in the mystery of Christ and of the Trinity.

Conclusion

Each religious institute must discern how these teachings can be realized in fidelity to its own particular history and charism. Institutes that have priests in their membership would have to ask where and how this fits with their charism. While these magisterial positions offer no systematic or univocal definitions of either priesthood or religious life, these positions seem to look for an apostolic factor in the practice of ordination among religious, even when this concerns life within a monastery.

Any changes made in the discipline affecting diocesan clergy and their relation to the churches for which they are ordained will have ramifications for the contribution of priests who are members of religious communities. As matters presently stand, the ideal proposed for diocesan priests remains that of the Gregorian reform and, thereby, in large part that of the medieval canons regular. The particular contribution of members of religious bodies follows from the charism of each institute. Consequently, it is necessary to ask how specific founding charisms were and are connected with the exercise of ordained ministry. In the process, a number of issues may emerge. First, there is the question of how necessary ordination is to fulfill this call and service. Secondly, one needs to examine how far suppositions about connections between ordination and ministries have infiltrated the process of foundation and ongoing development in religious communities.

HISTORICAL THEOLOGY

If this is the position of magisterial teaching at the present time, how is the question dealt with in theology? Before looking at current thought, it seems useful to recall theologies of priesthood and of religious life that have merged in the course of history. This is, in fact, a necessary background both for understanding today's theologies and for retrieving founding charisms.

Augustine

Even before Augustine of Hippo, Eusebius of Vercelli (d. 371) had instituted the common life for the clergy of his diocese.[24] But it is to Augustine that the church owes the tenacity of this tradition. As Kevin Seasoltz has explained in the preceding chapter, when Benedict composed his rule for monastic life, he was diffident about the presence of priests in the monastery.[25] Augustine was of a similar opinion, so when he was ordained bishop, he left the garden monastery that he had founded at Hippo.[26]

He then did something, however, that had a profound and lasting effect on clerical and priestly life in the Western church. Augustine invited all the clergy to live a communal life in the bishop's house, and he put together a rule of life for them.[27] The influence of this practice continued throughout the Middle Ages and endures today, not only in the rules of certain congregations, but also in conceptions about priesthood and priestly life. The ideal surfaces in the conciliar decree on priests, *Presbyterorum Ordinis,* both in the section on elements of the common life among priests[28] and in the section on their call to poverty.[29] Earlier redactions of this document had been stronger on both counts, with one version referring to the Jerusalem community as providing an ideal of poverty for priestly life and not just for religious.[30]

For Augustine, the ideal basis for pastoral work was a life lived in imitation of the apostolic life of the early Jerusalem community. This can be clearly seen in his two sermons to the people of Hippo on the life of the clergy, which were occasioned by a scandal involving a priest who made a will before he died, disposing of properties to which he still claimed a title. This was opposed to all that Augustine believed and to the image of common life that he wished to convey to the people for whom he and his priests were pastors. A life of poverty, where none had any possessions of his own, was the very ground of this life, and it was the aspect of the early Jerusalem, or apostolic, community on which he put most emphasis.[31] The clerical state, more an onus or burden than an honor, is assumed *propter populum,* that is, on account of the people, and so must be lived in holiness.[32] To profess holiness is to profess the common life, where one is supported by fellow clergy and can model the Christian ideal put forward in the Acts of the Apostles.[33]

The reason that Augustine wanted the clergy of Hippo to live the monastic life lies in the relationship that he saw between monasticism and the church.[34] The holiness of the church and its union with Christ its head is exemplified in the ideal of the Jerusalem community on the one hand and in the Pauline image of the body made up of many members on the other. The monastery is a more noble member of the body, from which all members profit in the exchange of love that constitutes the life of the body. Augustine also used the imagery of *militia* in speaking of the church and its members. Among the leaders of this militia, he placed both monks and pastors. Whether he spoke of the unity of the body or of the army of Christ, he found the ideal in the monastic community and found it most fitting that pastors exemplify this ideal in their own lives together. This was the beginning of groups of clerics known as "canons regular."[35]

Anselm of Havelburg

In responding to the evangelical awakening of the Middle Ages, and in looking especially to the reform of the clergy, the different groups of canons regular took their inspiration from Augustine. Apart from their clerical identity, what exactly identified their lives and what distinguished this way of life from that of monastic communities is still disputed.

Pastoral work and particularly preaching, both of which did not require priesthood in the prevailing practice of the church up to that time, had a more common and canonically recognized place in the lives of the canons than of the monks. The Praemonstratensian, Anselm of Havelburg, saw this as the distinctive difference between the two. He anticipated the thought of Thomas Aquinas when he expressed the view that the mixed life of contemplation and action is superior to that of contemplation alone. He located its origin in Christ himself as teacher, in a rather unusual exegesis of the gospel story of Jesus' visit to the house of Martha and Mary.[36]

Three states of life can be distinguished in that story: the teacher, the listener, and the one who serves others. If Mary has chosen the better part, it is because she has chosen to listen to the teaching of Christ. In the figure of Christ the teacher, then, Anselm finds the model for the role of the canons and defines the characteristics that make them different from the observants of a monastic rule. In another work, alongside the story of Martha and Mary, he pursues this same theme in the difference that he finds between Peter, the apostle and preacher, and John, who in contemplation rests on Jesus's breast or stands back in contemplation at the door of the empty tomb.[37] This is, in fact, to find in Christ the teacher a model for pastoral and priestly ministry, which can be fostered in the common life of the canonical communities that follow the rule of Augustine.

On the other hand, many canons did not engage much in pastoral work. The polemical works about the respective rights of monks and canons to take on pastoral ministry is not a good guide to the identity of the latter. Some, in fact, saw them as a new type of contemplative community in which, withdrawn from the world, they could pursue the way of perfection.

For the author of the anonymous work *Liber de diversis ordinibus,* the major difference in how a community lives a rule of life was in its location, that is, either in a withdrawn place or in a highly populated area.[38] Monasteries can be found in either situation, as can communities of canons regular. Those who live apart from the general populace can devote their lives more peacefully to prayer. Those who live among the people have to respond to pastoral needs and so must bear with some disruption of the rhythm of their common life. Given the concern of the author with location, there is one interesting difference in what the book says about monks and canons: any monk who lives outside a monastery is not worthy of his profession, whereas this can be tolerated in a canon who is caught up in pastoral care.

Even the defender of the canons' mission to preach, Anselm of Havelburg, in a letter to a fellow bishop, found some advantage in the life of those communities that live a more withdrawn life with time aplenty for prayer and study. In a rather idyllic description of the common life lived under such conditions, he compared it to life in the manger of Bethlehem:

> In my manger of Havelburg, I live myself as a poor man of Christ, together with my brothers who are also the poor of Christ. Some construct a wall with towers to ward off the enemy; others stand on guard to fend off the attacks of the pagans; others devote themselves to the divine office, daily awaiting martyrdom; not a few through fasting and prayer purify the souls which they wish to restore to God; finally, still others dedicate their lives to reading and holy meditation, bent on imitating the example of the saints. But all of us are naked and poor, all of us follow Christ naked and poor according to the full measure of our strength.[39]

A New Priestly Ideal

For both monastic life and canonical life, the question arises as to what role priesthood played in a community without external apostolic obligations, and what reason could be given for the practice of ordaining some members to the priesthood.[40] Perhaps the monastic ideal of ritually expressing one's inner affinity with Christ in his sacrifice and consecration—an ideal more abundantly embraced by the Carthusians than by others—applied to canons as well as to monks in the evolution of the link between religious life and priesthood.

Dom Jean Leclercq has documented situations in which monks were more frequently ordained to priesthood.[41] In doing this, he points out two significant factors. First, the conferring of priesthood rarely came early in the life of a monk. When given at the initiative of superiors or bishops, it was usually a recognition of the virtue and devout contemplative life of the ordained.[42] Rather than being the conferring of an ecclesiastical honor on the person, the ordaining of a holy person was an honor for the clerical state. Second, the purpose of such ordination was to enable the monk in question to celebrate the sacrifice of the mass, even in private, and no pastoral work was attached. To allow the monk to say mass alone was to give him more freedom for a life of solitude and prayer. This is what Leclercq calls an *ascetic* as distinct from a *pastoral* priesthood, but it could as readily be called a *contemplative* one. Hugh of St. Victor, himself a canon and not a monk, sums it up well:

> That these monks may be able to live internally and with greater quiet, the orders of divine ministry are given to them by special concession, not to exercise a charge among the people, but to be able to celebrate internally the communion of the sacrament of God.[43]

Thomas Aquinas

St. Thomas Aquinas made a comparison between the religious life and the episcopacy on the basis of the pursuit of perfection. The background to the theological comparison he made was the ministry and the life of the mendicant friars, especially the Dominicans. For Aquinas, perfection was measured by the degree of one's charity.[44] He described religious life as directed to the pursuit of perfection for the sake of one's own salvation, whereas the ministry of the bishop was one of dedication to the salvation of others.[45] Religious, by reason of how he described their state of life, are committed by vow to a lifelong pursuit of the perfection of charity and are taken up with observances, prayer, study, and discipline that lead to their own holiness. Ordination, however, is ordered to the service of others in ministry and requires that one be able to lead others on the way of charity.

Since a bishop is called to a full and lifelong engagement in this ministry, the candidate for this order has to be one who has already attained a high or perfect degree of love of God and neighbor. Indeed, unless it proves impossible for him to exercise his episcopal ministry, it is not right for a bishop to give up the exercise of the episcopacy to join a religious community.[46] If the candidate is a religious, however, he will combine the observance of his rule of life with his ministry, as far as that is possible, since it contributes fittingly to his personal holiness.[47]

Aquinas considers presbyters and deacons as persons committed to a lesser ministry than that of bishop, for it is held in dependency and subordination. Being less engaged in ministry, they have a lesser obligation to pursue perfection.[48] This indeed reflects a historical situation in which clergy often had pursuits other than ministry, and where it was still an open question as to whether the duty and right to preach went with ordination to the priesthood. As is well known, Aquinas defined priesthood in sacramental terms, primarily as the power to consecrate the body and blood of Christ in the Eucharist, acting in his person. While holiness of life befits such a sacramental task, Aquinas equated the relation of the minister to Christ, not with imaging Christ in his person, but rather with imaging Christ's action in the priest's sacramental action.[49]

The unfinished *Summa* of Thomas Aquinas lacks a treatise on orders. There is enough in his work, however, to show that his vision of the church and of ministry is marked by the Pseudo-Dionysian vision of order and hierarchy while distinguishing between the spiritual hierarchy of monk, baptized, and catechumen, and the ecclesiastical hierarchy of bishop, presbyter, and deacon, Aquinas held that the two converged in the person of the bishop. His *Ecclesiastical Hierarchy* describes the bishop or *hierarch* as one "divinely inspired and godlike, one learned in all sacred knowledge, and in whom the whole hierarchy is plainly perfected and recognized."[50]

In line with this thinking, Aquinas believed that the apostles and the prelates, as a sacred authority, order the life of the church and that the grace of Christ comes to others through them. This Pseudo-Dionysian vision was modified, however, because of the centrality of the Eucharist in the church and because Aquinas defined the sacrament of orders in terms of eucharistic action. The Eucharist is the central sacrament and action of the church, containing both the reality and symbol of Christ's body and blood and the spiritual reality of the mystical body, in which all are united in Christ and in anticipation of glory.[51] The sacrament of priesthood confers the power to celebrate the Eucharist. Preaching, the power to absolve, and the *cura animarum,* or pastoral responsibility for designated persons, come with the jurisdiction given by the bishop, to whom these functions properly belong.

Thus did Thomas Aquinas distinguish between the power of order, whose summit is the priesthood, and the power of jurisdiction, belonging to bishops and, in a particular way, to the pope. It was the principle of hierarchy adopted from Pseudo-Dionysius, however, that served to join rather than separate the canonically distinguished powers of order and of jurisdiction exercised by the bishops, helped by other clergy, in the work of sanctifying the faithful.[52]

In examining the thirteenth-century quarrel between secular clergy and mendicants over the right of the mendicants to preach and hear confessions,[53] one is struck by the practical reasoning of Thomas.[54] He is concerned in this dispute, not with eucharistic ministry, but with the ministry of word and penance. He clearly addresses the pastoral need for preachers and confessors who live holy lives and who are well versed in doctrine and the knowledge of the Scriptures in a way that many parochial clergy were not. These ministers are not attached to a local church; rather, with the proper jurisdiction from prelates, they can come as needed to the aid of local priests and the faithful. Thomas is also ready to offer scriptural warrants for such a ministry, pointing to passages in the New Testament that show that the early church knew of just such ministers of the Word who belonged to no particular church.

As for the life of the friar, the main relation between his religious life and his activity as preacher or as teacher lay in what Aquinas had to say about the comparison between contemplative and active life.[55] The essence of the active life is service in charity to one's neighbor, but the finest form of service is contributing to another's spiritual welfare. The highest form of religious life is found in institutes founded to teach and to preach. There the contemplative and active lives converge in one, and they do so in a way that is closest to the perfection of bishops.[56] This is in keeping with his thought that *doctrina* combines both the contemplative and the active lives, contemplating the truth and teaching the truth.[57] He dubs the foundation of religious orders for the purposes of preaching and of hearing confessions "most fitting" *(convenientissum)*[58] and sees that their members' religious observance makes them apt ministers,[59] whose work is a good and needed supplement to that of parochial clergy.[60] On the other hand, it is not religious life itself that gives the right to teach and to preach, but the reception of order or of the proper jurisdiction from higher prelates.[61]

St. Thomas's view in all this seems to be that the care of souls, inclusive of the ministry of the Word, comes from jurisdiction. It is fittingly given to those ordained to the priesthood, but it can also be given in a supplementary fashion to others, who may meet needs in a way not often within the capacity of a local pastor. The care of souls is first and foremost the charge of the bishop, in which he has some helpers in lower orders and among religious. On the other hand, religious who are founded for the ministry of the Word and are committed to the observance of the evangelical counsels and to study and prayer are fitting participants in what is essentially an episcopal ministry.

While there is no clearly theological connection between ordained ministry and religious life, there is a relation among contemplation, embracing prayer and study, and an active life of service. Given the pastoral need or advantage for the friars to act with authority when engaged in preaching and teaching, ordination could provide a sound authoritative basis for the work, but so also could jurisdiction. Both give the necessary authorization to share in the episcopal ministry, in the teaching and preaching of the Word.[62] That hearing confessions is added to this in question 188, article. 4, corresponds to the pastoral facts of the era. A new discipline of penance was being forged, one that did not require public penance, that could be more frequently administered, and that was very practically joined with the preaching of the Word that brought believers to contrition and confession.

Bonaventure

As is well known, Francis and his first followers did not see themselves as a community of priests, though they did engage in preaching and in bringing people to penance and conversion. In approving their way of life, Pope Innocent III had also given authority to their preaching by allowing them the small tonsure *(corona parvula)*. Rather than a clerical tonsure, this seems to have been a kind of *ad hoc* solution adopted by Innocent to save them from the suspicions often directed against lay preachers at the time. In the course of the thirteenth century, however, church authority put more and more restrictions on lay preaching, as well as on whatever practice there was of laypersons hearing confessions.[63] As a result, the ministries of preaching, teaching, and confessing practiced by friars required ordination, and this affected the entire composition of the order.

Bonaventure does not stand for the whole Franciscan tradition, but as theologian and as master general, he put his own twist on its meaning and implementation.[64] In explaining why Francis himself had revised the original rule, Bonaventure gave three reasons: to imitate the virtues of Christ as do the cenobites, to contemplate Christ as do the hermits, and to imitate Christ in saving souls as in the exercise of priestly ministry.[65] According to Bonaventure, the ministry of preaching and of hearing confessions becomes a task of the order through religious profession,[66] this then being a community goal and purpose, which of its nature required both ordination and learning. The relation of the friars to the Holy See was also important to Bonaventure on this score, in keeping with his ecclesiology, which described the pope as the first and supreme pastor of every particular church.[67] This was Bonaventure's practical and theological response to the quarrel over the rights of mendicants to exercise the ministry of Word and penance.

Bonaventure's vision of order comes to the fore in the *Breviloquium* in his treatment of the sacrament of order.[68] As the divine principle, bringing redemption and restoration to a fallen world, the Word Incarnate instituted the sacraments as remedies for sin. Since creation and redemption are brought about through the Word according to the order of divine wisdom, this order needed to be reflected in the dispensation of the sacraments. Hence, the power to administer the others is confided to some persons through the sacrament of order. The power of order in sacramental dispensation itself, however, fits within a greater dispensation of order. Tonsure serves as the sign that sets off the candidate from the rest of the people. It represents a total dedication to the service of God, cutting off temporal appetites and elevating the mind to God. After tonsure comes the ordination as psalmist, for through the psalms one is instructed in divine praise. Together, the seven orders combine the powers to purify and to illumine, leading to the priesthood, which is the power to confect the sacrament of the altar, in whose participation both purgation and illumination of the soul are perfected.

This view of order shows how Bonaventure fits the sacramental into a vision of spiritual order. It also shows how he has subsumed the tonsure into this vision as a preparation for priestly ordination, something that fits his understanding of the Franciscans as a clerical order. The view is perfected in the way in which he relates the sacrament to the power of the episcopacy, itself hierarchically ordered through bishops, archbishops, patriarchs, and the pope.[69] The episcopacy, in fact, is that eminent or excellent power to which all powers in the church are subject and by which all things are regulated. Thus, it belongs to the episcopacy to ordain, to lay on hands in confirmation, to conse-crate nuns and abbots, and to dedicate churches.

Situating the priesthood in the church in this way, the power of order is subjected to the power of jurisdiction. Both, however, are harmoniously blended into what is ultimately a spiritual understanding of power, ordered to the perfecting of the spiritual life. Order is not be conferred, and neither order nor jurisdiction ought to be exercised, except by those in whom the spiritual hierarchy of perfection parallels the ecclesiastical hierarchy.

This spiritual perception of the place of the sacrament of order in the church harmonizes with the Franciscan ideal of following Christ. As a fol-lower of Francis, Bonaventure found poverty in the discipleship of Christ as the key to the evangelical way of life. He expresses this clearly in his writings on the Franciscan order, which explain and defend the way of poverty. To be poor was first of all to be poor in the following of the poor Christ. To be poor was to love the poor with the compassion of Christ. To be poor was to possess nothing, to work with one's hands, to beg. To be poor was to be open in heart to the wonder of the world. To be poor was to count oneself as nothing in rela-tions with others.

All of this comes out in his writings on the way of the friars and on Francis. In the *Itinerarium mentis in Deum,* however, the completion of this life in contemplation becomes clear. It is exemplified in Francis' reception of the stigmata on Mount Alverna, which showed his complete oneness with the crucified Christ. What is also shown there is the way to contemplation and union with the crucified Christ along the sixfold way of purification and illu-mination. The relation to creatures is that of forgoing attachment to them in order to find in them the revelation of the divinity.

It is in this context that Bonaventure's theological statement on poverty in the work *De Excellentia Magisterii Christi*[70] can be placed, a statement to which he wishes clerics, bishops, and religious to carefully attend in order to truly understand *doctrina* and evangelical perfection. Commenting on the beat-itude *Beati pauperes spiritu,* he asserts that poverty is the very foundation of all good in heeding the teaching of Christ and following him on the way of truth.

There are two aspects to poverty. The first and most fundamental pos-ture is that of thinking nothing of oneself, *nihil se reputare.* In this sense,

poverty is practically synonymous with humility and underlies all one's relations with God and with others. The second aspect is the readiness to renounce
all worldly goods. In this way the avarice of attachment is removed and,
thereby, that which hinders one in the following of Christ and his teaching.
This may be said to constitute Bonaventure's theological statement on the primacy of poverty in the search for evangelical perfection and the preparation
for contemplation. It is more fundamental to religious life than that which
either he or Aquinas includes under the vow of poverty when they explain the
three vows of poverty, chastity, and obedience.

In the theologies, then, of both Aquinas and Bonaventure, there is a
strong practical element. This derives, in fact, from the origins of the ministry
of the Word in the lives of the mendicants, albeit in different ways for
Dominic and for Francis. From practice, both Thomas and Bonaventure knew
of the need for preachers of the Word who do not have a fixed and localized
cura animarum. They both were ready to find justification for this type of
ministry in the New Testament, to give it a firm ecclesiastical hold through the
jurisdiction given by the bishops or the pope, and to find theological justification for it within a concept of order and within a theology of the states of life.
How much Bonaventure changed the original Franciscan ideal of evangelical
life and preaching in the process is left to the discussion of historians of the
Franciscan order.[71]

French School

Historians contend that three major factors played a part in Pierre de
Bérulle's foundation of the French Oratory.[72] First and foremost, in light of the
state of the church in seventeenth-century France, he wanted to put his efforts
into the reform of the clergy. Second, his basic theological intuition in this
enterprise was what he saw as the intimate union between the priest and Christ
the mediator. Third, he wanted a society of priests at the service of the diocese
and its bishop and could not find an institutional formula of religious life that
would suit the purpose of the priests of the Oratory. Nonetheless, he consistently raised the question of their making vows that committed them to
priestly work in the service of the church and related this new foundation to
the history of religious orders.

Sacrifice, in communion with the sacrifice of Christ, is at the heart of his
vision of the priesthood. This is not, however, understood in a narrow sacramental or liturgical sense, albeit the celebration of the mass is at the center of
the priest's ministry and of his life. Sacrifice is understood as a gift of self and
an act of mediation on behalf of others. Both aspects are operative in the entire
ministry of the priest, in Word and pastoral care as well as liturgy. They are also
the key to a priestly spirituality founded on communion with Christ as priest
and victim in his work of mediation.[73] The influence of Pseudo-Dionysius is

notable in Bérulle's theology and in his spiritual teaching. The perfection of the priesthood in the order of mediation has to carry with it a perfection in the spiritual order, so that it constitutes a higher calling in the church.[74]

Bérulle's view of the factors involved in priestly ministry and life is well represented in a text now readily available in English, "A Letter on the Priesthood."[75] In this letter, there is a clear picture of Bérulle's understanding of the difference between priests and laity in the church, of the priest's role, and of his exalted call to holiness. Bérulle looks back sadly to a time when there was great holiness in the entire church, a time, that is, when it was well guided by priests. These were men who "radiated only holy things and dealt only with holy things, leaving worldly things to the worldly." It was God's purpose that authority, holiness, and doctrine be God's mark on the clergy. The writer laments that in his time the three are pulled asunder, authority residing in prelates, holiness among religious, and doctrine being left to the schools. God has thus by providential disposition preserved these marks in the church, but the reform undertaken by the Oratory is intended to unify them again in the clergy.

> This is why, writes Bérulle, we are gathered together: in order to reclaim our inheritance, to recover once again our rights, to enjoy our legitimate succession, to have the Son of God as our portion, to share in his Spirit, and through his Spirit to share in his light, holiness and authority, which are communicated to prelates by Jesus Christ and through them to priests.

When he reflects on the history of the church, he finds a strong affinity between his ideas of priestly holiness and the dedication expressed in religious communities that bind themselves to the service of God by solemn vows.[76] In that sense, then, the history of the priesthood and that of religious life are really inseparable when it comes to finding ways of realizing the holiness implied in the priestly vocation. Apparently, therefore, it was natural for him to think about asking the members of the Oratory to make vows that would express this dedication.

However, because he had a high regard for the place of bishops and the local church in the scheme of things, he did not want a form of religious consecration that would commit the new institute directly to the service of the Holy See.[77] Though he admired the dedication of the Jesuits, this aspect of their lives made them an unsuitable model for his purposes. He considered affinities with the Italian Oratory and some other clerical bodies but never resolved the matter canonically. Whatever else vows achieved, they had to bring about a stronger dedication to the service of the bishop in the service of the local church. The first vow that he instituted was to renounce church benefices, and the second, to obey the bishop, and under him the superior of the institute. After consideration of the suitability of the traditional religious vows, Bérulle turned to a vow of servitude. This he interpreted as a complete gift of self in the service of God, in communion with Jesus Christ and with Mary. Because of what it expressed, this seemed to give him some intellectual and spiritual satisfaction, but it was not the kind of vow that could readily be given canonical and outer form. Thus, it disappeared after the death of Bérulle himself.[78]

Monsieur Jean-Jacques Olier, upon whose ideas the Sulpician community was founded, consolidated Bérulle's ideal of priestly holiness by writing of the special union of the priest with Christ, priest and victim. Olier's major influence on priestly life came through his conferences on the seven clerical orders, published posthumously as a treatise by Monsieur Tronson.[79] In Olier, as in Bérulle, the understanding of priesthood is not purely sacramental, but embraces the entire work of priests for the sanctification of the faithful. At the beginning of the part of the treatise dealing with the priesthood, Olier singles out as the foundation of the priest's eminent dignity its sublime participation in the sovereignty of God over creatures.[80] Participation in the holiness of God, in union with the Son, Jesus Christ, is at the heart of priesthood and sacrifice. Sacrificing his Son as an act of divine sovereignty in restoring holiness to the world, God now unites the priest with himself and with the victim, Jesus.[81]

As far as his powers are concerned, the priest shares with God the power to produce the Son in the sacrament of the altar and in the lives of the faithful.[82] He also shares the power to give or send the Spirit for the sanctification of the church. Finally, he has the power to give the Eternal Father himself in giving Jesus Christ in the Communion of the church. All of this calls for a profound holiness of life—a holiness that is nourished by the adoration of Christ in the Blessed Sacrament.

Union with Christ pervades the priest's entire spiritual life. Writing, for example, of patience, Olier says that clerics, "being perfect Christians chosen from the midst of the church to assist before the tabernacle of God," have special reason to practice this virtue. This is because "in Jesus Christ and with Jesus Christ, they are both priests and victims for the sins of the world." While this gives importance to their celebration of the sacrifice of the mass, it is a union that pervades their entire lives, for they are in their persons and in all things "sacraments and representations" of Jesus Christ.[83]

The sublimity of this calling is likewise portrayed by John Eudes, who in the course of his life left the Oratory to found the society of priests known as the Congregation of the Hearts of Jesus and Mary. Eudes describes priests as other Christs, "walking among men" and representing his authority and perfections. He calls on the *Celestial Hierarchy* of Pseudo-Dionysius to speak of them also as visible gods. In that work, St. Dionysius invests you with these three attributes: You are gods because you take the place of God in this world and are clothed with His qualities, His prerogatives, and powers. You are children of gods because you are children of your bishops who in turn are gods in yet a higher degree than you. You are fathers of gods because you are fathers of Christians who likewise are gods, though in a lower degree than you.[84]

The last sentence shows that in the writers of the Oratory there is both an appreciation of the dignity of all Christians and a vision of the connections between the priesthood of the ordained and the priesthood of the baptized. For example, in an exercise for faithful assisting at Holy Mass, Jean Eudes writes eloquently of their call to be one with Jesus Christ as priest and as victim and of Christ's desire to dwell in them through sacramental communion.[85] This does not take away from ideas on the higher calling of priests. It does, however, put these thoughts more in balance, for it indicates to what end priesthood and ministry are ordered.

In sum, the contribution of the French School derives from a sublime vision of the priesthood, which of its nature constitutes a higher calling and requires a higher degree of holiness. They were not unaware, Bérulle especially, of how religious bodies, a rule of life, and vows had contributed in the past to the holiness and to the reform of the clergy. Though the canonical provisions of their era were an obstacle to finding a form of vowed life that would meet with their purposes, they nonetheless took elements from religious life and from its history to give a constitution and a way of life to members of the Oratory.

The Sulpician ideal exercised a strong influence in the later foundation of clerical missionary institutes. Such founders as Alphonsus Liguori (Redemptorists) and Eugene de Mazenod (Oblates of Mary Immaculate) wanted a reform of the church in times of distress. One of the particular objectives of the reform was bringing the gospel to the poor, whom they saw as abandoned by society and church alike. Preaching and a reform of clergy could be promoted by bringing a group of zealous priests together. Like other founders, in due course they found that binding their followers by the evangelical counsels and vows served both their mission and their personal sanctification. Both reflected the Sulpician ideal of the priesthood and the ideas of Bérulle. However, they employed these ideals in going beyond the service of the local church. The communities they forged did not replace the diocesan clergy. Rather, in the face of the needs of poor people in various parts of the world, they lived their charisms through the exercise of ministries that complemented the work of stable, local clergy, free to move beyond the confines of any one diocese. They never quite resolved the tension, either in theory or in practice, between the ideal of missionary mobility and the desire for life in stable communities of religious practice that was, in large part, modeled on monastic ideals and forms of life.

Conclusion

At this stage, it is possible to list some of the theological talking-points that emerge from this look at traditions and to see how present theology treats similar issues. Our survey of historical theology has presented four different views of the priesthood that served to link priesthood and religious life as well as four corresponding views of religious life.

The theologies of priesthood were: the Augustinian, the contemplative, the mendicant, and the Sulpician. First, there is the vision of Augustine that the clergy at the service of a local church ought to mirror in their own communal life the Jerusalem community, which served as the ideal for all Christian life. Second, there is the contemplative theology of priesthood. In the confusion of sorting out the perspectives of the monks and the perspectives of the canons regular in the Middle Ages, what stands out is the contemplative, largely monastic, perception of the eucharistic celebration of a devout ascetic who has reached the realm of contemplation. In the monk-priest, there is a convergence of the sacramental and personal representation of communion in the sacrifice of Christ. Third, there is also the view of priesthood associated with the mendicant way of life, developed by Aquinas and Bonaventure. Ordination is the needed authorization to preach and to hear confessions among Christ's poor, an authorization that comes in a particular way through the jurisdiction exercised by the Bishop of Rome. In Aquinas, this relates to his understanding of the episcopacy as a call to lead others to perfection and to his views on the superior nature of the mixed life. In Bonaventure, it relates to the ideal of the spiritual life, which, on the one hand, he saw exemplified in Francis and on the other in the person of the bishop, in whom ecclesiastical and spiritual hierarchy converge. Finally, there is the Sulpician view of the priest as mediator, priest, and victim along with Jesus Christ. The priest is a sacramental representation of Jesus Christ, not only in his liturgical action but also in his pastoral ministry and in his person.

In these theologies, one is struck by their attention to the practical necessities and realities of ministry.[86] None of the authors examined was caught up in pure theory. They all relate the practice of their time to what they saw as church tradition. For Augustine and for Bérulle, the need was for a devout and reformed clergy in a local church. For Thomas Aquinas and Bonaventure, the need was for a group of preachers and ministers of penance not tied to a fixed pastorate or "care of souls." The missionary congregations that found inspiration in Bérulle or Olier were able, in turn, to adapt their thought to the work of missionaries, who at that time were free of fixed benefice.

The theologies of religious life that mixed with these perceptions of priesthood were the Augustinian, formulated first by Augustine and then by the medieval Augustinian canons; the monastic; the mendicant; and the modern missionary view, which drew in some measure on all the preceding. The first put forward the vision of the common life, lived in poverty. The second expressed a vision of withdrawal from the world, to give oneself to the service of God in prayer, contemplation, and liturgy. The third was a missionary view of a community of poor preachers, whose main purpose was to bring the discipleship of Christ to fruition among the faithful through example, preaching, teaching, and hearing confessions. The fourth seemed to want to combine the missionary purpose of the mendicants with the common life in the Augustinian tradition and with the desire to withdraw for personal sanctification found in the monastic ideal. In each of these views of religious community, evangelical poverty played a significant role. Each likewise accommodated the exercise of priestly ministry to its particular view of the goal of the evangelical life in following and making Jesus Christ known.

THEOLOGIES OF RELIGIOUS LIFE AND PRIESTHOOD TODAY

Some questions inevitably emerge from this tradition in relation to contemporary ecclesiologies, theologies of priesthood, and theologies of religious life. The starting point of pastoral and practical necessity that emerged in looking at how past theologies developed is also vital in contemporary developments and their assimilation of traditions.

The theologies of priesthood written today are highly historical in format and exposition. Account is taken of various developments in church ordering, seeing them in relation to various ecclesiastical, cultural, and philosophical currents.[87] The effort at systematization is a highly uncertain one, despite the vast quantity of writing guided by newer theological perceptions and new realities within church communities. The priesthood is usually related to the local church, while the pastoral role exercised by priests is related to particular communities of faithful. This results in a situation where the role of the ordained who are not so located has little meaning in the system. For priests who are religious, they either must fit their ministry into the direct service of parish or diocese, retreat to a purely sacramental understanding of the priesthood, or leave open the question of where they belong in the order of ministry.

Since the issue of priesthood and religious life involves both *ways of life* and *ministry,* it is helpful to open this section by looking at an important author who relates these topics, namely, Hans Urs von Balthasar. After that, some pertinent directions in the treatment of priesthood and ordination, as well as developments in the theologies of religious life, will be considered. It will then be possible to outline the praxis of retrieving the charisms of religious bodies and see what this means both to their ministry and to the place of ordination among clerical religious.

The Contribution of Hans Urs von Balthasar

In contemporary theology on the states of life in the church, one of the more fascinating voices is that of Hans Urs von Balthasar.[88] The fascination lies not so much in his resolution of questions as in the way that he raises them and in the boldness of his attempt to find a balance that respects each calling. His questions may serve in some measure to sort out the issues already raised.

Even before the Second Vatican Council, von Balthasar looked for a theology of the states of life that would recognize the call to holiness and participation in the mystery of Christ in all of them, without privileging any one of them in this regard. There are two foundations for his thinking. The first is laid with his idea of the "suprasacramental." By this term he does not mean what comes without sacrament. Rather, he refers to that holiness to which all sacraments are ordained and in which all members of the church come together, through whatever means and along whatever path. The second foundation is the image and reality of sending. As the Son was sent by the Father to serve others, so all the members of the church are sent for the service of others, according to their particular charism and state of life. On these foundations he builds theologies for the particular states of life of the ordained, of the married, of religious, and of secular institutes.[89]

In line with this, he offers reflections on the spirituality of officeholders in the church. While their status does not give them any superiority over others, they could not rightly live out their charism without aspiring to close union with Jesus Christ. For this reason, von Balthasar believes that the way in which order and the development of religious life in the church have meshed is both inevitable and providential. He underlines the eschatological significance of religious life as a particular charism, connected with order or not. This means not only that it points to the fulfilment of the kingdom in glory, but also that in the present it is an evangelical and prophetic style of life, calling human and ecclesiastical endeavor into question in the light of the gospel and of the promise of the kingdom. The vocation of the married life lies in the fact that it is a human and natural calling, caught up by grace into the service of God's kingdom and the enrichment of the church.

One of von Balthasar's overriding concerns was with the emergence of secular institutes for laypersons. He saw them as one of the signs of the times and as holding great potential for the mission of the church, especially since the church and the gospel had lost the place and influence in the Western world that they had had for many centuries. The hope for the future lies now in the presence of believers in the midst of secular life as a leaven. Indeed, in recent decades this state of life has been given recognition by church authority and even has found its place in the proceedings of the special Synod on Consecrated Life in 1994. The quest for adequate canonical formulations is not without troubling connotations, lest these institutes be simply subsumed into the traditional categories and legislation affecting religious life. Their charismatic and prophetic service, however, helps us expand our views of the nature and qualities of the evangelical life. This, too, may have some implications for institutes that have characteristically joined ordination with religious profession.

Given von Balthasar's concerns, certain theological factors emerge. These can be considered under the two headings of priesthood and religious life. Then it can be asked how they relate.

Theologies of Priesthood

First, order and priesthood are placed within the context of church community and are related to other charisms and ministries that are possessed and exercised by other members of the baptized. The Pseudo-Dionysian (even in its Thomistic form) and the Sulpician models of priesthood are both inadequate because they separate the ordained ministry too radically from other ministries and defy efforts at a collaborative and communion ecclesiology. The desire to place ordained ministry within the context of the church has led theologians to concentrate on the role of the ordained within the local community, be this diocese or parish. An ecclesiology centered in the local church as sacramental realization of the mystery of Christ is often the key to a theology of ordained ministry.[90] In this regard, a study of the historical development of ordination rites and contact with Orthodox ecclesiology have been vital contributions.[91] On the other hand, ministries not rooted in the stability of a local church are not allowed for in the theology of order, even though this kind of service has been integral to the life of the church since New Testament times.

Second, priesthood is no longer seen simply as the sacred power of sacramental celebration joined with a power of jurisdiction in the government and pastoral care of the church. It is described as a charism, endowed for the service of the church and given sacramental expression for the benefit of the life and ordering of ecclesial communities.[92] With a greater sensitivity to the variety of charisms in the church, one can see the ordained ministry as integrated with other charisms, and not tied uniquely to ordination. When the call to religious life is likewise seen as charismatic and religious bodies are spoken of as having a collective charism, priesthood and religious life fit together into an ecclesiology of service and communion.

Third, the call to holiness associated with priesthood finds a more balanced expression. While priestly ministry that is not grounded in a virtuous life remains grotesque, it need not be seen as a call to a higher degree of sanctity or one that gives a priest domination over others. As the Second Vatican Council taught, the call to holiness and to participation in the Pasch of Christ is rooted in baptism. It is a call lived out with the aid of different gifts of the Spirit in different states of life and in different forms of service for the building up of Christ's body and the proclamation of his name.

Fourth, the reservation of the right to preach to the clergy, given firm juridical and theological expression in the development of the mendicant orders, is now opened to fresh consideration.[93] Leaving aside the question of the homily at liturgy, it is quite clear that the charism of public teaching and preaching is not inextricably associated with ordination. Requiring ordination for the ministry of preaching, assumed by both the mendicant and modern forms of apostolically ordered religious life, does not have solid scriptural or theological foundation. It is rather a disciplinary decision that was made at a particular time when there was the threat of heresy associated with lay preaching. This does not diminish the conjunction of sacrament, preaching, and pastoral care in the ministry of the ordained enunciated by the Second Vatican Council. It simply says that there are sacramental, Word, and pastoral ministries that are not tied to ordination and that are to be given proper practical and canonical recognition in the life of the church.

With all this said, however, one of the questions that has continued to defy clear theological explanation is the council's statement—since then frequently repeated by the magisterium—that the ministerial priesthood and the baptismal priesthood differ not only in degree but in kind.[94] In its decree on the ministry and life of priests, the council associated this difference with the sacramental link of order to the headship of Christ over the body of the church.[95] Some theologians have tried to relate this to the charism of oversight of church activity, but this hardly does justice to the sacramental dimension. Pope John Paul II continually associates it with the nuptial imagery of bride and bridegroom, taking the sacrament of order as sacramental representation of Christ's relation to the church as bridegroom. From a canonical perspective, this distinction raises the issue of what in the ministry of the church is to be restricted to the priest.

What needs to be looked at in facing this issue is the specific contribution of the sacrament of order to the church, not what makes its holders distinct from others. All sacramental theology is ecclesiological. Each sacrament has to be considered primarily as an expression of the church as a community in Christ and in his Spirit. What the individual receives, by way of gift and charism, is received as a member of the church. In looking thus at ordination, what needs to be worked out is what it says about the nature and vitality of the church. One has to ask, not what powers it gives to recipients, but what the sacrament signifies about the nature of the church, especially about its apostolic tradition and its catholic communion.[96] While this is today most readily related to the local church, the practices and theologies of the past lead us to ask what the ordination of ministers not tied to local churches may mean in this regard.

Meaning of Ordination

The variant meanings present in the liturgical act of ordination have not been given sufficient consideration in current theology. The insight that places ordination within a local church, and for the service of the local church, is correct and important. This was the meaning of ordination in the church's early centuries. But when ordination was given for specific activities, such as sacramental celebration or preaching the gospel, rather than for ministry within local churches, the action took on new meaning. Is this an aberration?

In some respects it certainly was, and, unfortunately, the postmedieval scholastic theology that gave it a basis spoke almost exclusively of the powers conferred. Some new insight into ordination might emerge if ordaining is seen as a *sending*. This is more clearly the case with a mission to preach among those who need to hear the Word or to bring the gospel to others. In response to charism and to need, a person may be sent from within one's own community to build up the faith and the communion in Christ of others. This, too, can be given a church-related sacramental expression. A biblical basis for this view can be retrieved from the apostolic ministry of Paul and others and from the sending of apostles and preachers for the founding or strengthening of other communities. While in the New Testament context it cannot be seen as evidence for the sacrament of order, there was prayer in community and a laying on of hands associated with such sending or commissioning. These are elements that could be retrieved into the sacramental economy of the church when ordination is more directly a sending to preach than it is an appointment to sacramental function.

On this score, polity could again risk associating preaching too closely with the sacrament of order, failing to recognize preaching as a charism given to some of the baptized. Ordination primarily for a ministry of preaching beyond the confines of the local church would, therefore, need a process of discernment to recognize the occasions when a sacramental and liturgical sending would be beneficial to the life of particular communities and to the communion between churches. Adaptability in ordination rites would be needed to fit these special circumstances.

Religious Life

Writings on the religious life since the Second Vatican Council are voluminous and touch on many subjects. Even in restricting attention to theologies of the religious life, the contributions are many and of very uneven quality. Some surveys given in the period immediately preceding the special Synod on Consecrated Life are helpful in sorting out trends and developments.[97]

In a survey done for the Union of Superiors General, Bruno Secondin finds three core issues in the development of religious life since the Second Vatican Council: (a) the specific identity of religious life; (b) the part taken by religious in the mission of the church; and (c) the relation of religious to the world. For his part, García Paredes presents the key questions about religious life under three other headings: (a) the stimulus given by religious life to the mission of the church; (b) religious life as communion; and (c) the charismatic identity of religious families. His last two points respond to the question of specific identity raised by Secondin, and his first embraces Secondin's distinct points of mission and relation to the world.

Using the image of consecration to explain the specific character of religious life was a choice guided by the documents of the Second Vatican Council. There, consecration was applied first to the incarnation and baptism of Christ himself, and then to the mystery of the baptism of Christians. On that basis, it was used of the priesthood and of religious life. Secondin points to the influence of Pie-Raymond Régamey, who endeavored in his post-Vatican II theology to explain what is specific about religious consecration.[98] It was Régamey's opinion that the theology of religious life could be totally based on this concept. He explained religious profession as a consecration. It configures the professed to Christ in the form of a witness publicly given and recognized, albeit in different forms according to the charism of each institute. More specifically he said that consecration made the professed living signs, in the service of the church, of the presence of heavenly goods in the world. As living public witnesses to this truth, they serve to keep it alive in the minds of all, a matter of great importance in face of the secularization of modern existence.

Other writers, while they kept the image of consecration, did not think that it sufficed as a concept on which to build a theology of religious life. Several, principally Leonardo Boff,[99] Thaddeus Matura,[100] and Jean-Marie Tillard,[101] found the notion of gospel radicalism particularly appealing as a way of expressing the fundamental impulse of religious or evangelical forms of life in the church.[102] As an expression of the radicality of all Christian life, it is even a quasi sacrament of the dedication to God as Absolute in the midst of human society. The images of *sequela Christi* and of the imitation of Christ help to spell out its nature. Matura writes:

> The entire scope of Jesus' radical demands can be summed up…in a few essential points: the primacy of Jesus, unconditional love of neighbor, freedom vis-à-vis possessions, and sharing with the poor.[103]

At the same time, he points to celibacy as primary in expressing a radical choice for the kingdom of God.[104] In this sense, it is essential to understanding the nature of religious life.

Tillard's work is more theological in the classical sense. His writing on religious life fits into his total plan, pursued in several tomes, of writing a communion ecclesiology. While he, too, builds on the notion of a radical following of the gospel in response to Jesus' call addressed to all believers, he links this in a stronger way with the idea of *koinonia* or communion. In the early Jerusalem community he finds an exemplary case of living out the radical call in community and in hospitality. He points to communities that pursue this urge together as prophetic and eschatological signs for the whole church. In communion with the bishops and all the baptized, they bring the urgency of the gospel into the world, according to the inspiration of the Spirit and in the charismatic freedom typical of each particular institute.

Despite its continued use in magisterial teaching and in the title of the special synod of 1994, the image of consecration is not strongly favored in theological writings as the foundation for a theology of religious life. The major problem with the image lies in the fact that it seems to lead inexorably to a comparative approach. Thus, the message of the synod, the propositions, and the apostolic exhortation speak of a *more* "radical" or "intimate" consecration through religious profession. This reverts to the language of greater and lesser callings that Vatican II actually wanted to avoid.[105] The image of consecration helped to give some sense of the rich variety of Christian life undertaken in communion with Christ's paschal mystery and mission, and rooted in baptism. Once it is qualified by adjectives such as *higher, deeper, more intimate* or *special,* however, it begins to belie its original purpose of grounding diversity within the universal call to holiness, service, and mission.

Making the idea of radically following Christ distinctive of religious life creates problems similar to those of consecration, since it also lends itself to comparison by way of the adjective *more* radical. While he finds much of worth in Tillard, Secondin notes that the way some authors use the category of sign risks an ahistorical approach to religious life, especially when they emphasize the transcendental reference of sign.

Given the problems with consecration and sign, Secondin seems to prefer approaches that highlight the radical and prophetic quality of following Christ in the religious life. One can detect in this the influence of the political theologies of Gustavo Gutiérrez and Johannes Metz, which favor the preferential option for the poor. This relates the following of Christ to the proclamation of the kingdom of God, couched in the Beatitudes and in the parables of Jesus. This following needs to be connected with reading the signs of the times, the option for the poor, and calling both church and society into question in the face of these signs. The twin notions of charism and sending by the Spirit are thus helpful in leading to an appreciation of the diversity of ways of life and of vocation in the church.

As they sought to retrieve their founding charisms after the Second Vatican Council, many religious put much emphasis on living in apostolic community. While this concern is still present in the convictions formulated by the Union of Superiors General before the 1994 synod, the notions of mission and service take priority.[106] In effect, the focus on apostolic community seems to have worn thin. It centered around the ideal of the Jerusalem church without giving enough attention to how the missionary goal of particular communities modified this in the course of time. Perhaps it helped to counter individualistic attitudes to religious life and to apostolic work or gave impetus to a sense of corporate responsibility and an awareness of life's witness value. It seems to be time, however, for this discussion to give way to more interest in mission and how it shapes evangelical life. In its final message the synod stresses this point, emphasizing it even for contemplative and eremitical communities of religious.

The relationship between religious and the world comes into a new perspective with the ready inclusion of secular institutes among contemporary forms of evangelical life. Von Balthasar saw their emergence as an important sign for these times. They show how those who choose for the evangelical life have to look to the needs of the world, take part in its concerns, and look for the ways in which to shape its future in the name of the gospel. Because of secular institutes, all of these concerns are seen by the superiors general and by the synod to belong to religious life as such. Furthermore, little distinction is made between female and male communities in what regards the essence of religious life and the works in which religious engage in virtue of their mission and charism.

Keeping these issues in mind, the specific role and identity of religious communities may arise from their respective contributions to the mission of the church. Mission is a factor even for those who favor the images of consecration and radical following. To give priority to mission is to use a practical rather than a theoretical norm in moving toward the future. Religious have professed a radical following of Jesus Christ and make an appeal to their founding charisms. If they now engage in the mission of the church in virtue of these inspirations, they will find their respective places by coming to grips with that mission in the urgency of its current forms. Each charism is enough to give identity to the way in which new challenges are taken up, whether in the form of continued evangelization, new evangelization, inculturation, prophetic option for the poor, or interreligious dialogue.

SIFTING OUT A PRAXIS ORIENTATION

Comparing these theological writings with the positions of the magisterium can lead to a fresh perspective that is less abstractly theoretical and more related to reflective practice. What is needed now is not so much a different theory or the evolution of different categories whereby to address religious life, but a praxis orientation. This orientation will enable religious priests to reconsider the commitments traditionally connected with ordination in the context of their commitment to their own original religious charisms.

In evolving a specific praxis orientation, a combination of the following factors may turn out to be key: (a) the option for Jesus Christ and the *sequela Christi* in the midst of human life; (b) the courage to be prophetic in relation to both society and church; (c) the practice of evangelical poverty as messianic; and (d) the search for a communion in life rather than simply for community life. An orientation along these lines would fit between (a) a discernment of the signs of the times and (b) a discernment of the institute's specific charism. There is not a progressive order of actions to be performed; rather, these two things constitute a framework within which religious communities fulfill their ecclesial vocation in response to the movements of the Spirit.

There are, thus, six points to be taken into account when developing a praxis orientation to evangelical life in the church today: (i) reading the signs of the times; (ii) the *sequela Christi;* (iii) the prophetic; (iv) evangelical poverty; (v) the mystery of communion; and (vi) the recovery of charism.

Signs of the Times

In the theological section of this chapter, it was noted that theologies developed in relation to practice and new needs. In addition, they took into account the ministries that religious took on because they seemed expedient or necessary. A praxis orientation relates theological reflection and response to gospel imperatives. It requires, in the first place, that the renewal of religious life and of special charisms respond to a call to serve the gospel of Christ in the world in which we live. Communities have continued in recent years to read the signs of the times. The recent general congregation of the Jesuits, for example, addressed questions of justice, interreligious dialogue, collaboration with the laity, and women in the church and society.

The practice has been there, though unarticulated as such, all through the history of religious life. Augustine wanted to respond to schismatic threats to communion. Dominic wanted to respond to the prevailing dualism that had infiltrated the life of the church in many ways. Francis responded to social ills that came with the new economy of his time. The Sulpicians and missionary congregations were concerned with the reform of the church and preaching the gospel to the poor in face of the turbulent changes in the society of their times.

In listening to what is happening in different places, one could conclude that the signs of the times with which religious today concern themselves are:

i. Human inequality, whether within societies or on an international level, which gives a new face to the quest for justice.

ii. The breakdown of human communities in their traditional forms and the subsequent loss of cultural identity.

iii. The role of cultures in transition as many subordinate groups delve into their past riches, calling forth a new cultural sensitivity and inspiring apologies such as that which John Paul II made to the Indian and African American people of Latin America.[107]

iv. The place of interreligious dialogue in the shaping of the world of the future, calling forth a Christian respect for other religions, long absent from its history.

v. The challenge of the gospel under the designation of the "gospel of life," when the world is faced with so much random destruction of human and other forms of living things.

vi. The role of women in society and in the church, without exclusion from any sphere of public life, seeing in Pope John Paul's recent apology a public and institutional step along the way.

If these forces shape the mission of the church and the apostolic objectives of religious, there could be enormous consequences—the emergence of new kinds of religious communities and, for many, a new face on old ones, even as they act in fidelity to their original call.

Sequela Christi

The option for Christ is the controlling factor in Christian faith and hope. The term *sequela Christi* is sometimes tied in with a messianic christology.[108] This seems to express the particular historical form of anticipating the reign of God in Christ and the hope of the coming of the Son of Man, taken as an apocalyptic expression and a harbinger of universal hope. This provides Christian life with roots in the given historical moment as well as an imaginative hope for the future. Images associated with this following of Christ are *kenosis,* the breaking down of barriers between peoples and communities, the readiness to live by uncommon values whatever the challenge, and ultimately by the wisdom of the Cross.

Prophetic

Some current literature about religious life underlines its prophetic character. This seems typical of writings in North America. The appeal to this aspect of communities and their work underscores the complementarity of the charismatic and the official in two different modes of life. From another angle, as in the synodal *Instrumentum Laboris,* this notion of the prophetic is subsumed, in some measure, into ideas about the role of religious priests or clerical institutes in particular churches that remain in service to the universal church. Such usage comes with the warning, which has been sounded earlier, about the danger of confining charisms to the exercise of the priesthood.

The way in which the prophetic may shape the future of religious life has been given particular attention by Sandra Schneiders.[109] Following Walter Brueggemann, she distinguishes between royal consciousness and prophetic consciousness, pointing especially to the role of prophetic imagination in shaping possibilities for the future.[110] She bases the distinction on a reading of the downfall of the Davidic dynasty, when the voices of the prophets went unheard. As happened among the people of Israel, there are those in the church who live by royal consciousness. They are content with the status quo and put their trust primarily in institutions to which they attribute a divine origin and a special divine guardianship. The prophets, on the other hand, are those who can read the signs of the times and point out the new ways in which it behooves the church to respond to God's covenant. In doing so, they not only identify personal failings that obstruct a faithful response, but also dare to show the flaws inherent in the very institutions on which the church relies, including both pastors and people. Prophets remain free enough to imagine different ways of being church and of proclaiming the gospel of Christ.

Since they profess evangelical poverty in its large sense, religious ought to have the freedom of the Spirit to take on a prophetic role in the church. This stance would allow them the distance and perspective needed to see what enslaves the very mission of the church and to find new ways of being church and missionary. They cannot meet this call, however, unless they are first critically involved in renewing the lives of their own institutes and critical of the royal consciousness that resists new forms of living, governing, and acting. Among other things, the accustomed differentiation between male and female communities, often based on their characteristic works, is open to challenge. Missionary tasks, preaching and teaching, and work for justice and the improvement of the life of the marginalized are all needs addressed by both men and women. Indeed, they are often best addressed by both together. Eventually this could mean not only that distinct communities opt to work together, but also that new forms of government unite men and women in a partnership of equality. A prophetic call for institutional forms that unite women and men who feel challenged to the same kind of work finds common ground in founding stories that merge.

Evangelical Poverty

The Jerusalem community as a model for following the poor Christ has had an ambiguous role. Either it is necessary to attend to this model less or to find in it the traits of the following of Jesus Christ found in a study of the synoptic gospels.

Central to the actions and teachings of Jesus is a concern for the disadvantaged in the world and in the reign of God. Jesus proclaims a new wisdom about living together on this earth. The aspect of struggle in embracing poverty has to emerge more clearly in religious life. It is expressed in the gospel in terms of wrestling with mammon because of what is done in its name to the poor. It is also expressed in a new discovery of the sacredness of life vouchsafed by the covenant, in whose name one is ready to accept being marginalized. Jesus did not throw the money dealers out of the Temple because they were violating a holy place, but because they made trade of preventing the people from bringing their own money and goods into it. Whatever the historical status of the gospel story, it clearly shows how Jesus addressed this kind of violation of the covenant with anger and rage. He had a secular reaction to those who invoked the Sabbath laws to prevent the healing of ills. The poverty and self-emptying of Jesus are thus contextualized in mission, as they must be for religious communities.

The practical aspects of living poorly need to be faced. As Aloysius Pieris suggests from the perspective of another continent, the very profession of holding all in common is not without dangers.[111] The assets of communities, once deemed necessary to their work, can actually create obstacles to change when it is felt that future works need to maintain and use these holdings. As Pieris puts it, from a historical perspective, the importance of learning from the poor Christ is taught to us by our founders, people such as Francis and Ignatius.

The evangelical way of the poor life is also open to the contemplative in several ways. In his work *The Journey of the Soul into God,* Bonaventure teaches that the poverty of Francis was a condition for his spiritual journey and that it was consummated in contemplative union with the Crucified Christ marked by the stigmata. This was, in effect, Francis' final act of witness to the reign of God wrought by the poor Christ on earth.

The very basis of solidarity with the poor, living in poverty and simplicity opens up new attitudes to this world. It generates reflective, contemplative, and unencumbered presence to things. This life stands at the root of the search for inculturation, of a mission on behalf of nonhuman forms of life, and of interreligious dialogue. Both the personal and the corporate implications of embracing evangelical poverty have great consequences for the future missionary work of religious institutes.

Communion

Beyond a concern with sharing life together, Tillard's writings give importance to the mystery of communion.[112] In this context it is of interest to note that the special Synod on the Church in Africa chose the model of the communion of persons in God to complement the model of the incarnation in fostering a better grasp of inculturation.[113] The bishops feared that the incarnational model missed the richness of diversity and, by focusing on the roots of cultures, risked becoming a static model. The mystery of communion in the

Trinity is, however, totally a mystery of diversity and relationality in diversity. Appealing to this model, they hoped to create a new openness to cultures and, in their case, to traditional African religions. A communion between peoples of different cultures, and even a communion with people professing other religions, is called for in the very name of the God whom Christians profess and proclaim.

When Tillard uses this model for religious life he is not insensitive to differences or to diversity in unity. Like many another, however, he seems preoccupied with the dangers of division in the church and, consequently, gives a large place to the need for communion with the church's episcopacy. The harmony between being prophetic and being in communion is important. But perhaps religious need to be on the side of the diversity called forth by charism and prophecy. Beyond concern with the internal forms of apostolic community, religious life is challenged to live not so much community but communion with the other.

Here there is much that affects the relation to other peoples, other churches, and other religions. There are those who would find in this call to communion a special challenge to contemplative communities. Contemplation is a call to be present to the Absolute and to the other. Those who practice it can bring to the church a new and fresh openness of being. This is a way of seeing the apostolic dimension of contemplative life and monastic communities, an element to which the synod drew attention.

Recovering Charism

The praxis options dictated by these features of the following of Christ in the religious life are determined, on the one side, by a reading of the signs of the times and, on the other, by fidelity to corporate charisms. When the conjunction is made, the accent is not on institutional factors put in place at the beginning, or even on precise works chosen. A concern with mission is expressed rather by listening to the foundational narrative of the community in a way analogous to that in which the church reads the gospel story of Jesus Christ. That is not a simple task. It involves a practical act of hermeneutics that engages the prophetic imagination.

Since religious bodies began with different objectives and forms of life in view, the question is not the same for all. For some, the immediate and primary purpose consisted of prayer and the common life, or a common life of poverty. How ministry relates to this is a question. For others, the simultaneous commitment to ministry and to a form of common life went together from the beginning, so that they are what can be called apostolic communities. The appropriate renewal of kinds of ministry and of forms of common life go together for them in the recovery of the founding charism. In this context, the issue of ordination to the priesthood may well take on a new appearance.

Ministries for which it was at one time assumed that ordination was necessary may well look otherwise in a changed ecclesial practice. A number of institutes also must deal with the fact that they have nurtured narrowly sacramental understandings of priesthood among their members in the past. They must now balance this with the need to relate ordination to mission and ministry, not to status or state of life. Noting this, however, is to move already to the discussions that have to take place within the particularity of each institute. It is orders or congregations or societies of regular clergy themselves who must assume primary responsibility to articulate these relationships satisfactorily.

CONCLUSION

One might draw many conclusions from what has been presented in this chapter. These final thoughts address questions concerning the relation between priesthood and religious life in the light of all that has been said.

Recent directives of the magisterium have been issued to religious communities that ordain members to the priesthood, calling upon them to discern and rediscover their charisms as evangelical communities. Their contribution within the exercise of the priesthood will come from the success and fidelity of that endeavor. This will enable them to renew both their contribution to local churches and their service to a more universal communion of churches.

The history and positions surveyed above show that the custom of ordination itself is not without question and that retrieving the founding charism of a clerical institute might cast doubt upon elements that have become customary. The reasons why ordination was considered necessary for certain types of apostolic work are historically conditioned. The same holds true for the motivation of apostolic groups that took it for granted that the goals they set could only be accomplished by clergy.

The connection between ordination and the local church, made by the Second Vatican Council, has been important in recent developments in ministerial practice. John O'Malley, however, has shown in the first chapter that ordination can have wider purposes and a more diversified meaning, a fact corroborated by the present contribution. This perspective needs to be taken into account, especially by religious communities, without, of course, slipping back into clericalism or an unbalanced sacramental view of priesthood.

In examining what it means to combine priesthood and religious consecration into one vocation various issues have to be faced by different bodies. In all cases, discernment of their evangelical charism by religious is the practical context within which to consider the practice of ordaining members and the exercise of ordained ministry. This, however, involves a number of practical questions. Is the focus put directly on the mission assumed or on the form of religious life adopted? Is the priority in the history of the body given to living together as an apostolic community according to a rule of life and inspired by the image of the early Jerusalem community or is it given to the goal of mission (for example to that of preaching)? Such questions may call for some rethinking of the clerical factor in the life and in the work of the congregation or order.

At the same time, discernment will not go unaffected by more open thinking on the purpose and form of ordination to ministry. Attention needs to be given to different meanings and modes of "sending." A wider view of ordination, one not too tightly tied with ordination to eucharistic celebration, will have its place in this process.

While the matter is still under consideration, there are some practical measures that religious may take. They may seem at first glance insignificant, but in the history of the church we have come to realize the significance of the insignificant. The most important practical action, one easily within everybody's reach, is the avoidance of ordination procedures that seem to make priesthood a status and an embodiment of powers, however spiritual. There can be nothing automatic about ordaining someone because he has reached an acceptable stage in his studies or in his spiritual development. That ordination is for an apostolate and the related mission ought to be crystal clear, whether it is for service to the local church assembled or in virtue of a sending to another church or another people.

Since ordination is tied to so many institutional suppositions, it could hinder developments involving the future of religious communities. In the first place, an undifferentiated ordination practice could hinder the retrieval for some religious of their original form of common life. Even those bodies in which it was, in the beginning, taken for granted that commitment to a special type of ministry meant ordination might find that the ministry can be better served in some cases by the nonordained. Greater cooperation with other nonordained ministers might take priority over ordination. Such cooperation fosters a better sense of fraternity within a community if ordination is not viewed as status distinction. In addition, keeping unnecessary status distinctions between male and female communities because of the assumed priorities of the ordained impedes service in some spheres of apostolic activity. Those committed to preaching, for example, could well ask themselves if ordination is really necessary to the kind of preaching that they do. Already, there is some cooperation between religious priests and religious women in the work of preaching or of giving retreats. Perhaps it could evolve even further, with more charismatic and prophetic freedom, if neither member of the team were ordained.

Clarifying the purpose and meaning of ordination itself can be helped by the practice of religious bodies. Ordaining some persons for a mission that is not directly tied to service in a local church (provided this is clear) opens up new vistas on the meaning of ordination that can help develop not only theoretical but also practical ecclesiologies. We now appreciate better the functioning of order within a local church in collaborative forms of ministry. Religious priests can promote fidelity to their own calling and tradition both by expanding the sense of communion and mutual service among local churches and by keeping alive a stronger sense of mission, which is not confined to them but for which they serve as prophetic reminder. In the past, as noted above, the relation of religious to Roman authority overshadowed the horizontal communion among churches. Today, the sending of members from one place to another would be done with a greater sense of the direct communion between churches.

The primary practical norm in all of this is fidelity to the founding charism and story of the religious body. The nature of evangelical life envisaged by any particular community affects the practice of ordination and future possibilities. For some bodies engaged in apostolic ministry it will be obvious that a particular form of religious life is the source of mission or ministry. For other apostolic bodies the balance between common life and mission is worked out in such a way that the former is seen to be in service of the latter.

In short, when placed within the context of a praxis orientation that recovers tradition and charisms, the practice of ordaining religious to priesthood takes on new perspectives. Various changes—practical and institutional—prove possible to those who engage in the church's present mission and in an openly charismatic retrieval of founding narratives with prophetic imagination.

NOTES

1. The word *praxis* is used to mean not only a relation to practice but also a simultaneous reflection on this practice.

2. Congregation for the Clergy, "Directory for the Life and Minisry of Priests," *Catholic International* 6 (1995): 62–98.

3. "Directory," par. 26, p., 69.

4. "Directory," pars. 14, 15, p., 66.

5. The ordained ministry itself is not to be seen primarily as an institution, but as a ministry and a charismatic call.

6. *Instrumentum Laboris* 20, *Catholic International* 5 (1994/II): 528.

7. *Ibid.*

8. On the relation between priests and diocesan priests in the local church according to present teaching, see Julio García Martín, "También los religiosos presbiteros pertenecen al presbiterio diocesano (Lineamenta, n. 39)," *Commentarium Professional Religiosis et Missionariis* LXXV (1994, I/II), 149–62.

9. *Instrumentum Laboris* 22, *Catholic International,* 529.

10. Among other places, an English translation can be found in *The*

Pope Speaks 40 (1995/2): 73–79; and in *Catholic International* 6 (1995/3): 135–39. For comment on the message and on the propositions, see Bruno Secondin, "Un primo bilancio complessivo sul Sinodo. Temi e problemi teologici," *Vita Consecrata* XXXI (1995/1): 52–65; Egidio Vigano, "Il Sinodo dulla vita consacrata," *Vita Consecrata* XXXI (1995/2): 201–16. A bibliography, mostly in Italian, of 834 titles dealing with the special Synod on the Consecrated Life has been published in *Vita Consecrata* XXXI (1995): 3–51, 196–200, 276.

11. *The Pope Speaks,* 76.

12. *Ibid.,* 77.

13. Synodal Message, *Catholic International,* 137.

14. *Ibid.,* 138.

15. *Ibid.*

16. These propositions are given in an Italian translation in *Il Regno-Documenti* 21 (1994): 662–73.

17. John Paul II, "Apostolic Exhortation *Vita Consecrata,*" Origins 25 (1996/41): 681–719.

18. *Ibid.,* 31.

19. *Ibid.,* 80, 98.

20. *Ibid.,* 84, 95.

21. *Ibid.,* 30.

22. *Ibid.*

23. *Ibid.,* 48, 49.

24. Pseudo-Ambrosius, *Sermo 56, De Natali S. Eusebii Vercellensis epistola,* PL 17:720.

25. *Regula Sancti Benedicti* LX. In *The Rule of St. Benedict in Latin and English with Notes,* ed. Timothy Fry (Collegeville, Minn.: The Liturgical Press, 1981), 272–75.

26. On Augustine, monasticism, and the different monasteries that he founded, see Adolar Zumkeller, *Augustine's Ideal of the Religious Life,* translated from the German (New York: Fordham University Press, 1986).

27. The primary texts are *Sermones* 355 and 356, PL 39:1568–75; and Possidius, *Vita Sancti Aurelii Augustini, Hipponensis episcopi,* PL 32:33–36.

28. *Presbyterorum Ordinis* 14 (hereafter cited as *PO*).

29. *PO* 17.

30. See R. Wasselynck, *Les Prêtres. Elaboration du Décret de Vatican II. Histoire et genèse des textes conciliaires* (Paris Desclee, 1968), 158–63.

31. *Sermo* 355, l. c., 1569; and *Sermo* 356, l. c., 1574.

32. *Sermo* 356, l. c., 1573.

33. "Professus est sanctitatem, professus est communiter vivendi societam." *Ibid.*

34. See Zumkeller, 103–44.

35. For overviews and considerable documentation on the canons regular, see Caroline Walker Bynum, *Docere Verbo et Exemplo: An Aspect of Twelfth Century Spirituality* (Missoula, Mont.: Harvard University Press, 1979); and Reginald Gregoire, *La Vocazione Sacerdotale, I canonici regolari nel Medioevo* (Rome: Edizioni Studium, 1982).

36. *Epistola apologetica professional canonicis regularibus,* PL 188:113lf.

37. *Liber de ordine canonicorum,* cap. XXXIV, PL 188:1113–16.

38. *Liber de diversis ordinibus et professionibus quae sunt in ecclesia,* PL 213:807–50.

39. *Epistola* 235, *Ab-abaldum abbatem* (a.d. 1154), PL 189:1319f. Translation is the author's.

40. As priests, some monks took on pastoral obligations not known in the earlier days of monastic communities. In chapter 2 of this volume, Kevin Seasoltz studies the Benedictine ideal and its evolution.

41. Two studies in English can be taken as representative: "The Monastic Priesthood According to the Ancient Medieval Tradition," *Studia Monastica* 3 (1961): 137–55; and "The Priesthood for Monks," *Monastic Studies* 3 (1965): 53–85.

42. Toward the end of the thirteenth century, William Durand in his edition of the Pontifical turned this on its head when he appealed to the priestly duty of celebrating the sacrifice of Christ as motivation for the pursuit of holiness. See the exhortation, *Agite quod agitis,* in M. Andrieu, *Le Pontifical Romain du haut moyen-âge* (Vatican City: Studi e Testi 88, 1941), 3:339. By that time too, ordination was being called consecration, with priority being given to the priest's sacrificial action over pastoral ministry. As older priests remember, this exhortation was a part of the ordination service of the Roman Pontifical until 1968.

43. *De Sacramentis Fidei* II, 3, 4: "Ut ergo intrinsecus quietius vivant [monachi] ordines ministerii divini per indulgentiam ipsis conceduntur, non ad exercendam praelationem in populo Die, sed ad celebrandam intrinsecus communionem sacramenti Dei" (PL 176:423). Jacques de Vitry saw both Cistercian monasteries and the abbey of the Victorines as havens of solitude and withdrawal from the evils of the world. See *The "Historia occidentalis" Jacques de Vitry: A Critical Edition,* edited by J. F. Hinnebusch (Freiburg: Spicilegium Friburgense 17, 1972).

44. *Summa Theologiae* IIa IIae, q. 184, art. 1.

45. Q. 185, art. 4, ad 1m: "Ad perfectionem religionis pertinet studium quod quis adhibet ad propriam salutem. Ad perfectionem autem episcopalis status pertinet adhibere studium ad proximorum salutem"; and q. 185, art. 8, c.: "Status religionis comparatur ad statum episcopalem sicut disciplina ad magisterium, et dispositio ad perfectionem."

46. *Summa Theologiae* IIa, IIae, q. 185, art. 4, c.

47. Q. 185, art. 8, c.

48. Q. 174, art. 5.

49. *Summa Theologiae* III, q. 83, art. 1.

50. *The Ecclesiastical Hierarchy,* trans. Thomas L. Campbell (Washington, D.C.: University Press of America, 1981), 19.

51. For the place of the Eucharist in the sacramental economy, see *Summa Theologiae* III, q. 65, art. 3.

52. Because he defined the sacrament of order in terms of the Eucharist, Aquinas did not look upon episcopacy as a sacrament, but in Pseudo-Dionysian terms it is an order and a hierarchy, a *principalitas,* both in the sense of eminence and in the sense of source or principal, within the church. On this, see Davis N. Power, *Ministers of Christ and His Church: The Theology of the Priesthood* (London: Chapman, 1969), 118–22.

53. On the concept of hierarchy operative in this quarrel, see Michel-Marie Dufeil, "Ierarchia: Un concept dans la polemique universitaire parisienne du XIIIe siecle." *Miscellanea Mediaevalia,* vol. 12, pt. 1, *Soziale Ordnungen im Selbstverstandis des Mittelalters,* ed. Zimmermann (Berlin: Walter de Gruyter, 1979), 56–83.

54. Thomas Aquinas, *Contra Impugnantes Dei Cultum et Religionem,* Pars II, cap. 1, 2, and 3. *Opuscula Theologica,* vol. 2 (Rome and Turin: Marietti, 1954), 8–37. In the Leonine edition of the *Opera Omnia* this work is found in vol. 41A.

55. *Summa Theologiae* IIa, IIae, q. 182.

56. Q. 188, art. 6. Of the duties of this form of life, he says, "quae et propinquissimae sunt perfectioni episcoporum." On this topic, see also the opusculum *De Perfectione Vitae Spiritualis,* edited in the *Opuscula Theologica* II, 111–53. In the Leonine edition, this is found in vol. 41B.

57. Q. 182, art. 3. On the comparison between the active and the contemplative life, see the entire four articles of this question.

58. Q. 188, art. 4 c.

59. Q. 187, art. 1, c.

60. Q. 188, art. 4, ad 5m.

61. Q. 187, art. 1, c; and q. 188, art. 4, ad 3m and ad 4m.

62. Dominicans had always avoided the fate that befell the followers of Peter Valdes by showing respect for the proper ecclesiastical authority. The Early Constitutions, article 32, say: "No one should dare to preach in any diocese when the bishop has forbidden him to preach, unless he has letters and a general mandate from the Pope." See *Early Dominican Constitutions,* in *Early Dominicans: Selected Writings,* ed. Simon Tugwell (New York: Paulist Press, 1982), 467.

63. Thomas Aquinas finds that there is a place for this as a *quasi-sacramentum,* when no priest is available, or when it is a matter of confessing venial sins, and no formal absolution is given. See *Summa Theologiae Supplementum,* q. 8, arts. 2 and 3.

64. There is a move among Franciscans today to return to a less clerical understanding of their community by going back to their origins with Francis, and to relate their ministry to this. See the subsequent chapter in this volume by Roland J. Faley, T.O.R.

65. Opusculum XIII, Quaestio I, Cur sanctus Franciscus novam Regulam instituit, *Opera Omnia* (Quaracchi ed.) VIII:338.

66. "Cum…praedicationis officium exercise regulari professione Ordini annexum sit et confessionis…." Opusculum XIII, Quaestio II, Cur Fratres praedicent et audiant confessiones, cum ordinarie non habeant curam animarum, *Opera Omnia* VIII:339.

67. …Sedes apostolica, quae immediate curam ecclesiarum habet, et a qua ceteri ecclesiarum pastores, tam maiores quam minores, gubernandi suscipiunt auctoritatem, tame mediate quam immediate, et a qua omnes canonum leges emanant, videns, in his novissimis temporibus." *Ibid.,* 338f. See also Opusculum XIV, *Opera Omnia* VIII:375.

68. *Breviloquium,* Pars VI, cap. XII.

69. He calls the Pope the "pater patrum," the "unus primus et summus pater patrum unus, primus et summus pater spiritualis omnium patrum, immo omnium fidelium…. *Ibid.,* par. 5.

70. *De Excellentia Magisterii Christi* III.

71. The effect of the practice of the Jesuits and of the Council of Trent on ordination has been considered by John O'Malley in chapter 1 of this volume, so that is not treated here.

72. Michel Dupuy, *Bérulle et le Sacerdoce. Étude historique et doctrinale. Textes inedits* (Paris: Lethielleux, 1969).

73. *Ibid.,* 123–36.

74. *Ibid.,* 145–62.

75. Pierre de Bérulle, "A Letter on the Priesthood," in *Bérulle and the French School: Selected Writings,* ed. William H. Thompson, trans. Lowell M. Glendon (New York: Paulist Press, 1989), 183–85.

76. Dupuy, 73–92.

77. *Ibid.,* 219–28.

78. On Bérulle's attitude to vows, see Dupuy, 229–42.

79. *Traite des saints ordres, publie par M. Tronson selon les ecrits et l'esprit de Jean-Jacques Olier* (Paris: Colombe, Ed. du Vieux Colombier, 1953).

80. *Ibid.,* 199.

81. *Ibid.,* 202.

82. Chapter II, entitled "De la dignite et de la saintete des Pretres par rapport a leurs fonctions et a la grandeur de leurs pouvoirs" in *Traité des saints ordres,* 203–17.

83. "Motives for Patience," in "Introduction to Christian Life and Virtues," *Bérulle and the French School*, 246. On the topic, see especially *Traité des saints ordres*, ed. Gilles Chaillot, Michel Dupuy, and Irénée Noye (Paris: Saint-Sulpice, 1984).

84. Jean Eudes, *The Priest: His Dignity and Obligations*, trans. William Leo Murphy (New York: Kennedy, 1947), 8.

85. "The Life and Kingdom of Jesus Christ in Christian Souls," *Bérulle and the French School,* 322–25.

86. This perception of the practical side of a theology of ministry where religious are concerned coincides with the observations of John O'Malley in chapter 1 in this volume.

87. In this field, the unparalleled contributions of Yves Congar and Edward Schillebeeckx cannot go unrecognized. Nothing comparable has been done in the English-speaking world, but one may mention the names of Bernard Cooke, Edward Kilmartin, and Kenan Osborne.

88. What follows is based mainly on the essays collected in Part Two of *Explorations in Theology*, vol. 2, *Spouse of the Word* (San Francisco: Ignatius Press, 1991), 301–457. Some of his more recent thought on office in the church and on spirituality of the baptized and the ordained is given in *The Glory of the Lord: A Theological Aesthetics* (San Francisco: Ignatius Press, reprint 1989) 1:556–604.

89. Demurral from his positions is often evoked by his use of the imagery of bride and bridegroom in explaining the sacrament of order and the way in which this is tied to a specific gender anthropology. This need not be embraced in order to be enlightened by his thought on the states of life.

90. In efforts at a systematic theology, the thought of Karl Rahner on symbol and sacrament has an enduring place.

91. The publication of *The Sacrament of Holy Orders,* ed. Bernard Botte, translated from the French (Collegeville, Minn.: The Liturgical Press, 1962) was a landmark in this attention to liturgies of ordination as theological source.

92. In this regard, the contribution of biblical studies was primary. For an early influential contribution, see AA. VV., *Le ministere et les ministeres selon le Nouveau Testament* (Paris: Ed. du Seuil, 1974). This is a helpful basis for a theology and discernment of vocation.

93. By way of example, see the small volume *Preaching and the Non-Ordained: An Interdisciplinary Study*, ed. Nadine Foley (Collegeville, Minn.: The Liturgical Press, 1983), with important contributions by Edward Schillebeeckx, William Hill, and Mary Collins.

94. *Lumen Gentium* 11.

95. *PO* 2.

96. *Ministers of Christ and His Church*, 166–80.

97. Most helpful is the article by Bruno Secondin, "La théologie de la vie consacrée. Etat présent et perspectives," *Vie Consacrée* 66 (1994, nos. 3 and 4): 225–70. See also L. Renwart, "Théologie de la vie religieuse. Chronique bibliographique," *Vie Consacrée* 63 (1991, no. 1): 49–62, and 64 (1992 no. 1) 47–66; José Cristo García Paredes, *Consecrated Life Today,* vol. 1, *Theological Synthesis* (Rome: OMI Documentation 1944); and idem, *Consecrated Life Today,* vol. 2, *Convictions and Proposals of the Union of Superiors General* (Rome: OMI Documentation, 1994).

98. P.-R. Regamey, *L'exigence de Dieu. Redecouvrir la vie religieuse* (Paris: Cerf, 1969); and idem, *Paul VI donne aux religieux leur charte. Exhortation "Evangelica Testificata" presentee et commentee* (Paris: Cerf, 1971).

99. Leonardo Boff, *God's Witnesses in the Heart of the World*, translated from the Portuguese (Chicago: Claret Center for Resources in Spirituality, 1981).

100. Thaddeus Matura, *Gospel Radicalism: The Hard Sayings of Jesus*, translated from the French (Maryknoll, N.Y.: Orbis, 1984).

101. His most important work on the topic is J.-M.-R. Tillard, *Devant Dieu et pour le monde. Le projet des religieux* (Paris: Cerf, 1975). A smaller book is translated into English, *There Are Charisms and Charisms: The Religious Life* (Brussels: Lumen Vitae, 1977).

102. García Paredes himself developed the idea of religious life as gospel radicalism. See José Cristo Rey García Paredes, "Jesus, A Radical Discipleship," in *Jesus a Radical Discipleship in the Context of the Philippines* (Quezon City: Claretian Publications, 1993), 1–186.

103. Matura, 185.

104. Edward Schillebeeckx followed the same line of thought in his critical and apologetic review of the norm of clerical celibacy in the book translated as *Celibacy Under Fire;* he related the idea historically to the origin of the friars.

105. This problem has been pointed out by Cardinal Lorscheider of Brazil in his review of the work of the synod. See Aloísio Cardinal Lorscheider, "O Sinodo dos Bispos sobre a Vida Consagrada e a sua Missao na Igreja e no Mundo (1994)," *Revista Eclesiastical Brasileira* (1995, no. 217): 5–31.

106. García Paredes, *Consecrated Life Today,* vol. 2.

107. *Osservatore Romano*, weekly edition in English, 28 October 1992, no. 43, 11.

108. For example, Tillard, *Devant Dieu*, 153–96; and García Paredes, *Jesus*, 1–20.

109. Sandra M. Schneiders, *New Wineskins: Re-imagining Religious Life Today* (New York: Paulist Press, 1986), esp. 266–84.

110. See principally Walter Brueggemann, *The Prophetic Imagination* (Philadelphia: Fortress Press, 1978).

111. Aloysius Pieris, *An Asian Theology of Liberation* (Maryknoll, N.Y.: Orbis, 1988), esp. 3–23.

112. Tillard, *Devant Dieu*, 197–279.

113. Proposition 28 of this special Synod on Africa. In *Il Regno* 39 (1994, no. 6, prop. 728): 334–42.

4

An American Experience of
Priesthood in Religious Life

Roland J. Faley, T.O.R.

Priests who are members of religious communities continue to play a vital role in the ongoing history of the church in the United States. At the same time, there has long existed a certain measure of ambiguity in their life as men related to their own community and to the dioceses where they serve. Practice and custom have dulled some of this ambiguity. And history in recent decades has evidenced a more understanding clime between religious priests and dioceses. But certain questions still remain and continue to play themselves out on the American scene and elsewhere.

The Second Vatican Council clearly separated religious life from the hierarchical structure of the church, while underscoring its indispensable place in the church's life.[1] The Dogmatic Constitution on the Church, *Lumen Gentium,* clearly sees priests together with bishops and deacons as the "divinely established ecclesiastical ministry," that is, the hierarchy of the church.[2] In addition, the description of the two offices is different. For religious, the life of contemplation is coupled with a diversified response to human need in the spiritual and corporal works of mercy.[3] Priests, on the other hand, are seen largely in liturgical and sacramental terms, constituting with the bishop, their leader and chief shepherd, a single presbyterate in the local church.[4]

What may seem to be a well-ordered presentation of two "ways of being" in the church brings to the surface as well the difficulties in defining the nature of religious priesthood. The clear model for priesthood in the council documents is diocesan.[5] This is seen not only in the emphasis on the sacramental dimension of ministry but also in the close-knit unity with the bishop. Many priests in religious communities identify with such a role and structure only partially. Whether in the ministry of teaching, preaching missions, or running soup kitchens, they are unquestionably part of a local church and make a valuable contribution to its life. They do this, however, basically as an expression of the charism of their institute rather than as a way to fit into the traditional hierarchical mold.

Vatican II, in speaking of the distinctive nature of religious life, sees it as neither clerical nor lay. but it indicates that people are called to this way of life from both of the aforementioned categories.[6] This specification, seemingly clear in itself, presents its own set of difficulties. In saying that religious are neither lay nor clerical and without specifying clearly what the *tertium quid* is, the council leaves religious today in a rather ambiguous situation wherein they "fall between the cracks." Certainly, the living of the evangelical counsels in community life gives specificity to the vocation, but it is not so clear how this is distinct from the lay state. Since the call to holiness in the church is universal,[7] does not religious life add an important dimension to this universal call without removing it from the lay state? The expression "lay brother," now somewhat dated, once gave expression to an important reality that should not be simply identified with a distinction from the clerical state. In his apostolic exhortation *Vita Consecrata,* issued after the synod of 1994, Pope John Paul II calls attention to the anomaly of certain religious institutes being named *lay,* while religious life is seen as a state in itself. He proposes that communities of religious brothers be called *religious institutes of brothers,* without any reference to *lay* character.[8]

To be both religious and clerical presents problems of its own. Belonging to any hyphenated state in life is not uncomplicated, as has become evident in the religious-priest question. On the one hand, the religious who feels his call to holiness is complete in following the evangelical counsels in a religious institute while fulfilling a ministry that does not require priestly ordination (e.g., teaching or social ministry) may well decide that the clerical state has no real part to play in his calling. The person who feels strongly a call to the sacerdotal ministry, on the other hand, may find that his religious life ends up in a subordinate or secondary position. In this regard, I remember interviewing a bishop who was also a Franciscan and asking him which was the primary calling of his life, a Franciscan friar or a bishop. He unhesitatingly responded, "Being a bishop, a successor of the apostles." I must admit that my own thinking on the subject had so altered over the years that I was somewhat taken aback. But there is no denying the fact that many members of religious institutes believe that, at least in practice, their priestly calling is primary.

This basic tension has come much to the fore on the American scene. As we shall see, there was a major shift in understanding in the postconciliar years in response to Vatican II's strong emphasis on the religious calling in and of itself. This tension has not been fully resolved with the passing of the years. This is partly due to the fact that the clerical state still offers a certain clarity and even status in American society that religious life does not. Vocations to the priesthood, while not nearly as numerous as in the past, continue to fare better than the calling to the brotherhood and the sisterhood, with some rare exceptions. This being the case, those clerical religious institutes that continue to have a novice class each year are faced with real questions as to why their order or congregation is being chosen. Which weighs in more heavily, priesthood or religious life? One is inevitably faced with the question as to where religious life for men would be today if priesthood were not seen as an important ingredient.

A HISTORICAL OVERVIEW

While a comprehensive picture of the role that priests of religious institutes played in American church history is beyond the intent of this chapter, it is vital to note that priest missionaries who were religious played an immense role in planting the seeds of faith in this country. The Jesuits labored in the Northeast and Midwest; the Franciscans and Oblates of Mary Immaculate, in the West and Southwest. The names of Jogues, de Brébeuf, Marquette, and Serra are woven into the fabric of American church history. The Benedictines, notably in the person of Boniface Wimmer, combined the missionary spirit and monasticism by birthing monasteries that became centers of faith and culture. Kevin Seasoltz has traced this development well in chapter 2.

If these early missionaries had difficulties in justifying priesthood as a component of their religious life, they have left scant testimony to that effect. They identified clearly with their order or congregation, which had missioned them, and in their work of evangelization, priesthood was an essential ingredient. This complementarity was characteristic of the first centuries of American life. Indeed, many of the early bishops in North America were themselves members of religious communities, a phenomenon that continued well into the nineteenth century. One thinks of Van de Velde of Chicago, Alemany of San Francisco, Concannon of New York, and Egan of Philadelphia.

Many of the tensions that eventually arose between religious institutes and dioceses were rooted in the religious priesthood. The fact is that religious priests were often seen as "competitors" as dioceses continued to increase. Sometimes the opposition was understandable; in other instances it was not. To an ever greater extent, tensions centered around parish issues. Parishes in the hands of religious were seen as encroaching on diocesan territory. The more solid the economic base of the parish, the greater the difficulty.

Much of this has been so ameliorated in modern times that it is more than a little surprising when religious are relieved of their responsibilities in a diocese today. Yet to the historian the comment of one provincial whose community was asked to surrender a parish in a large diocese in recent times has a familiar ring: "We have been told we are no longer wanted. It made us feel as if we are a commodity to them. We were there when they needed us, and now we are treated like outsiders who have to leave."[9] Regardless of one's stance on the merits of this or similar cases, there is no doubt that priestly parochial ministry has often been conflictual in a church "world" that has both diocesan and religious clergy.

There is a lengthy history of bitter conflict between bishops and clerical religious orders, especially in the early years of diocesan life in the United States. J. P. Marshall sees this as centering around two major issues: the control of education by religious institutes, which restricted diocesan vocation recruitment, and the exempt status of religious, which affected their control of land, churches, and money.[10] Controversy between religious and bishops extended from New York to San Francisco. Archbishop John Hughes of New York was in conflict with the Jesuits over property and ownership rights. Archbishop Blanchet of Oregon was involved in a lengthy feud with the Oblates of Mary Immaculate. Archbishop Peter Kenrick of St. Louis had a battle with the Jesuits over expenses incurred at St. Louis University. Sometimes pastoral issues became incendiary and led to bitter dispute. Archbishop Joseph S. Alemany of San Francisco, himself a religious, led his diocesan clergy in opposition to the Jesuits, once again, because of the magnetic pull exercised over parishioners by the Jesuits to the detriment of local territorial parishes. As Alemany put it: "There are other churches in this city besides St. Ignatius, and they are much in debt and are entitled to the support of their respective faithful; if the Jesuit Fathers wish to ignore this, no written agreement can satisfy me."[11]

If history is any indication of a climate, then it would have to be said that the religious priest in a diocesan setting often found himself and/or his institute at odds with the local church. Very often the emotional state ranged from cool to distant, with some notable exceptions wherein relations were excellent. This rarefied air was all too common and was caused by a variety of factors. Where there were hard feelings, the causes were frequently found on both sides; no one was totally free of guilt. But whether the religious were involved in education, a social ministry, or parish work, the relations with the diocese impacted the way they saw their own life and their role in the church. It is important to look at the factors that brought this about.

EXEMPTION

The relationship between a local church and the religious who engage in ministry within it has for centuries been characterized by a legitimate autonomy of the religious institute. This autonomy, which eventually became known as *exemption,* was rooted in historical and apostolic realities conceding to religious the right to organize their own internal affairs, to govern themselves, and to determine the scope and extent of their ministry. This was an acknowledgment of their right to determine their specific contribution to the church, following, of course, upon their official recognition by the church itself. This autonomy, with its clearly defined independence of episcopal authority, gave the broader church, especially in the person of its visible head, the pope, the right to draw on religious institutes to meet pastoral needs in various parts of the world. This privilege of religious exemption was jealously guarded by the religious orders and congregations up to and including the Second Vatican Council, where there was some expressed intent to limit it.

All of this must be balanced against the prerogatives of the local bishop that have to be recognized as well. It is the bishop who accepts religious in the diocese and approves their apostolate. In ministerial service, it is the bishop who is responsible for the overall pastoral coordination of the diocese. Therefore, while religious have the right to direct their own ministries, they are not free to alter them dramatically or introduce new ones without episcopal approval. It is the bishop's duty to see that the integrity of religious belief and practice is safeguarded.

In theory all of this seems clear enough; in practice, however, it is has been fraught with difficulties. Exemption can easily give the impression of a certain clerical elitism. This was voiced clearly by Jerome Hamer, O.P., in the mid-1960s, long before he became the cardinal prefect of the Congregation for Religious and Secular Institutes. Diocesan authorities, he said, often feel that the religious is primarily devoted to his institute and only peripherally to the local church. Very often the religious arrive with a distinct spirituality, particular devotions, an independent financial base, and a network of societies, organizations, schools, and the like that contribute to the notion of a "church within a church."[12] For their part, more in the past than in the present, bishops have made demands upon religious that have resulted in compromises with the institute's basic spirit and been destructive of some very fundamental values. And it must be admitted that there were other times when religious simply acquiesced to such requests and willingly paved the way for a weakened identity.

What does this diocesan relationship mean for the religious who is also a priest? It certainly results in a measure of ambiguity. In the way priesthood is generally defined in the church, he is part of the presbyterate of the diocese. To a greater or lesser degree, he is engaged in the sacramental or parochial ministry in which his diocesan brothers are involved. He is part of a shared sacramental calling and would be quite upset if his voice were not heard in some way within diocesan structures. And yet he knows that he is different. He is a religious, and increasingly since the council this has been underscored as the authentic "glue" of his life.

For many institutes of consecrated life, it is now clearly stated: "first a religious, and then a priest." This can only mean that the integration of a religious into the local presbyterate is necessarily limited. The fact is that when religious identity is submerged in the interests of diocesan service, then different values can begin to shape the understanding of the vows, prayer, and community. Since religious must retain their identity and since superiors, in making assignments, are held to see that authenticity prevails, this is certain to color the difference inherent in what it means to be a priest in a religious institute.

This is not to argue the fact that religious life can offer an enrichment of the priesthood. Religious offer a type of spirituality, of service, and a variety of devotions that are prized by many dioceses. The praises sung about the presence of religious in parishes is affirming and gratifying. But this only helps to point up the problem. Because religious are different, their view of priesthood and ministry varies as well. In some way, as we have seen, they are considered an island unto themselves, and, even up to the present time, that can lead to contentious eruptions within a local church. Most of the time things go quite well, but the difference is there nonetheless. In the midst of a generally placid scene, contention can serve to underscore inherent problems within a local church.

THE HYPHENATED PRIEST

What results from this split in his ecclesiastical personality is that the priest religious in his both/and situation has particular tensions that arise from his "hyphenated" state. If he is a parish priest, he recognizes in some form the tensions that have been cited. It should be noted that the positive relationship between bishops and religious was greatly enhanced with the publication of the Vatican document "Mutual Relations Between Bishops and Religious in the Church" in 1978.[13] What can happen, and not infrequently does, however, is that the religious tends to identify to an ever greater degree with his diocesan counterparts, and this often to the detriment of his religious calling. Because of the preponderance of diocesan structures, which become so much a part of his life, he may find himself increasingly involved in diocesan concerns, whether in terms of parish life, liturgy, finances, schools, or diocesan procedures. It is with the local presbyterate that much of his time is spent, and their problems are to a great extent his own. There is nothing negative about all of this in itself. But we are undoubtedly faced with the fact that many religious priests have given the priestly ministry such a dominance in their life that they are hardly distinguishable from the diocesan clergy.

This is not meant to demean diocesan life, blessed as it is with many men marked by an authentic spirituality and deeply felt pastoral concern. This is simply to say that it is a different way of life. It is interesting to note that some religious priests will respond with great interest to the concerns of the presbyteral council but will consider the religious council of the diocese or the office of vicar for religious as pertaining only to women religious.[14] What might have been by original intention a friary begins to look increasingly like a rectory. The rhythm of daily life is not determined by the community's constitutions as much as by the demands of the parish. This means a difference in life-style and outlook that can erode a primitive vision and yet be deemed acceptable because it can still be said that "the people see a parish run by religious in a different way."

It should be said that not all religious institutes fit into the same mold. For that reason, it is particularly difficult to speak of religious priesthood in a global sense. Some institutes are called religious only in a broad sense, since they are basically diocesan priests living in community for some defined purpose. The Sulpicians, for example, were founded as diocesan priests living in community for the mission of educating future priests. Other institutes were founded to assist the diocesan clergy when a pronounced need was present. It is understandable that such communities identify strongly with diocesan priesthood and have done so since their founding. Such is clearly not the case, however, with the greater number of religious orders and congregations founded with a mission or a spirit that went beyond diocesan limits.

The diocesan model of priesthood was predominant at Vatican II, and it is not surprising that the religious priest finds difficulty in identifying with this dominant model. Yet, in many instances, he still experiences the doctrinal understanding of what it means to be a priest. Whether it be parish ministry, the preaching of missions, or the work of evangelization at home or abroad, he still sees the sacerdotal ministry as an enrichment of his calling, even if it is not seen as primary. Such is not the case, however, if priesthood is simply an adjunct to the principal focus of his apostolate. Years ago it was common for a Benedictine, Franciscan, or Dominican to be ordained and then destined for a classroom for the greater part of his life. He was accorded whatever "privileges" might be attached thereto and served in parishes occasionally as need decreed. But it could never be said that his primary calling was sacerdotal. In fact, as a teacher, whether in high school or college, he often stood shoulder-to-shoulder with nonordained brothers of his own institute or laypersons who were performing precisely the same function.

This "nonsacerdotal" role of many religious led inevitably to questions regarding the necessity of priestly ordination in accomplishing the task at hand. Long before the council, the question was raised and, for many people, not satisfactorily answered. While priesthood was not irrelevant and even within religious life had a status of its own, it was, however, for many religious an adjunct. There are memories of those rows of altars in every friary or monastery, very often in the crypt or the undercroft of the main chapel, where "private" masses requiring no more than the presence of a server were celebrated daily. The theological underpinnings of this practice emphasized the public nature of every mass that was offered and its value as part of the "treasury" of the church, but the situation remained rather anomalous. While some priests welcomed a Sunday assignment in a parish or a summer substitution in a metropolitan area where pastoral needs were abundantly present, others remained close to their task assignment without the benefit of a vibrant and engaging experience of priesthood.

After Vatican II the problem became even more acute. In its document on religious life (in many ways somewhat better than that on priesthood), the council called religious to a return to their founding spirit or charism.[15] This resulted in one of the most remarkable responses to the call of the council seen in the postconciliar era. Institutes of men and women religious undertook detailed studies on the founder and the founding spirit. The updating of constitutions and, in some instances, of the rule of life itself consumed years of effort and was pursued on a churchwide basis. This process of updating resulted in a deeper awareness of the sense of prayer and community and the living of the vows. It also brought about some dramatic changes in the direction of ministry and apostolate. At the same time it was not without its repercussions on priesthood in religious life.

What the council succeeded in doing was to highlight the religious vocation. For institutes that were by definition *clerical,* that is, composed of priests and brothers, it was the notion of the common "brotherhood" that came to the fore. The first and primary vocation was to be a Franciscan, Dominican, Jesuit, or Redemptorist. It was not a question of the value of priesthood or its sacramental dimension; rather, it was a call to see it within the broader framework of religious life, and not vice versa. While the council had given considerable attention to the episcopacy, to complement Vatican I's emphasis on the papacy, the same cannot be said of its treatment of priesthood. In the Constitution on the Church, priests are given one paragraph,[16] while an entire chapter is dedicated to religious.[17] The postconciliar church did not engage in developing a theology of priesthood, but work on the meaning and significance of religious life moved ahead at a remarkable pace.

All of this had an effect on religious priesthood. More and more, the commonalities of the religious state became prominent. Brothers and priests were of equal status, theologically if not juridically. Questions of precedence no longer had meaning. Concelebration, which was initially welcomed as a liturgical expression of a common priesthood, frequently became seen as divisive in separating brothers and priests. Initially brothers were still prohibited from holding canonical office in the community, even though they were now admitted as councillors; in the course of time, this too broke down as more and more congregations requested special permission of the Vatican for brothers to act as local superiors. Eventually, if the community could demonstrate that distinction of brothers from clerics was not the mind of the founder (as in the case of the Franciscans), then a more general permission was granted for the naming of brothers as ministers, even to the point of its becoming part of constitutions.[18] This leveling process extended to all noncanonical offices by decision of the institute itself. The result was that administrative offices on all levels were filled by religious, with no weight given to whether they were clerical or lay.

As right and just as all of this was, it did not contribute to a better understanding of what it means to be a religious priest. Now not only was there a limited engagement in priestly ministry, but also within the community itself there was scant recognition of the distinctiveness of priesthood. Those religious whose work was dominantly clerical felt this less than others but did not escape it entirely. The preaching ministry, for example, engaged the talents of many priests in religious orders and congregations for centuries. However, preaching today is restricted to the church's clergy only in the context of the liturgical homily. Preaching in other circumstances is not so limited. It may be done by other qualified and theologically prepared people. Retreat work, which once was the exclusive domain of the priest, is now done by brothers, sisters, or laypeople. Where at one time a retreat master was requested of a clerical institute without specifying the person desired, today the contrary is the case. Therefore, while there may be degrees of difference in this whole question, with some religious priests affected more than others, it is unquestionable that postconciliar developments have not thrown into strong relief the specific character of the ordained religious.

It is the religious who is a pastor or associate pastor who experiences the least ambiguity in reference to priesthood. His sacerdotal duties are more clearly defined and, like his diocesan counterpart, he finds more than enough to do to make his day full. As we shall later see, this is not to say that there are not problems of identity surrounding priesthood in the present day. But the fact remains that, whether or not many of his reponsibilities may be shared with others and prescinding from the theological questions, most priests today experience little ambiguity in their daily ministry. The danger for the religious priest in all of this, as has been previously stated, is that his identity with priesthood may tend to override his religious vocation. In a real sense, it is possible to find a greater distinctiveness and clarity in the exercise of a ministry that, especially in terms of its sacramental dimension, still remains viable. Since this is a life shared with the diocesan clergy, the pastor's point of reference is often found in the local presbyterate rather than in the religious community.

If religious life and priesthood had developed jointly, the seam that joins the two may have been less visible. The fact is that, from the time of early monasticism, religious life evolved along strongly lay lines, as has been made clear in the previous chapters. Priesthood, where it existed, was seen to be at the service of the religious community and did not play a dominant role in shaping monasticism. The Middle Ages moved in different directions. Because of the role of preaching in his founding intention, St. Dominic gave priesthood a dominant role in his order from the beginning. His contemporary and friend Francis of Assisi adopted a contrary stance. While he reverenced priests and in no way excluded them from the community, his emphasis fell on the brotherhood, in which a spirit of total equality was to obtain. In the post-conciliar period, Franciscans have repeatedly opposed efforts to define them as a *clerical* institute.[19] As Vatican II makes clear, religious life grew out of baptism and therefore binds one to all the baptized. As an enrichment of the baptismal commitment and a living out of basic gospel values in a unique way, it finds its own distinct place in the church. Gradually, priesthood was woven into the fabric of the life itself, leading eventually to the canonical category of clerical religious institutes. The council's emphasis on that which binds religious to all the baptized has not left the identity of the religious priest untouched.[20]

In brief, as far as religious life is concerned, the priest finds himself in a distinctly different situation from the brother, whose identity is connected solely with his life as a religious, as a person called to live the evangelical counsels in a specific religious institute. In this vocation he finds his total *raison d'être*. His nonclerical ministry is simply an expression of what the religious institute is about. The priest sees himself in similar terms, but there is another dimension of his life connecting him with the church's hierarchy. As a priest, he may or may not be directly involved in sacerdotal pastoral ministry. But the "character" of priesthood will remain with him until death. It is in fitting this twofold dimension of his life into a unified framework that a social, and even psychological tension is often present.

THE FEMININE PERSPECTIVE

The religious calling is shared by men and women in the church. In many ways this has bound them together in a common pursuit and on many levels has brought them together in ministry as well. Since Vatican II, common initiatives have come more to the fore. This is particularly evident in the work of the national conferences of religious. In most countries there is a single conference of men and women religious. In others, as in the United States, the conferences are separate but work jointly in a variety of undertakings. Various offices, formerly separate, have now been joined, and the two conferences of leadership in U.S. religious life hold their national assembly together every few years. This has been a productive initiative, inspired by the nature of their life and a better understanding of their common calling.

It is on the local level where joint ministries are very much in evidence. Women religious today are involved in an extensive variety of parish and diocesan ministries on a broader scale than ever existed in the past. In religious education and formation, social outreach, marriage preparation, liturgy, and finances, women religious are central to the church's life today. This has led to multiple forms of collaboration between men and women religious both within the parish and on the diocesan level. This has proved to be a positive and complementary approach to ministry. At the same time we must admit that it has perhaps dulled the clarity of the distinctive community charism.

The issue of priesthood, however, often stands as a reef on a rather tranquil sea. The rise of feminism on the American scene has placed in bold relief major differences between the sexes, as well as marked areas of inequality which form part of the social fabric. Women have undertaken a determined struggle to obtain equality of opportunity in the professions and the work force in general. They have highlighted the extent to which women have been abused physically and mentally by men both in the home and beyond. The term *sexual harassment,* largely unheard of a decade ago, has become commonplace in today's world. Feminism has a clear agenda, much of it positive. If voices that are too strident and guilty of overstatement often prove to be counterproductive, the basic fact remains that a greater sensitivity to women's concerns has come to the fore in recent years.

This whole effort has had its repercussions within the church and, more specifically, within religious life. The desire of women to play a greater role in the church's decision-making process was inevitable in light of the greater awareness present within society as a whole. In a church that is repeatedly termed *patriarchal,* there has been an ever growing sentiment that the present situation is anomalous and in dire need of change. Coupled with this, of course, is the whole question of priestly ordination, on which church authority has been adamant in its opposition to change. The voices in favor, however, have not been stilled, and the issue continues to arouse no small amount of controversy.

Women religious have played an important part in the development of women's concerns in the church, as will be demonstrated at length by Doris Gottemoeller in the subsequent chapter. The ordination question has often proved to be a very sensitive issue, with religious priests often finding themselves at the center of the maelstrom. Notable at any gathering of men and women religious is the evident compatibility between sisters and brothers. Even though not necessarily taken up with the feminine agenda, brothers share a certain commonality with women religious in terms of vocation, without the added considerations of priesthood. The difference lies, of course, in the fact that brothers do not embrace priesthood because of a personal decision; for women it is not an option.

It is in the celebration of the Eucharist that sensitivities come most to the fore. From the woman's side, there is a desire to "equalize" the male-female liturgical image by giving greater prominence to women and downplaying the visual aspects of a male priesthood. Thus, when women and religious priests come together, concelebration is generally frowned upon. A position of prominence for at least one woman at or near the altar is seen as at least neutralizing a very lopsided presence. None of this offsets the fact that the Eucharist, which stands at the heart of the Christian experience, is seen by many women religious as part of hierarchical patriarchy and is, therefore, a very painful experience.[21]

All of this has prompted a very mixed reaction from priests who are religious. They often feel that they are being held accountable for a problem that is not of their making. In addition, they feel no inclination to apologize, even implicitly, for their priestly state. It is important to note that religious and priestly formation has placed the Eucharist at the very heart of the spiritual life. Even if often weighted in favor of the mentality of their times, founders (and foundresses) reverenced the priesthood and saw the Eucharist as a principal source of the community's life. All of this has unquestionably created a certain defensiveness among priests regarding attitudes of women religious today, sentiments that often go unspoken in public but are vocalized among priests themselves. One can note a marked hesitancy on the part of some priests to accept a liturgical engagement involving women religious. When there is a joint meeting of men and women, the liturgy almost invariably becomes a central issue. It must be sensitively prepared and every possible unifying step taken. This can easily overshadow the spiritual significance of what is being done.

This is not to generalize or to speak in absolutes. It is not at all difficult to cite instances where the best possible climate obtains between women religious and priests of religious institutes. There are also those priests who are ardent spokesmen for women's concerns. At the same time the tension is still present and remains unresolved. Admittedly the problem is structural and not personal, and insensitivity can be present on either side. The single point to be made here is that religious priests feel a certain hurt and pain in this whole question, which can often lead to a defensive posture. It is not solely a women's issue.

A PERSONAL JOURNEY

Since this chapter centers on the experience of religious priesthood, I would like to reflect on my own life experience over the last fifty years. I am a religious and a priest, very much in love with both realities. I embraced both as a calling before Vatican II and have lived through the changes of the postconciliar church. As we stand on the brink of a new millennium, I have no idea of what the future holds, but the twentieth century has afforded us enough change in our mission, life, and thinking to move us toward the edge. My reflections are certainly not those of all my contemporaries in religious life, but I am willing to wager that they are comparable to what has been the experience of many priests in religious institutes.

If I were to reflect on my earliest vocational inclinations, I would have to say that my interests were in writing and drama. At an early age I very much wanted to go to the West Coast and write movie scripts or be a playwright. My pastor, who competed with neighboring pastors in recruiting vocations for his diocese, very much wanted me to enter the local seminary. When I voiced my own interests, he unflinchingly told me that a life in Hollywood would certainly lead to perdition, and therefore I had better focus my attention elsewhere, specifically the diocesan priesthood. My high school years were spent being educated by Franciscan friars in whom I saw excellent role models, and by the end of my years there I had decided I wanted to be a priest in the Franciscan order. When I told my pastor that I wanted to be a priest, he was overjoyed. His face fell, however, when I told him that I wanted to be a Franciscan. His only rejoinder was, "Why don't you go to Hollywood and write movie scripts?"

As I look back on my early years as a Franciscan and try to sort out my sentiments on the twofold vocation, I can only say that I felt intensely drawn to being a priest. I knew that I wanted to do that within the framework of community life and as a vowed religious. St. Francis cast no less a spell over me than he has countless others in the course of eight centuries, but I would have to say that in that period of my life priesthood was much to the fore.

The formation that we received in the 1950s only reinforced my priorities. While we spent the year of novitiate in plumbing the Franciscan spirit, the major emphasis of almost a decade of studies was on priesthood. During the year of novitiate, there was no distinction made between those preparing to be brothers or clerics; we were all Franciscans. Immediately after profession, however, we found ourselves on separate tracks. The brothers were off to develop manual or domestic skills and the rest of us went to the classroom. From that point on, the two groups saw each other only in passing. The clerical students were clearly marked for the sacerdotal state; they studied with diocesan seminarians and developed strong bonds of friendship with them, which certainly bettered understanding between the two forms of life. The study of both philosophy and theology prepared one for that momentous step into the priestly world.

The psychology of this type of formation is particularly evident in the "rites of passage" that moved us ahead. The major moment of religious formation came with the pronouncement of solemn or final vows. This occurred approximately three years after initial profession. It was the culminating moment in the life of a young religious, his definitive commitment to his religious institute. And yet it was clearly overshadowed by the "better things to come." It was juridically required before any major hierarchical order could be conferred and, thus, became a stepping stone to priesthood. From that point on, the clerical students were clearly on their way to that ultimate and culminating moment.

In conferring various ministries on the priestly candidate, the church builds on that note of expectation and anticipation. By the time we were ordained deacons (in the days before the permanent diaconate), we knew that the end was in sight, that we had "run the race" and "finished the course." Priesthood, then, conferred in the beauty of spring's splendor, with friends and family from near and far, bringing with it the exercise of a very sacred power, was clearly the climactic moment. And one very much looked forward to exercising that ministry, even though as a religious, one reckoned with the likelihood that it might be quite limited.

In my case the initial disappointment was particularly acute. Since I had been designated for biblical studies, academics took precedence over an initial pastoral introduction. More semitic languages were in the forefront of my postordination summer. Once again I was back in the classroom, lamenting the fact that my strong desire "to serve" had been subverted. The completion of my scriptural studies in the early sixties found me destined for seminary teaching, where I remained for more than a decade.

My calling as a religious certainly conditioned my whole priestly vision. My spiritual life was rooted in the Franciscan tradition; my community life meant more to me as time went on; and the vowed life of poverty, chastity, and obedience, while never as demanding or curtailing as it might have been, was precisely the way I wanted to live my life. Priesthood, however, was still primary. I was educating men for that calling, and everything surrounding it took on special significance. As part of a seminary staff, I realized that the fruit of my labor was seen in young men kneeling before the bishop on ordination day and pledging themselves to this ministry.

It was also true, however, that not all of my religious confreres saw their priestly ministry in this light. Many were teaching the secular sciences on a college or high school level and had very little opportunity to be engaged in parish ministry. After years of clerical preparation, which ranged from confessional practice to rubrics in administering the sacraments, they now had little or no opportunity to do specifically priestly work. They frequently questioned themselves as to why it was necessary to be ordained in order to be a professor of mathematics or chemistry. They came to grips with the question and answered it as best they could. But for many it remained something of an anomaly, especially when they asked the question, "To what did I really feel called?"

In those days my own order in the United States had very few parishes. But those who were engaged in this ministry found it very rewarding. Yet, there was very little in the parish setting that resembled a Franciscan way of life. It was not uncommon for a friar to be stationed by himself or at most with one other friar. This made community life and prayer a near impossibility. But it offered genuine opportunities for ministry, with the result that priesthood became the dominant motif. In many an instance, a pastor could not envision himself returning to community life or being involved in an institutional apostolate. Priesthood was the overriding concern, and the longer the friar remained in the parish, the more entrenched he became. And so, living memory offers two scenarios: one of friars who wondered seriously about how necessary priesthood was in their life and another of friars who found it controlling and indispensable.

Within the community itself, even with all the recognition given to total equality, the fact is that such did not obtain. The "lay" brothers, as they were then called, were barred from offices requiring canonical jurisdiction, which was linked with priesthood, and therefore could hold no positions of authority within this hierarchical structure. They were excluded from being even local superiors, which would have meant that they had authority over the priests in the house. Such was literally inconceivable. So, brothers were structurally relegated to a subordinate position. Initially in years past even their right to vote within the community was restricted. At the mother house of our order in Rome, the brothers took their place at table in a descending grade, after the priests. Canon law had norms of precedence that accorded first position always to those in priestly orders. So, even if priesthood was not exercised in any striking way, it still had its privileges. If one were going to rise to any position of prominence in the community, one had to be a priest. And all of this was coupled somehow with the realization that the order's founder, Francis of Assisi, was not himself a priest.

There was no doubt that many a lay brother felt this keenly, even though most adapted humbly to their subordinate state. For some religious orders, priestly precedence was built into the founding structures. The priests were involved in the preaching ministry or scholarly pursuits, and brothers facilitated this pursuit by looking after the material and domestic needs of the community. Such was not the case with the Franciscans, who were founded on the note of equality and were forced to admit that later canonical strictures were not in harmony with the original spirit. But the *de facto* separation was there and continued to prevail until the time of the Second Vatican Council.

Vatican II urged religious to return to their original spirit. What this did was to give religious life a prominence over priesthood within religious institutes that it had not previously enjoyed. A spirit of equality returned to many a monastery and friary, even though the adjustment was not immediate. The issue of precedence, which traditionally placed priests before brothers, became something of a dead letter. While my own experience was largely limited to Franciscans, the same spirit was also having its effect on other communities, even those which from their origin had been hierarchically structured. Not only did brothers now vote, but they also could be elected councillors on any level of the institute's life and, with the necessary dispensations, could be named local superiors as well.

All of this unquestionably impacted priests of the community. For some it made the quandary even more pronounced. In one's assignment within the community, there was often nothing distinctly priestly. With the decrease in vocations, the classroom, to an ever greater extent, was being shared with lay-people. The preaching mission became open to women religious and theologically prepared laypeople, so it was no longer "Father" who gave the annual retreat or even preached the parish mission. As ministry became more diverse and centered on the needs of the poor, the presence of the religious was a vital factor, but whether they were or were not priests had little or no significance. If one adds to all of this the changing life of the friary or monastery, with its leveling effect, it is not difficult to understand the ambiguity regarding identity that was brewing. The place of priority that priests had traditionally held no longer obtained. Brother councillors or superiors were making decisions that directly affected priests' lives. Many welcomed these changes, seen to be linked with the basic spirit of the community, as well as in line with the traditional ethos regarding the equality of all. Others were not so elated and found themselves questioning the very meaning of their lives. Once again religious priests in parish ministry fared better than most because their role was still quite clearly defined, even though the definition of ministry was constantly expanding.

There is a sense in which the concelebration issue highlighted the problem. Initially the concelebrants were vested in albs, exited the pews or choir stalls at the determined moment, and were visually distinct from the brothers, who remained in their traditional places. It was priesthood that came to the fore, and, considering the eucharistic setting, there was solid theological justification. For some, there was simply no question in following the lead that the church had set forth. For others, however, it was symbolically jarring, effecting a separation within the broader brotherhood in the liturgical act that should most unite all professed religious. This led to controversy and conflict, with some priests remaining with the brothers and refraining from concelebration and others holding tenaciously to what was seen as a "threatened" position. It took some time for the problem to be worked out satisfactorily, but it is cited here as a concrete example of the postconciliar tension regarding the priesthood.

There is still another impact of Vatican II on the lived experience of priests—both diocesan and regular. With the change of language, the emphasis on a contemporary theological and scriptural background, the great demand for preaching skills, and the need for greater gender inclusiveness, many priests, both religious and diocesan, were brought to the realization that a basically sacramental ministry, with its *ex opere operato* theology, was no longer enough. In celebrating mass, one had to be more than a rubricist; a sense of liturgy was required. Mass facing the people brought about a visual and personal contact with the congregation that had never been experienced before. Preaching had to be rooted in the scriptural readings over a three-year cycle, which required a contemporary understanding of God's Word. There was a new way of catechizing, of preparing couples for marriage, and of preparing people for ministry. This required abilities that made many preconciliar priests feel very inadequate. Psychologically, problems arose that made priests opt out of parish ministry completely. Moreover, the rapidity with which change took place proved to be unnerving and disconcerting. Communion in the hand, as I personally recall, became the breaking point for some religious priests, who felt at that point they could not possibly continue.

It would be wrong to think that the positive changes that the council introduced are to be seen in a dim light. They were unquestionably a necessary and salutary antidote to the status quo mentality that had long dominated. They raised important and basic issues and, in moving us forward, actually enabled us to see our authentic past more clearly. But the changes required major adjustments for people whose view of religious life and priesthood was as fixed and certain as dogmatic truth itself. The fact is that some priests in religious life did not succeed in making that transition. In their minds much of this adjustment touched the very core of their vocation and was not as simple as donning a new suit of clothes. This resulted in much personal anger for the individual; polarization within the religious house, province, or institute; and very trying times for those called to leadership.

I experienced this personally in two different ways. In being elected to the office of minister general of our Franciscan order, I knew firsthand the difficulties that some priests were experiencing, from changes both within the order and without. I could see that much of this was due to the fact that as we strove for greater clarity as an order, we were creating for some people a deep sense of ambiguity. And where identity is no longer clear, resulting from a paradigm shift, then the value of the life itself is called into question. What had been for me personally a liberating and very positive experience of growth after the council had not been the same for others. And this required on my part a sensitivity that was not easily acquired.

Another of the ways in which this change in my understanding of religious life was manifested was in the number of very qualified and academically capable candidates who upon entering the order reached a decision that they wished to remain brothers and not study for the priesthood. Many of these men felt that their vocational objective was fully realized in becoming a religious and in performing nonclerical ministries. Needless to say, this created quite a sense of surprise, if not consternation, on the part of members of the community who had long seen the priestly calling within religious life as the "pearl of great price." On the other hand, there were those who had been brothers for decades, living the very task-oriented life of the lay religious, who now wanted to pass to the clerical state and study for the priesthood. To what was this unexpected turn of events due? An authentic calling to the priestly life? A dissatisfaction with the earlier "second-class" category of brothers? A change of ministerial perspective? Were all such people capable of handling the seminary curriculum? Many superiors were faced with these two conflicting views, both rooted in a certain ideology, which saw the religious vocation in two distinctly different ways.

My own experience as minister general of our Franciscan order received broader confirmation when, upon completing my term of office, I became an executive with the national conference of men religious of the United States. Many religious orders composed of priests and brothers were finding that questions centering on the priestly life were present in their own ranks as well. There was an ongoing tension within the single vocation between the religious and priestly dimension. A survey was taken within the conference, and a series of workshops for the leaders of men's communities throughout the country examined the issue for the first time. An indication of the changing times appeared in this national organization during the 1980s. From the time of its inception in the 1950s, the organization had only priest religious as presidents. In the 1980s, two brothers were elected successively to head the entire conference. This was seen in a very positive light; it is cited here only as an example of the extent to which the accent on religious life, and not priesthood as such, had come to the fore.

Along similar lines, there has been an ongoing concern over the extent to which a new emphasis on parish ministry has exerted a strong magnetic pull on religious institutes in the postconciliar era. In former times the larger parishes in a diocese were entrusted to the local clergy. However, as their numbers began to dwindle, attractive offers were made to religious orders and congregations to staff prominent parishes. Some communities that had long been weighted in favor of institutional ministries and whose members were now interested in parish opportunities responded positively to such offers. For more than one community it has proved to be a mixed blessing. In more recent times, there is a reticence to assume further obligations, not only because of shrinking numbers, but also because of the extent to which parish demands can erode commitment to the fundamental values of the institute and blur the distinctive religious image.

A QUESTION OF CLARITY

In responding to the religious priesthood question, there is no escaping the fact that there is a lack of clarity in the minds of many people today about both the nature of the priesthood and the nature of religious life. The factors that have brought us to this point are many and diversified, and the points of view on the issue are very distinct. The 1994 synod of bishops, dedicated to the consecrated life, saw the emergence of a broad variety of views on healing the ills of religious life. These ranged from overcoming the idea of any inherent contradiction between mission and consecration,[22] to a call to a greater simplicity of life,[23] to an urgent plea to save the ship of religious life before it crashes on the reef of spiritual and moral disintegration.[24]

Somewhere between the extremes of unwarranted optimism in favor of a new, evolving and presently unknown form of religious life and the rhetoric of the death throes of religious consecration, there must be a middle ground. The same applies to priesthood. Between a priesthood with "another Christ" theology and a leveling of important distinctions by a priesthood-of-the-faithful mindset, it is vitally important to establish certain parameters of identity. Anyone who works in a Catholic seminary realizes that the role of the priest has become too blurred. Very well-intentioned and open-minded seminarians struggle with the question of priestly identity. And religious life faces similar problems. The question can be legitimately posed: If all Christians are called to the way of perfection, then what is my vocation in a religious institute? In addition, much of the church work that I formerly performed as a priest is now done by laypeople. Thus, in neither my life nor my work do I find any real distinctiveness.

Therefore, the future of priesthood in religious life will hinge greatly on the extent to which we strive honestly and without bias for genuine clarity in what it means to be a religious and what it means to be a priest. That is, I would suggest, not as difficult a task as it may seem. There is a role that religious have played in the church for centuries that is not eliminated by a universal call to holiness. By their vowed life, their commitment to community, and their corporate ministries, religious have stood strongly within the church as a living testimony to important features of the gospel life. One need not speak of a "higher state" or a separated state of life. Religious simply live with intensity a dimension of the gospels that is a reminder to all Christians of their responsibility to be chaste, poor, and obedient in a following of Christ adapted to their own state of life. They live out in community fashion that unity of Spirit that was found among the early Christians and that is reflected in the Acts of the Apostles. In their ministry they make present the gospel Christ "contemplating on the mountain, announcing God's kingdom to the multitude, healing the sick and the maimed, turning sinners to wholesome fruit, blessing children, doing good to all."[25] In itself this is not and cannot be an ambiguous calling. It is distinctive, not lived by the masses, and is situated squarely within and not above the faithful as a whole. Honesty compels us to ask if the shortage of vocations is not due, at least in part, to a self-created obscuring of the life. This is not to return to an outdated mindset, nor is it to set aside important gains that renewal has provided. It does not preclude our addressing the needs of the times, nor does it mean that we retain time-honored ministries with inflexibility. It simply repeats what prophetic voices have been saying repeatedly in recent years: that there is an overwhelming need for the presence of religious men and women in a culture that is hell-bent on being swept away by values that are antithetical to the gospel. The times point to the unquestionable value of highlighting the evangelical counsels.

Similar thoughts are relevant to priesthood. In the matter of the priesthood of the faithful and the ministerial priesthood, it is a question not of either/or but of both/and. Ministries performed by the nonordained, especially those that are eucharistic, only enrich the church and highlight our corporate heritage and responsibility. But this is not to denigrate the role of the priest, accentuated for centuries, as the presider who, in the name of the community, renders visible and tangible the one eternal offering of the one eternal Priest. Rather than standing in contrast to lay ministers, he is the one who shares his learning and his love with others dedicated to service. And as much as we may think to the contrary, in a long-lived tradition that shows no sign of dying soon, he is the one to whom many people turn with their cares and concerns. It is true that he no longer functions as a "lone ranger," but his position is still very much assured. The more that clarity on the ministerial priesthood is attained once again, the more the religious priest will be seen in proper perspective. The celibacy question certainly colors the thinking of the seminarian, who in the present discipline must make a commitment prior to ordination. It is not part of the religious priesthood issue, where celibacy pertains to the fabric of religious life itself.[26] Where greater clarity on the issues of both religious life and priesthood is attained—and my thesis here is that it is not unattainable—the understanding of the meaning of priesthood within consecrated life can only be made clearer.

As religious life developed in the church, priesthood became an important part of that life. There was no inherent incompatibility. If priesthood is viewed as a component of the religious calling—situated squarely within it and not as an appendage or as the overriding and determining factor—priests can render a valuable service to God's people. Priesthood that springs from the heart of the institute and is simply a further expression of its charism is neither a threat nor an imbalancing factor. Rather, priesthood is enriched by being refracted through the prism of the Jesuit, Franciscan, or Passionist tradition. Preaching, instruction, and liturgy are seen differently by those who are part of a centuries-old tradition. In short, where a true integration of priesthood and religious life is sought, it cannot help but make a difference. Clarity will then make for better choices. As priesthood is seen as an expression of the religious charism along very determined lines, as opposed to a generic form of priesthood, some will be drawn to it, and others will not. As the religious calling emerges more clearly, the priesthood within it may speak to some people quite eloquently; for others it may add nothing to what they see as their basic call.

After a reading of the present volume's contents, the question is posed anew: What meaning in concrete terms might all of this have for leadership in religious institutes at this moment in history? The answer, it would seem, lies in a willingness to face the problematic that such a study of both history and theology presents. A few key questions suggest themselves.

CHALLENGES AHEAD

What can we do to situate priesthood within the charism of the institute? Do we articulate priesthood as one of the various expressions of the founding spirit? Do we continue to move people toward ordination "on track" without raising the issue of its meaning or necessity in terms of the founding charism? Are we inclined to encourage the intellectually endowed religious to think of ordination as his goal, or does the religious calling take precedence? What questions are raised when a religious decides to study for the priesthood after many years as a brother? Do we see the staffing of parishes as the centerpiece of our ministries? Do we have the courage to say "Enough" and to withdraw from parishes in the interest of apostolates more directly linked with our charism? Although our parish residences may carry a distinctive name, how much different are they from the diocesan rectory? In leadership, do I wrestle with the issue of what our special contribution to the church today might be? And then do I have the courage to work toward implementation? Are we as leaders just too overwhelmed by a sense of lethargy and love of the status quo to attempt "to move the boulder"? Perhaps the most important question is also the most sensitive, and it has already appeared in the present volume in various ways. In a church dominated by a hierarchical vision and diocesan structures, are we willing as religious to take possession of our lives in what was historically a distinctly different form of church life? Are we willing to lay claim to everything that *exemption* signified in the past? Or shall we continue to be the submissive "sleeping giant" of the contemporary church? Can we recapture the courage of our founders?

A biblical perspective might help. The Bible invariably plans for the future by looking to the past. The People of the Land understood their life by recalling Sinai, but Sinai raised its own questions of origins that made the people reach back to the patriarchs to gain enlightenment. The early church got its moorings by recapturing Jesus and presenting him in a new light in what we call the gospels. The death of the Lord was the living object of reflection in that we term *Eucharist*. In facing the future, we are always children of our past. In an age of an almost exclusive focus on the present, we must draw on our traditions. This is especially true of those called to religious life. It is in remaining true to that initial vision that the blending of religious life and priesthood in the present age resides.

NOTES

1. Constitution on the Church, no. 44 in *The Documents of Vatican II*, ed. Walter M. Abbott, S.J. (New York: The Guild Press, 1966), 74–75.

2. *Ibid.*, no. 28, pp. 52–55.

3. *Ibid.*, no. 46, pp. 77–78.

4. *Ibid.*, no. 28, pp. 52–55.

5. Decree on the Ministry and Life of Priests, esp. no. 4, in Abbott, 538–40.

6. Constitution on the Church, no. 43, 74–75.

7. *Ibid.*, no. 5, pp. 17–18.

8. The apostolic exhortation *Vita Consecrata*, *Origins* 25, no. 41 (1996): p. 701, no. 60.

9. *The National Catholic Reporter*, October 14, 1994, 5.

10. J. P. Marshall, "Diocesan and Religious Clergy," in *The Catholic Priest in the United States*, ed. John T. Ellis (Collegeville, Minn.: St. John's University Press, 1971), 388. On tensions between hierarchy and religious in general, see Patricia Wittberg, *The Rise and Fall of Catholic Religious Orders* (New York: New York University Press, 1994), 78–97.

11. *Ibid.*, 389–96.

12. Gerard Huyghe et al., eds., *Religious Orders in the Modern World, A Symposium,* (Westminster, Md.: The Newman Press, 1965), 91.

13. *Acta Apostolicae Sedis* 70 (1978): 473–506.

14. I have treated diocesan and religious relations in an earlier article: Roland J. Faley, "Diocesan Need versus Religious Charism," *CMSM Forum* (spring 1993): 17–20.

15. Decree on the Appropriate Renewal of Religious Life, no. 2, in Abbott, 468–69.

16. Constitution on the Church, no. 28, in Abbott, 52–55.

17. *Ibid.*, chapter 6.

18. *Constitutions and General Statutes of the Third Order Regular of St. Francis*, Title IX, pp. 93–95. In speaking of the qualifications of the local minister, no mention is made of priesthood.

19. Constitution on the Church, no. 44, in Abbott, 75–76.

20. Shades of this struggle can be seen in the Third Order Regular constitutions where the general chapter defines the order as an "evangelical fraternity" (par. 1, art. 1) with a reluctant nod given the canonical designation in paragraph 3, article 1, where the order "is enumerated by the church among the clerical institutes of pontifical right."

21. Mary Collins, "Is the Eucharist Still a Source of Meaning for Women?" in *Living in the Meantime*, ed. Paul Philibert (Mahwah, N.J.: Paulist Press, 1994), 185–96.

22. *Origins*, 22, no. 19 (1994): 328–31.

23. *Ibid.*, 323–24.

24. *Ibid.*, 331–32.

25 Constitution on the Church, no. 46, in Abbott, 77–78.

26. See chapter 5, in which Kevin Seasoltz alerts us to some of the more recent decisions affecting the rites of ordination that tend to demean the vow the religious makes to be perpetually celibate.

5

The Priesthood: Implications in Consecrated Life for Women

Doris Gottemoeller, R.S.M.

This chapter can be dubbed an exercise in *speculative theology: If* the prohibition against the ordination of women were to be removed, what would be the implications for women in consecrated life and for their congregations? Some readers might answer that it is useless to speculate, either because the possibility is too remote or because the implications are too obvious. However, the work of the Spirit frequently takes us by surprise. If at some point it should be decided that women can be ordained, women's congregations would immediately be faced with a number of critical choices. An analysis of this hypothetical situation can be a useful tool, I believe, for sharpening our understanding of the charism of the consecrated life, whether for men or for women.

The choices that would face women's congregations can be illustrated by a number of interrelated questions: Should my religious congregation promote ordination for some/all of its members? Should this be ordination to the diaconate and/or to the priesthood? As a corollary, should we admit previously ordained women to membership? Each congregation would further have to ask, how would the ordination of some or all of our members affect our corporate identity and corporate mission? Is this what we choose? Before addressing these hypothetical questions, let's look at the context in which they occur today. There are five factors that condition the way in which women religious might respond to questions concerning their ordination.

First of all, women's religious life in the United States has become increasingly parochialized. The report of the Future of Religious Orders in the United States project first drew attention to this phenomenon of parochial assimilation. In their executive summary, authors David J. Nygren, C.M., and Miriam D. Ukeritis, C.S.J., point out that "The increasingly widespread insertion of religious into diocesan and parochial positions, to the point where such commitments take precedence over involvements in the lives of their congregations, is a growing phenomenon in the United States. This trend…has had a dramatic effect on most religious orders and probably most significantly among women. It can easily lead to a compromise of the prophetic role of religious."[1]

This transition occurred so subtly that it went unnoticed for a long time. Prior to the Second Vatican Council women religious working in parishes were almost exclusively employed in elementary schools. Although these schools were technically under the direction of the pastor (and, where they existed, parish councils or school boards), they were popularly regarded as "Mercy" or "Josephite" or "Notre Dame" schools. The respective religious congregations assigned the sister principal and faculty, and, if lay teachers were needed, the principal hired them. A well-informed Catholic *knew* which parishes had Mercy schools, which had Josephite schools, and so forth. Within the religious congregation, there was a sense of corporate mission to, or responsibility for, specific parish schools. This sense of congregational identification with a school began to erode when the number of lay teachers came to equal or exceed the number of sisters.

As qualified lay teachers became more available, parishes looked to sisters to fill roles for which they were deemed uniquely qualified, especially religious education of children and adults and a variety of pastoral services such as outreach to the elderly and homebound, music ministry, or liturgy preparation. Then, as the number of clergy declined and the number of parishes with a single priest grew, pastors looked to sisters to move into the new roles of pastoral associate or even pastoral administrator (in priestless parishes). An unforeseen effect of this parochial assimilation is that the typical parish has little or no sense of the distinctive charism of each religious congregation, no sense of the congregational mission or spirituality that supports *their* sister. Carried to its logical conclusion, women religious can come to be regarded as generic religious, interchangeable parish functionaries.

Another factor contributing to the way women religious look at the possibility of ordination is their movement into professional chaplaincy roles on college campuses and in hospitals, prisons, and other special situations. The 1995 annual report of the Catholic Campus Ministry Association (CCMA) indicates that 239 sisters currently serve as campus ministers (13% of the national total).[2] The Certification Policy Manual of CCMA identifies numerous personal, theological, and professional competencies expected of a campus minister. According to Donald McCrabb, executive director of CCMA, a master of arts in theology or the equivalent is a minimum expectation. Similarly, the March 1996 Statistical Report of the National Association of Catholic Chaplains (NACC) shows that 1751 sisters comprise 49 percent of its total membership of 3,546 chaplains. The NACC also publishes personal, theological, and professional standards and certifies Catholic chaplains. In a hospital setting, the chaplain is more than twice as likely to be a sister as a priest.

A third factor conditioning the attitude of women religious to ordination is the restoration of the permanent diaconate. Permanent deacons have become a new class of ministers in the church in the years since 1968, but a recent national study demonstrates that their role is still not clearly differentiated from other roles. The study reports that "In their written-in comments more than a few deacons complained that they are too often thought to be either 'incomplete priests' or 'more advanced laity.'"[3] Many deacons wonder whether ordination is necessary for what they do, and the majority of lay leaders surveyed do not think that ordination is necessary for the ministries performed by deacons in their parishes. Despite these ambiguities, the study concludes that the restored order of the diaconate has been highly successful. Certainly the rate at which it has grown indicates its widespread acceptance. While the total number of priests, sisters, and brothers has declined in the United States over the past decade, the number of permanent deacons has increased dramatically: from 7,204 in 1985 to 11,371 in 1995.

For our purposes, another statistic is also significant: The Vatican's 1993 *Statistical Yearbook of Churches* reported that, worldwide, 349 parishes are entrusted to deacons and 1,068 to religious women.[4] Comparisons between deacons and sisters are inevitable. The profile of American deacons developed in the national survey indicates that they are similar to sisters in active ministry in several ways. The median age of deacons is sixty; the majority are Caucasian, college-educated, middle-class, deeply spiritual, and highly motivated toward ministry. But sisters note that permanent deacons are permitted to preach, to serve at the altar during liturgy, and to administer some sacraments—ministries from which women are excluded—although in many instances their educational, professional, and spiritual preparation for ministry is significantly less than that of the sisters with whom they serve on the same parish staffs. Not surprisingly, situations of tension and conflict arise.

Fourthly, over the last decade official church documents have repeatedly emphasized the need to include women in all phases of decision making and administration in the church. Beginning with the 1985 apostolic letter "On the Dignity and Vocation of Women" (*Mulieris Dignitatam*) and continuing up to the recent postsynodal apostolic exhortation on consecrated life, *Vita Consecrata,* the pope has reiterated again and again that women's gifts are essential to the life of the church. The following are a few representative passages: "Only through openly acknowledging the personal dignity of women is the first step taken to promote the full participation of women in church life as well as in social and public life."[5] "Above all, the acknowledgement in theory of the active and responsible presence of women in the church must be realized in practice."[6] "Today I appeal to the whole church community to be willing to foster feminine participation in every way in its internal life."[7] "It is therefore urgently necessary to take certain concrete steps, beginning by providing room for women to participate in different fields and at all levels, including decision-making processes, above all in matters which concern women themselves."[8]

The United States bishops sounded the same themes in their 1994 statement, *Strengthening the Bonds of Peace.* "We commit ourselves to enhancing the participation of women in every possible aspect of church life."[9] The net effect of these constant reiterations of the need for women to participate in church life is to draw attention to the gap between the ideal and reality. Women are expected, invited, enjoined to participate in all aspects of the life of the church, including decision making, and, at the same time, most significant decisions are firmly in the hands of the clergy. It is a situation of impasse that the collective imagination and will of church members seem unable to break through.

Finally, the interest of women religious in ordination is shown by their longstanding participation in the women's ordination movement. The initial conference of the Women's Ordination Conference (WOC), held in Detroit in 1975, was largely organized by sisters, and the overwhelming majority of the attendees were sisters. WOC cofounder Dolly Pomerleau claims that without women religious, the organization would not exist.[10] Over the course of years the leadership of WOC has passed into the hands of laywomen, but sisters are still disproportionately represented in the membership, on the board, and as participants at national gatherings. WOC treasurer and board member Maureen Fiedler, S.L., reports that the financial support of women's congregations and of individual sisters continues to be significant. So much is this the case that working for the ordination of women is popularly regarded as a *sisters' issue.* The reasons for this identification of the issue with sisters are understandable. Sisters form a cadre of women in the church who are especially qualified by education and ministerial experience to care deeply about the issue. We have forums for dialogue that help shape and reinforce opinion. No systematic study has been done, however, to establish what percentage of sisters favor ordination of women or on what basis.

The commitment to women's ordination that many sisters express may be based on a variety of reasons: their sense of a personal call to priestly ministry; their conviction that the theological arguments offered in the 1975 *Inter Insigniores* and the 1994 *Ordinatio Sacerdotalis* are not persuasive; their desire to respond to the pastoral needs, especially for the Eucharist and the Sacrament of Reconciliation, that they experience in their daily ministry; or their feelings of frustration and injustice at a fundamentally gender-based exclusion. The current tension within the women's ordination movement between continuing to espouse ordination to the priesthood as a goal versus working for a "discipleship of equals" in which the priesthood is radically recast is reflected among sisters as well.

The net effect of the factors we have identified is that many Catholics assume that sisters in general want to be ordained or that ordination is a natural evolution in their ministerial commitment. Such assumptions can easily become self-fulfilling prophecies, so in what follows we will examine some of the possible implications of ordination for religious congregations of women. My premise is that we are discussing ordination to the priesthood and diaconate as they are presently understood and experienced in the Catholic church. It could be argued that the present theology of the priesthood/diaconate should be radically revised or that many specifics of practice such as the selection of candidates, formation programs, assignment policies, roles, and accountabilities should be changed. Indeed, the argument might follow that admission of women to orders would be a powerful means to effect such revisions. For the sake of focusing on one issue at a time, however, I will not undertake to critique the present theology of orders or practice of clerical ministry. My thesis is that the consequences for an individual congregation of ordaining one of its members would be extremely significant, bearing directly on its corporate identity and mission. Thus, I would urge any congregation to undertake a thoroughgoing discernment leading to chapter action before promoting one of its members for orders or admitting someone in orders.

IMPLICATIONS OF ORDINATION TO THE PRIESTHOOD

One can imagine four interrelated consequences of introducing the possibility of ordination into a women's congregation: it would change the fundamental equality among members; it would require a specific formation for those to be ordained; it would bring a new set of ecclesial accountabilities; and it would alter the corporate identity of the congregation.

First of all, ordination would change the fundamental equality of membership. In the past some women's congregations had two classes of members, choir sisters and lay sisters. The former enjoyed superior education, served in public ministries such as teaching and nursing, and were obliged to the choral recitation of the office (either the Divine Office or the Little Office of the Blessed Virgin Mary). The latter generally had minimal education, served in domestic ministries in the convent, and had a simpler prayer regimen. In some cases the two categories were further distinguished by variations in their dress and were separated at community events such as meals and recreation. This history is behind the injunction in Vatican II's Decree on the Appropriate Renewal of Religious Life *(Perfectae Caritatis)* that "care be taken to produce in women's communities a single category of sister" (no. 15).[11] However, most American congregations had already eliminated the two categories prior to the council.

In addition to the separate categories of membership, women's congregations also formerly emphasized distinctions based on seniority and office. Sisters sat in rank in chapel and refectory; convent duties and privileges were allotted on the same basis. One of the most freeing aspects of our post–Vatican II renewal has been to create a sense of the fundamental equality of all members. Chapter and renewal processes have emphasized participation by all in articulating directions and setting vision for the congregation. There is a danger that the introduction into a congregation of ordained members might seem to re-create a sense of two classes or tiers of members. Indeed, as is clear from the preceding chapters, this is the experience of some men's congregations that have ordained and nonordained members.

This concern is heightened by the fact that the ordained would be obliged to a specific education and formation that not all would share. The requirements for ordination in the United States are set forth in the *Program of Priestly Formation*.[12] The document acknowledges that the priestly life and work of religious will differ from that of diocesan priests, but asserts that there is a fundamental unity. "Religious and diocesan priests share an increasingly pluriform but common priesthood; their needs for priestly formation *as such* do not differ. Theological literacy, ministerial skills, the ability to reflect theologically on experience, a grasp of the global mission of the Church—these ought to be part of the preparation of every priest." At the same time, "the distinctive charism of a given religious community and its ramifications into the spirit, lifestyle, and work of members of that community are real factors in the maturing and incorporation process of a seminarian who is a religious."[13]

Not only is there a prescribed education and formation process for priests, but also there are prescribed institutions in which it is carried out, namely, seminaries. The seminary provides a residential setting in which the seminarian undergoes an integrated program of spiritual, intellectual, and pastoral formation over a period of several years. Some men's congregations maintain their own seminaries or their own formation programs within a freestanding diocesan seminary or a collaborative "union" model. *The Program of Priestly Formation* recognizes the legitimacy of maintaining what is distinctive to a religious congregation in its seminary program.[14] The challenge for women's congregations contemplating ordination would be to envision the impact on their corporate identity of having some members formed and educated in a seminary program. The program is not necessarily more rigorous— or even as rigorous—as many other graduate programs. There is, however, a specificity of intentionality and method that might serve to set those who complete it apart from the rest of the community. The experience of a sister who spends several years in medical school might be something of a parallel. Not only has she undergone a very intense preparation for a particular ministry, but she has also entered into a "fraternity" of practioners that confers a new identity with its own peer expectations and pressures.

The sister-priest would also assume a new set of accountabilities. With the new capacity conferred by sacred orders come new relationships and responsibilities.[15] The pastoral exhortation on priestly formation, *Pastores Dabo Vobis,* summarizes these as follows:

> The ministry of priests is above all communion and a responsible and necessary cooperation with the bishop's ministry, in concern for the universal church and for the individual particular churches, for whose service they form with the bishop a single presbyterate. Each priest, whether diocesan or religious, is united to the other members of this presbyterate on the basis of the sacrament of holy orders and by particular bonds of apostolic charity, ministry and fraternity. All priests in fact, whether diocesan or religious, share in the one priesthood of Christ the head and shepherd; "they work for the same cause, namely, the building up of the body of Christ, which demands a variety of functions and new adaptations, especially at the present time," and is enriched down the centuries by ever new charisms.[16]

The exhortation recognizes that religious priests play a special role in the diocese, enriching the presbyterate by their particular charisms and broadening the horizon of Christian witness. But the need for unity is clear: "For their part, religious will be concerned to ensure a spirit of true ecclesial communion, a genuine participation in the progress of the diocese and the pastoral decisions of the bishop, generously putting their own charism at the service of building up everyone in charity."[17] If a women's congregation were to accept responsibility for a parish, as do many men's congregations, it would find itself even more tightly bound into diocesan accountabilities. Perhaps the question of new and potentially conflicting accountabilities is best seen in the limit case, appointment to the episcopacy. Some men's congregations have regularly seen their "best and brightest" called to episcopal ordination, thus effectively removing them from congregational leadership and participation. Is this a consequence that women's congregations are willing to accept?

The consequence of ordination that supersedes all the others is the challenge to corporate identity and mission. Religious life has come through a period of intense change and significant diminishment, with resulting anomie within religious congregations and confused perceptions among onlookers. Nygren and Ukeritis point out that "at the present time many congregations lack a sense of corporate identity....Lack of clarity regarding the group's mission focus offers little to attract the commitment or capture the passion of potential new members."[18] The extent to which outsiders share our confusion or fail to grasp the meaning of our lives can be illustrated by the question I have heard several times from reporters, "If priests are allowed to get married, do you think sisters will too?" These inquirers have no idea of the distinction between the vocation of religious and of diocesan priests and no idea of religious life as a way of life in which celibacy is an integral component. They think that religious observe celibacy as a sort of price for working in the church rather than as the heart of our religious commitment.

It seems to me that the paramount task for each congregation is to clarify for itself, and recommit to, its specific identity, rooted in its own charism. Religious life is not a cluster of more or less arbitrary obligations, but an integral way of life in which the various components mutually reinforce one another. The witness of celibate community is a powerful expression of ministry; ministry engenders passion in prayer; prayer purifies the heart of attachment to material things; renunciation of material things brings us closer to the poor and needy, and so forth. At the same time each congregation needs to clarify and recommit to a corporate mission, a vision so powerful that it shapes the public perception of the congregation and guides individual and corporate choices of ministry. Only then can the decision to embrace ordained ministry as an option for some members be made in the context of this corporate identification and commitment.

Interestingly, at the end of Vatican II, *Perfectae Caritatis* stated that "there is no objection to religious congregations of brothers admitting some members to holy orders, to supply needed priestly ministrations for their own houses, provided that the lay character of the congregation remains unchanged and that it is the general chapter that makes the decision" (no. 10). By and large, most congregations of brothers have chosen not to exercise this option. When and if the option presents itself, what choice will sisters' congregations make? Will they be willing to compromise their lay character?[19]

IMPLICATIONS OF ORDINATION TO THE DIACONATE

The considerations raised relative to ordination to the priesthood also apply, with appropriate qualifications, to ordination to the diaconate. However, there are two factors that mandate an independent assessment of the implications of women religious being ordained to the diaconate. The first is that ordination of women to the diaconate might be a real option in the relatively near future. The second is that we can examine the contemporary experience of the permanent diaconate among men.

The Canon Law Society of America's (CLSA) study, "Canonical Implications: Ordaining Women to the Permanent Diaconate"[20] concluded that a decision to ordain women to the permanent diaconate is possible and may even be desirable for the United States in the present cultural circumstances.

The study was, in part, a response to the Vatican's own commentary on *Inter Insigniores,* which stated that the possibility of ordaining women deacons "must be taken up fully by direct study of the texts, without preconceived ideas; hence the Sacred Congregation for the Doctrine of the Faith has judged that it should be kept for the future and not touched upon in the present document."[21] Several successive drafts of a pastoral letter on women's concerns, prepared by an *ad hoc* committee of the National Conference of Catholic Bishops (NCCB) between 1988 and 1992, also called for a study of the issue of ordaining women as deacons. The following are other pertinent conclusions of the CLSA's study:

- The diaconate is presented in canon law as a sacrament, a grade in the sacrament of holy orders. It is a permanent or character sacrament, and those ordained deacons stand in a different kind of relationship within the community and not just a difference of degree. Ordination provides sacramental grace for the witnessing presence of the ordained, but does not impede or denigrate the proper role of laypersons in the church or in the world.

- The supreme authority of the church is competent to decide to ordain women to the permanent diaconate. It would require a derogation from Canon 1024, which restricts all ordinations, including that to the permanent diaconate, to males. This can be done by legislation or individual indults to episcopal conferences.

- It would not be necessary to adopt ordination of women to the permanent diaconate throughout the entire church; as with the ordination of men to the permanent diaconate, this is a question properly left to decisions by the episcopal conference and individual diocesan bishops.

- Women ordained to the permanent diaconate would be bound by the canon law which applies to men ordained to the permanent diaconate, and women who are members of religious institutes would be bound by the law which applies to male religious who are clerics. Some adjustments would be required in some specific provisions concerning clergy which are currently expressed in masculine terms.

- Women ordained to the permanent diaconate, moreover, would be able to exercise ministries and to hold offices from which they are not excluded, but which are in keeping with the services women currently provide in the church. They would be given the added assistance of sacramental grace as a result of ordination in the same manner that men already involved in church service have received this sacramental aid through their own ordination as permanent deacons.

What reflections do these conclusions suggest? One might be that ordaining women to the diaconate inserts a wedge into the absolute barrier against ordination of women, the first "foot in the door," so to speak. On the other hand, the permanent diaconate is promoted as just that, as *permanent*. Accepting ordination to a permanent, stable office in the church implies a call to, discernment around, and acceptance of that office. Another reflection is that actions and activities that are permitted are often uncritically assumed to be desirable, especially if they have not been permitted in the past. Hence the necessity of a careful discernment about the desirability of change in a particular instance (or for a particular individual or congregation).

The experience of the permanent diaconate for men, as documented by the NCCB National Study of the Diaconate, has been cited above. Here are a few more points that might be relevant to the discernment of a women's congregation regarding ordination. The first applies to accepting candidates into the congregation who have previously been ordained deacons. The study indicates that diocesan preparatory programs do not presently emphasize the church's social ministry or the social teachings of the church.[22] Deacons gave only mediocre ratings to their formation preparation when asked if they were prepared "to use social referral agencies like Catholic Charities and the family life bureau." They did not demonstrate a knowledge of the social encyclicals or the bishops' pastoral letters on justice and peace; sixty percent were not familiar with the term *the consistent ethic of life*.

Women's congregations that have integrated the church's social mission into their own will want to insure that candidates are willing and able to make this commitment. Similarly, the study shows that the permanent diaconate is overwhelmingly a parish-based ecclesial service. Issues of accountability and role clarification are largely determined through the single channel of the pastor.[23] If religious women deacons follow in this mode, it will contribute further to the parochialization of their life. Add to this the significant identity issues experienced by deacons (Are they overqualified laypersons or underqualified priests? Is ordination even necessary for the ministries they perform?), and the possibility of further erosion of the identity of women's religious life is real.

CONCLUDING THOUGHTS

My effort in this chapter has been to distinguish the question of the ordination of women religious from the question of the ordination of women in general and to show that the possibility raises specific questions of congregational identity and mission. I believe that if the possibility becomes a reality, a congregation's discernment about its future direction should precede any sister's request to seek ordination. My bias is that a religious congregation risks losing a lot by including ordained members. On the other hand, there will surely be instances where the needs of the church and the prompting of the Spirit will lead congregations to embrace this change. In these instances the choice may be a means of refocusing congregational vision and revitalizing its energies.

The recent Synod on Consecrated Life strongly affirmed the unique and indispensable value of consecrated life to the church's life and holiness. Religious life offers a prophetic witness not only, or even primarily, because of the work that religious do, but also because of the radical commitment to Christ that it embodies. At the same time, the synod recognized that religious congregations are not part of the essential structure of the church. Religious life belongs to the charismatic life of the church, which means we have a certain freedom to commit ourselves to spiritual and corporal works that are outside the mainstream of church priorities. A strongly felt and deeply lived corporate spirituality, apostolic creativity, and willingness to invest corporate resources are hallmarks of dynamic religious life. The church will be poorer if religious sacrifice these for the sake of parochial ministry.

NOTES

1. David J. Nygren, C.M., and Miriam D. Ukeritis, C.S.J., "Religious Life Futures Project: Executive Summary" (Chicago: De Paul University Center for Applied Social Research, 1992).

2. CCMA Executive Director Donald R. McCrabb reports that this number has shifted downward from 24 percent in 1989. The number of ordained has remained constant (around 50 percent) but the number of laywomen has increased. Memorandum to the author, May 6, 1996.

3. "NCCB National Study of the Diaconate," *Origins* 25, no. 30 (1996): 501. Survey respondents included deacons, their wives, their priest supervisors, and parish lay leaders.

4. Cited in *Origins* 25, no. 30 (1996): 501.

5. The apostolic exhortation *Christifideles Laici, Origins* 18, no. 35 (1989): 585.

6. *Ibid.,* 586.

7. Pope John Paul II, "On Fully Fostering Women's Roles in the Church," remarks delivered at his Sunday audience just prior to the opening of the Fourth World Conference on Women in Beijing, *Origins* 25, no. 13 (September 14, 1995): 201.

8. The apostolic exhortation *Vita Consecrata, Origins* 25, no. 41 (1996): 699.

9. *Origins* 24, no. 25 (1994): 419.

10. Opinions cited here were expressed in a personal conversation among Dolly Pomerleau, Maureen Fiedler, S.L., and the author.

11. In the same paragraph the decree makes a similar statement about lay brothers in clerical congregations: they "should be brought into the heart of its life and activities."

12. National Conference of Catholic Bishops, *The Program of Priestly Formation,* 3rd ed. (Washington, D.C.: United States Catholic Conference, 1982).

13. *Ibid.,* 6.

14. *Ibid.,* 65–66.

15. The legal symbol of this new accountability is incardination. According to canon 265, every cleric must be incardinated into some particular church or into an institute of consecrated life. As a commentary on this canon states, "Every cleric without exception must be subject to a definite ecclesiastical superior. The law prohibits a cleric from being unattached or in an itinerant status at any time. The fundamental reason is that clerics by definition are public servants; no one should be inducted into the clerical state except for the necessity or utility of the Church (John E. Lynch, C.S.P., *The Code of Canon Law: A Text and Commentary,* commissioned by The Canon Law Society of America, ed. James A. Coriden et al. [New York: Paulist Press, 1985], 191). Thus, the ordained religious has a double obligation to obedience, in virtue of religious profession and of ordination. See the subsequent chapter in this volume by Kevin Seasoltz regarding the development of this relationship with local bishops.

16. *Origins* 21, no. 45 (1992): 726.

17. *Ibid.,* 754.

18. Nygren and Ukeritis, 35.

19. I have argued elsewhere that its "lay character" is a valuable characteristic of apostolic women's religious life, in "The Identity and Mission of Apostolic Women's Religious Life," an intervention at the Synod on Consecrated Life, published in *Origins* 24, no. 19 (1994).

20. Washington, D.C. 1995. Excerpts are published in *Origins* 25, no. 20 (1995).

21. Cited in the CLSA study, 3–4.

22. "NCCB National Study," 502.

23. *Ibid.,* 503.

6

Institutes of Consecrated Life and Ordained Ministry: Some Canonical Issues

R. Kevin Seasoltz, O.S.B.

The complex history of religious institutes and their relationship with the hierarchical church is reflected in the canonical legislation that has attempted to regulate those relationships. Longstanding conflicts between religious and bishops were certainly not resolved by the detailed legislation concerning religious institutes in the 1917 Code of Canon Law, nor have they been either resolved or eliminated by the 1983 Code. In fact, some of the tensions have greatly increased in light of the remarkably changed position of women in Western society and because the new Code has set out what has been called a bill of lay rights (canons 203–31) and has sought, where possible, to eliminate all discrimation against laymen and laywomen.[1]

Experience since the promulgation of the 1983 Code has already given us some assured sense of the strengths and weaknesses of the new legislation; some of the problem areas are already quite evident. Such problems need to be clarified so that religious institutes will be aware of both their rights and responsibilities regarding these basic issues as they negotiate a path into the twenty-first century, a path that is apt to cross through very rugged ecclesial and secular terrain. In plodding their way forward, religious institutes must take with them their legitimate patrimony, assured by both the gospel and their distinctive rules and constitutions. They must not allow that legitimate heritage to be eroded or taken away, because it is a heritage that has been given in trust not only for the benefit of contemporary religious but also for those who will follow along the path in the future.

Christians are those who have made a commitment to Jesus Christ; hence they are committed to the values and the way of life set out in the gospel. Their primary responsibility is to uphold gospel values. But the members of institutes of consecrated life are Christians who have vowed themselves to live out Christian values as they are interpreted by their rules and constitutions; hence their responsibility is to live according to those rules and constitutions and to uphold the values inherent in those documents. In this somewhat anxious period in the church's history, their principal concern should be, not to adapt their lives as readily and easily as possible to canonical directives from the hierarchical church, but rather to discern carefully whether new legislation is consonant with the values set out in the gospel as well as in their rules and constitutions, which have in fact been approved by Roman authorities.

The members of institutes of consecrated life must keep their legitimate patrimony from being eroded by canonical legislation that in some instances might be incongruent with their tradition, in other instances might be simply irrelevant, and in still other instances might call for refinement in the light of an informed canonical hermeneutic. Obviously, competent work on such particular legislation can be done only by those who are formed in the tradition of an institute, conversant with developments in the theology of religious life, and trained in canon law and abreast of current canonical developments.

It is a truism that we interpret the world from our own vantage point. Hence, Jesuits rightly interpret the 1983 Code and subsequent legislation from a Jesuit point of view, which is apt to be colored very much by ministerial concerns. Dominicans interpret it from a Dominican point of view, influenced very much by the friar's commitment to preach the Word of God. Benedictines interpret it from a monastic point of view, dominated by commitment to a cenobitic way of life under a specific rule and an abbot. In other words, the history, particular legislation, and cultural and theological context of each institute should form the framework in which appropriate new legislation is interpreted, assimilated, or possibly rejected.

Certainly not every canon in the 1983 Code nor every new directive issued by a Roman dicastery carries the same weight. Some are expressions of Christian dogma; others are expressions of theological opinions that are defensible but not authenticated by the magisterium of the church; still others are expressions of prudential decisions conditioned by ecclesial and cultural contingencies. Hence, each piece of legislation should be interpreted according to its proper nature. Some should be observed at all times, others should be adjusted to theological developments, and some should be changed or disregarded as prudence dictates.[2]

Many of the canons in the 1983 Code pertaining to institutes of consecrated life are doctrinal rather than dogmatic; hence, they should be evaluated by theological criteria and interpreted from theological sources. On all doctrinal points, the canons of the new Code should be interpreted in light of the documents of the Second Vatican Council, not vice versa.[3]

Likewise, the canons that affect institutes of consecrated life must be interpreted in light of the gospel and the particular rules and constitutions of each institute because it is to the gospel and their rules and constitutions that religious have vowed their way of life. The experience of institutes of consecrated life, their theology, and canon law should condition and complement one another so that they not only promote fidelity to a past tradition but also assure the implementation of the mandate of the Second Vatican Council that there should be in the church and all its institutions an ongoing process of reformation.[4]

In light of this background, several issues will be addressed in this chapter that seriously affect institutes of consecrated life and the exercise of ordained ministry both within the community and in the wider ecclesial context: the nature of religious exemption and autonomy; the power of jurisdiction and empowerment for church functioning and mission as distinct from the power of orders; and the legislation and rights pertaining to the installation of ministers and the ordination of the members of institutes of consecrated life as well as other liturgical matters.

EXEMPTION AND AUTONOMY

Perhaps the most important canonical right belonging to an institute of consecrated life that needs to be preserved and protected today is its right to lawful autonomy. This insures that an institute is free from unauthorized external controls in its efforts to be faithful to its distinctive charism and its duly approved rules, constitutions and customs, and free as an expression of the charismatic dimensions of the church to relate properly to the hierarchial structures of the church. Autonomy is to be carefully distinguished from canonical exemption whereby the pope, by virtue of his primacy in the universal church, and with a view to the common good, withdraws an institute of consecrated life from the governance of local ordinaries and subjects them to himself alone, or to some other ecclesiastical authority (canon 591). The canonical institute of religious autonomy, as we shall see, was something that developed and was clarified only gradually in the course of church history, often as a result of controversies with local bishops.

In the first centuries of monastic life extending from the time of Anthony (c. 251–356) to the time of Benedict (c. 480–c. 550), individuals, either alone, if their charism was anchoritic or eremitical, or in the company of others, if their charism was cenobitic, responded to a particular charism that required total dedication to seek God. As anchorites or cenobites, monks were primarily laypersons; consequently, they had little official contact with diocesan bishops. Hence, there was no question of exemption, for the monks were no more subject to the local bishops than were the rest of the laity. The early monks organized their lives without benefit of canon law. Their baptismal response to God was focused by their fidelity to a particular charism, a gift of the Spirit, enabling them to follow Christ in a distinctive way. The directives and structures for their life emerged from their own understanding of their charism. Hence, their monastic life was organized, not by the principles of canon law, but by the responsibilities and rights that flowed as exigencies of their charism. In other words, these structures constituted a precanonical institution, that is, a network of intersubjective rights and duties that had their source in the charism itself.[5]

After the death of Anthony, monks functioned as teachers of Christian doctrine; they often enjoyed popularity as models of orthodox Christian life. Hence, they sometimes achieved a religious and a doctrinal role that brought them into conflict with the bishops of the church. The fourth and fifth centuries were periods of great Christological controversies, with the monks identifying sometimes with one side in the controversies and sometimes with another. Such controversies were naturally on the agenda of the church councils held at that time.[6]

At the Council of Chalcedon in 451, canons were drawn up to clarify doctrine, and decrees were passed to bring the monks into line.[7] While acknowledging their status as monks, the council decreed their subjection to the local bishop. Religious life, therefore, received its first official recognition in the church and was canonically incorporated into the structures of the church, but it was clearly made subject to the hierarchy constituted by the bishops. In Africa, even after 451, some monks remained outside the jurisdiction of the local bishop, but they constituted exceptions rather than the rule.[8]

The historical origins of exemption are to be found in a bull of Pope Honorius I placing a threatened monastery outside the jurisdiction of Bishop Probo of Tortona while integrating both the monks and the monastery within the higher jurisdiction of the pope himself. On 11 January 628, the abbot of the famous monastery of Bobbio received the bull granting the first exemption of religious in the history of the church. The monastery was founded by the Irish monk Columban; Abbot Bertofolo was his second successor. He sought and received the privilege of special protection from the Apostolic See.[9]

Coming from Ireland where church life was organized around the monasteries rather than the diocesan bishops, the Bobbio monks were predisposed to seek the pope's special protection in addition to that of the king, which they had enjoyed from the time of the monastery's foundation. The papacy itself was pleased to encourage the monastic life of the thriving community as a bulwark against the Arian heresy.[10]

Bobbio's privilege of exemption was reconfirmed and extended by Pope Theodore I on 4 May 642. He gave the monks the clear right to elect their own abbot, and the abbot was given the privilege of using *pontificalia*. Hence, the exemption of the monastery meant not only protection from outside influences but also a strengthening of the jurisdiction of the abbot himself.[11]

The exemption of the monastery at Bobbio was the first in a long line of such privileges granted to monasteries and, eventually, to other religious institutes. The Council of Chalcedon had envisioned the relationship between monks and diocesan bishops as a rather simple one, but that relationship underwent development of a complex nature in the course of church history. Legislation governing the relationship between religious institutes and the hierarchical church was on the agenda of almost every ecumenical council convened from Chalcedon until Vatican II and was seriously debated by the preparatory commissions set up to formulate the canons of both the 1917 and 1983 Codes of Canon Law.[12] Naturally, the relationships were increasingly complicated by the clericalization of monasticism and by the clerical character of so many religious institutes of men from the late Middle Ages down to the present time.

David Kay expresses the situation clearly:

From Bobbio onwards a new relationship began to develop between religious institutes and the bishops, who were bypassed wholly or in part in the cases where religious had received an exemption from their jurisdiction and were placed directly under the jurisdiction of the Pope. There thus became explicit a third canonical coordinate in the axis of sacred power structuring religious life; no longer could one speak of religious and bishops alone; in future one would also have to speak of the highest common factor added to the canonical equation governing religious institutes; it now read: Pope, bishops and religious. What has been called a third coordinate in the structuring of consecrated life is commonly expressed today in institutes of pontifical right, but this is a concept dating from Leo XIII's Apostolic Constitution *Conditae a Christo* of 1900 only, and it is canonically distinct from the ancient concept of exemption.[13]

In fact, four major stages of development of the institution of exemption may be broadly distinguished. (1) From the time of Bobbio in 628 and the Abbey of Cluny in the period extending from the early tenth to the middle of the twelfth century, exemption served to guarantee tranquil monastic life. (2) Between the time of Cluny and the development of the mendicant communities in the early thirteenth century, exemption served as an effective instrument in the Cluniac and Gregorian efforts to reform both religious life and the church as a whole. (3) From the early thirteenth century until the Council of Trent (1543–1563), exemption served as an assurance of independence for the centralized apostolates of the mendicant orders. (4) From the Council of Trent until Vatican I, despite the decline in the effectiveness of exemption proportionate to the decline in the strength of the papacy, exemption continued to function as a canonical institute right up to the time it was incorporated into the 1917 Code of Canon Law.[14]

The Council of Trent had tried to bring conflicting laws governing the relationship between religious and local ordinaries into harmony with the pyramidal ecclesiology that was in place at the time;[15] that legislation was in effect until the 1917 Code of Canon Law. Following the promulgation of the 1917 Code, commentators tried to clarify the delicate relationship between religious, especially exempt religious, and the hierarchy. Authors wrote in detail about the degrees of subordination of religious to the jurisdiction of bishops and their freedom from such jurisdiction. However, the legislation of the 1917 Code was interpreted in isolation from the history and theology of religious life, as well as the particular legislation of each institute. It became increasingly clear that the universal legislation on exemption cannot be properly interpreted apart from the legislation proper to the religious institutes themselves. All of the laws, both universal and particular, must be carefully considered together.[16] It is therefore imperative that episcopal vicars for religious as provided for in the 1983 Code must know the legislation of both the Code and the religious institutes in the diocese where the vicar serves.[17]

The bishops of the Second Vatican Council were in agreement that the legislation concerning the relationships between themselves and the religious in their dioceses needed to be discussed and carefully restructured canonically. The Constitution on the Church, *Lumen Gentium,* solemnly affirmed religious exemption as a canonical institute (no. 45): "With a view to providing better for the needs of the whole of the Lord's flock and for the sake of the general good, the Pope, as primate over the entire church, can exempt any institute of Christian perfection and its individual members from the jurisdiction of local ordinaries and subject them to himself alone."[18] It was affirmed in weaker form in the Decree on the Pastoral Office of Bishops in the Church, *Christus Dominus* (no.35, 3): "The privilege of exemption whereby religious are reserved to the control of the Supreme Pontiff, or of some other ecclesiastical authority, and are exempted from the jurisdiction of bishops, relates primarily to the internal organization of their institutes. Its purpose is to ensure that everything is suitably and harmoniously arranged within the institute, and the positive development of the religious life promoted. The privilege ensures that the Supreme Pontiff may employ these religious for the good of the universal church, or that some other competent authority may do so for the good of the churches under its jurisdiction. This exemption, however, does not prevent religious from being subject to the jurisdiction of the bishops in the individual dioceses in accordance with the general law, insofar as this is required for the performance of their pastoral duties and the proper care of souls."[19]

Unfortunately, the council did not produce an adequate statement on the rights of religious themselves vis-à-vis the local ordinaries, nor did it set out a clear statement of the theological and spiritual meaning of that autonomy that is essential to the freedom and proper development of religious institutes; it is generally agreed that the decree on the up-to-date renewal of religious life, *Perfectae Caritatis,* is one of the less impressive documents of the council.

Consequently, following the council serious tensions developed between local bishops and religious, especially concerning the exercise of ordained and other ministries in accord with the prophetic character of various religious institutes.

On 14 May 1978 the Congregation for Religious and Secular Institutes and the Congregation for Bishops issued the document *Mutuae Relationes* in an attempt to resolve some of the difficulties.[20] It affirmed that the pope and bishops together should see to it that, under their vigilance and protection, religious institutes should develop and flourish according to the spirit of their founders. It allowed that certain institutes should be exempted from the jurisdiction of the local ordinary for the sake of the general good of the universal church and for the promotion of religious life.[21] The document underscored that, of its nature, exemption is not an obstacle either to pastoral coordination or to good relations among God's people.[22] Building on earlier pronouncements, it affirmed that exemption relates to the internal organization of religious institutes. Exemption was described as a privilege that ensured that the pope or some other competent authority could employ religious for the good of the church.[23]

As already noted, exemption and autonomy are certainly not the same. The 1983 Code of Canon Law concedes that the pope may exempt institutes of consecrated life from the governance of local ordinaries and subject them either to himself alone or to another ecclesiastical authority (canon 591). In more significant terms it addresses the issue of autonomy as a necessary consequence of the identity of consecrated life as described in canon 573. According to canon 578, the intentions of the founders and their determinations concerning the nature, purpose, spirit, and character of the institute that have been ratified by competent ecclesiastical authority as well as the wholesome traditions of such institutes are to be faithfully observed.

Canon 576 insists that competent authorities are to ensure that institutes grow and flourish according to the spirit of the founders and wholesome traditions. The following canon acknowledges that there are many different institutes of consecrated life with gifts that differ according to the grace given them. This legitimation of pluralism indicates that these two canons were drawn up with the principle of subsidiarity in mind. Following the promulgation of the 1917 Code of Canon Law many religious institutes lost much of their distinctive character because they were forced to conform to rigid, standardized norms when drawing up their proper constitutions.[24] It should be noted here that in many cases the founders of religious institutes were in fact very prophetic people who were major reformers in the church and who often had serious differences with local ecclesiastical authorities. Counseled by the Code to follow the spirit of their founder, religious institutes should be no less prophetic today.

Canon 586 of the 1983 Code summarizes the church's affirmation of autonomy and establishes the framework for any discussion of work or ministry in a religious institute. It states: "For individual institutes there is acknowledged a rightful autonomy of life, especially of governance, by which they enjoy their own discipline in the church and have the power to preserve their own patrimony intact as mentioned in canon 587. It belongs to local ordinaries to safeguard and protect this autonomy." What needs to be stressed is that autonomy affects the whole life of an institute, not simply its so-called internal workings. It is artificial to make a clear distinction between the autonomous internal governance and relationships of the institute and the work and ministry of the community, presuming of course that an institute has been faithful to its distinctive identity.[25]

In light of their autonomy, whatever religious do should be marked by their proper identity. To maintain that autonomy pertains to the inner life of the institute but not to its apostolates is neither valid nor helpful, for it reflects an anthropological and cosmological dualism also inherent in the canonical distinction between contemplative and active religious communities and between religious and secular institutes. In practice every religious life is a mixed life, just as every human life has both active and contemplative dimensions; difference is apt to be a matter of degree or emphasis. If religious are living a life of Christian faith, there is no area of life that is secular or unredeemed by the death and resurrection of Jesus Christ. To speak of apostolic communities as though they were distinct from monastic communities is really to abuse the term *apostolic.*

As studies in Scripture, Christology, and ecclesiology have shown, the term *apostolic* covers both senses of that mission that is essential to the identity of both Christ and his church: the inner building up of the community and the proclamation of the Word of God in the gospel. This interdependence of the life and mission of the church and all its members sets the foundation for the missionary and apostolic character of every religious institute; it also demands that every Christian, including all religious, be open to the world, since a mission to the world is an essential part of the church's life. To the extent that religious institutes are in fact open and faithful to the Word of God, they are apostolic, and their very life is an apostolic ministry in the church and the world.[26]

Canon 678 notes that "religious are subject to the authority of bishops, whom they are obliged to follow with devoted humility and respect, in those matters which involve the care of souls, the public exercise of divine worship and other works of the apostolate." In interpreting that canon, however, one must keep in mind that the bishops themselves are obliged to respect the prophetic charism of the religious institutes and to foster the development of those charisms. In the case of clerical religious institutes, that charism regularly involves the exercise of ordained ministry.[27]

Just setting out the pertinent canons of the 1983 Code shows how difficult it is to keep the tensions between a religious institute and a diocese poised. Difficulties often arise because of differences in assessing the same situation. At times misunderstandings occur because religious feel called to witness to certain Christian values that are not popular in a local diocese. Since the Second Vatican Council, special difficulties have arisen because of the involvement of religious in work for justice and peace. In canon 672 the Code notes that religious are bound by the provisions of canons 285 and 287, which regulate the involvement of clerics in political parties and labor unions. It follows then that religious "are forbidden to assume public offices which entail a participation in the exercise of civil power" (canon 287, paragraph 3) and that they are not "to have an active role in political parties and in the direction of labor unions unless the need to protect the rights of the church and to promote the common good requires it in the judgment of the competent ecclesiastical authority" (canon 287, paragraph 2). If one respects the principle of subsidiarity, the competent ecclesiastical authority should be the major religious superior.

The document on "Religious Life and Human Promotion," issued in January 1981, affirmed that religious should be concerned to establish the kingdom of God in the very structures of the world by inserting gospel values into human history, but not in the sense that they become directly involved in party politics. The document further noted that active involvement in politics is something to be undertaken by way of exception; each case should be carefully examined so that, with the approval of both the local bishop and the religious superior, decisions can be made that benefit both the civil communities and the church.[28]

Certainly the members of religious institutes have played a significant nonviolent role in witnessing to and working for peace and social justice in the contemporary world since the Second Vatican Council. In their witness, however, especially in controversial areas, they should remember the cenobitic character of their commitment, which means that they act not simply in their own name but also in the name of the community. In these matters, involvement should be authorized by the religious superior, who in turn should inform the community of such authorization and, where it seems appropriate, also the diocesan bishop.[29] In this way misunderstanding, unjust judgments, and alienation can be avoided.

Canon 611 stipulates that the consent of the diocesan bishop to erect a religious house of any institute brings with it certain rights, in particular the right to lead a life according to the character and purpose of the institute and to exercise the works proper to the institute according to the norm of law, with due regard for any conditions attached to the consent. If the conditions are such that an institute cannot be faithful to its distinctive charism, it should not open the new house. In this matter, as in other matters involving the presence and ministry of a religious institute in a diocese, whether it is in a parish, school, or retreat house, the agreement and its conditions should always be carefully drawn up in a legal document that binds both the diocesan authorities and the members of the religious institute. As a result of such canonical clarity, religious and diocesan bishops should be in a better position to exercise their shared responsibility in the apostolate by the way of mutual agreement and consultation.

THE APOSTOLIC EXHORTATION *VITA CONSECRATA*

Pope John Paul II has dealt with this issue of autonomy and exemption in his apostolic exhortation *Vita Consecrata,* issued on 25 March 1996.[30] There he encourages institutes of consecrated life to be creative in retrieving the charism of their founders in response to the new needs emerging in today's world. He has invited them to pursue competence in their personal work, to develop a dynamic fidelity to their mission, and to adapt their life and work to new situations and different needs in complete openness to God's inspiration and the church's discernment.[31] However, such efforts to be creative and to respond to new needs sometimes bring institutes of consecrated life (in particular their ordained members) into conflict with the hierarchical church. The pope emphasizes the need for every institute to be faithful to its rule and constitution because they provide individuals with reliable criteria for determining appropriate forms of witness capable of responding to the needs of the times without departing from the institute's own proper mission and goals.[32]

In his apostolic exhortation the pope stresses the importance of cooperation between consecrated persons and local bishops so that there might be organic development of pastoral programs in the local churches. He stresses the rightful autonomy of each institute and the responsibility of local ordinaries to preserve and safeguard that autonomy.[33] He also insists that in coordinating their service to the universal church with their service to particular local churches, the members of institutes of consecrated life may not invoke either rightful autonomy or even exemption in order to justify ministerial choices that in fact undermine the organic communion so essential to the life of the church.[34]

The pope reminds the members of institutes of consecrated life that in descerning which initiatives are proper and which are counterproductive, their ministerial efforts should be carried out in a climate of open and courteous dialogue between bishops and the superiors of the various institutes. Bishops should respect the vocation and mission of each institute; each institute should respect the ministry of bishops and the concrete pastoral programs that they have set out for their dioceses. In this regard, mutual respect is an expression of that charity that builds up the organic communion of the whole church.[35]

In an important section of his exhortation, the pope writes:

> Everything must be done in communion and dialogue with all other sectors of the church. The challenges of evangelization are such that they cannot be effectively faced without cooperation both in discernment and action of all the church's members. It is difficult for individuals to provide a definitive answer; but such an answer can arise from encounter and dialogue. In particular, effective communion among those graced with different charisms will ensure both mutual enrichment and more fruitful results in the mission in hand. The experience of recent years widely confirms that "dialogue is the new name of charity," especially charity within the church. Dialogue helps us to see the true implications of problems with greater hope of success. The consecrated life, by the very fact that it promotes the values of fraternal life, provides a privileged experience of dialogue. It can therefore contribute to creating a climate of mutual acceptance in which the church's various components, feeling that they are valued for what they are, come together in ecclesial communion in a more convinced manner, ready to undertake the great universal mission.[36]

It must be acknowledged here that the members of institutes of consecrated life are often much better equipped than local bishops to participate in dialogue because of their experience of cenobitic life, their frequent involvement in chapter and council meetings, their training in discernment processes, and their close ministerial collaboration with laypeople, both men and women. The pope's reflections on the role of dialogue in arriving at decisions involving the ministry of religious in local dioceses will not be easy to implement but will often require much patience and charity on the part of both bishops and religious. What must be stressed is the clear fact that, in discussing the relationship between religious institutes and local bishops, Pope John Paul II never proposed a facile solution to complex problems whereby religious should simply be subject to the authority of local bishops.

EXERCISE OF JURISDICTION BY THE NONORDAINED

In 1988 Alba House published a collection of essays entitled *Who Are My Brothers?*[37] It is a study of the relations between clerical and lay religious in men's congregations in the United States of America that was sponsored by the Conference of Major Superiors of Men. One of the essays, by Justin Der,

O.F.M. Cap., deals with the canonical issues of rights and relationships in such communities. More specifically, it deals with leadership roles in those religious institutes that have both clerical and lay members.[38]

The 1983 Code of Canon Law asserts that, in itself, the state of consecrated life is neither clerical nor lay. But in canon 207, paragraph 1, the Code affirms that, by divine institution among Christ's faithful, there are in the church sacred ministers, who in law are clerics, and that there are others who are called laypeople. Institutes of consecrated life are legally divided into clerical institutes and lay institutes, and generally function as one or the other. A clerical institute is one that, by the design of the founder or because of legitimate tradition, is under the governance of clerics, implies the exercise of sacred orders, and is recognized as such by the authority of the church (canon 588, paragraph 2). A lay institute is one that is recognized as such by legitimate authority because, by its nature, character, and purpose, its proper role, defined by its founder or by lawful tradition, does not include the exercise of sacred orders (canon 588, paragraph 3). Clerical institutes of men, however, need not be composed exclusively of clerics, nor need every member of the institute be ordained as a priest. Hence, there are some clerical institutes in which the majority of religious are ordained; the Jesuits would be an example of such an institute. But there are also clerical institutes in which many of the members are not priests; the Cistercians and Benedictines would exemplify such an institute. Clerical religious institutes have the right to have a church and to carry out liturgical ministries in accord with the general law of the church (canon 611, paragraph 3).

In the 1917 Code as well as in the present Code, the exercise of liturgical ministries is the basic determining factor for being a clerical institute. The 1917 Code described an institute as clerical if the greater number of the members were ordained (canon 488). Although not stated in that Code, commentators generally understood that the fact that priests exercised the governing postions in their institutes was an additional reason for classifying them as clerical. Likewise, it was understood that once an institute was classified officially as clerical, it remained so until its classification was formally changed, even though the greater number of its members were no longer priests.[39]

Basic to the differences between clerical and lay institutes is the fact that internal jurisdiction is exercised by ordained members. The 1983 Code clearly affirms that major superiors and chapters of religious institutes and of societies of apostolic life that are clerical pontifical institutes possess the power of governance for both the external and the internal forum (canon 596, paragraph 2). This means that major superiors in such institutes are ordinaries, a term used in the Code for those who are set over a particular church or community with the authorized power of governance.[40]

One of the canonical difficulties today is determining the meaning of the term power, *potestas*. There are a number of areas in the 1983 Code affecting religious life that involve the exercise of power, *potestas*. These include the following:

1) The power to dispense from disciplinary laws in certain cases (canons 14, 87).
2) The power to dispense from observance of a feast day or a day of penance (canon 1245).
3) The power to dispense from private vows and oaths (canons 1197, paragraph 2; 1203).
4) The power to grant dimissorial letters (canon 1019, paragraph 1).
5) The power to dispense from irregularities and impediments for admission to holy orders (canon 1047).
6) The power to grant faculties for hearing confessions (canon 969, paragraph 2).
7) The power to grant permission to establish an oratory (canon 1223).
8) The power to bless a sacred place (canon 1207).
9) The power to grant permission to use a sacred place for another purpose (canons 1210, 1212).
10) Permission to reserve the Eucharist in an oratory other than the principal oratory of a church (canon 936).

THE EXERCISE OF JURISDICTION

Clearly the exercise of most of these faculties belonging to a religious superior is not jurisdictional. The 1917 Code affirmed that only ordained members of the church could exercise jurisdiction in the church. That position, however, was occasionally altered by the Holy See when it gave nonordained religious superiors, both men and women, faculties to act both validly and licitly in certain matters that had previously been reserved to the ordained and were of a jurisdictional nature. For example, superiors were given the faculty to permit a member in temporary vows to leave definitively from the institute. This faculty was eventually incorporated in the 1983 code (canon 688, paragraph 2). Two very different schools of thought concerning the nature, source, and exercise of power in the church—known as the German school and the Roman school—have developed since the Second Vatican Council. The German school maintains that only the ordained can possess or exercise sacred power in the church; the Roman school maintains that the sacrament of baptism disposes all the faithful to receive and exercise sacred power in those instances that are specifically granted by the highest authority of the church.[41]

In 1976 the commission entrusted with the revision of the Code of Canon Law asked the Congregation for the Doctrine of the Faith whether laypersons could participate in the legislative, judicial, and executive aspects of jurisdiction and, if so, which functions they could exercise. The congregation responded that laypersons were excluded only from those offices that required ordination, and that specific instances would be determined as occasion arose.[42]

This complex issue was eventually dealt with in canon 596 of the 1983 Code. The first paragraph of that canon states that superiors and chapters of institutes have the authority over the members that is defined in the universal law and in the constitutions. Clearly the power of nonclerical religious is considered a public ecclesiastical power similar to jurisdiction; nevertheless, the wording of the second paragraph of canon 596 does make it clear that the power mentioned in paragraph one is not exactly the same as the power of governance mentioned in paragraph two: "In clerical religious institutes of pontifical right they have in addition the ecclesiastical power of governance, for both the external and the internal forum." Thus, despite the debates of the German and Roman schools of thought concerning the meaning of *potestas,* the 1983 Code notes at least three situations in which nonordained religious superiors may actually exercise jurisdiction: they may grant an indult of exclaustration to their members (canon 686), they may grant an indult of departure for those in temporary vows (canon 688, paragraph 2), and they may issue a decree of dismissal after following the proper procedures (canon 699, paragraph 1). These canons are in accord with canon 129, paragraph 2, which states, "Lay members of Christ's faithful can cooperate in the exercise of this same power *(potestas regiminis)* in accordance with the law."

Most of the authority exercised by a religious superior is not in fact jurisdictional. The great majority of older religious institutes in the church were founded without any distinctions between the clerical and lay members of the community. This is evident from the early history of the monastic and mendicant communities; apart from the Dominicans, they were established with absolute equality of membership. At times the governance of monasteries was in the hands of laymen so that the clergy could be free to engage in apostolic activities for the good of the church. These lay members exercised not only so-called dominative power but also true jurisdiction over the members of the community—what we would today call the power of governance *(potestas regiminis).*

There is, then, a sound historical precedent for the desire of many institutes to receive church authorization to determine, in accord with their constitutions and tradition, who shall govern their communities without reference to ordination. Each religious institute, in accord with the mind of the founder and the traditions of the community, should be able to determine its own identity as lay, clerical, or mixed. It should also be able to determine the best possible way it will be governed. Religious institutes are usually the best judges to discern who is gifted with the charism of leadership from within their ranks. The members should be able to choose the persons most capable of leadership without concern for their status in the community. The ability to lead a community supersedes the importance of ordination.[43]

In his apostolic exhortation, Pope John Paul II reflected on the status of religious brothers in the church. He noted that in such religious institutes nothing prevents certain members from receiving holy orders for the service of the religious community, provided the practice has been approved by the general chapter. The Second Vatican Council, however, did not explicitly encourage such a practice because it wanted institutes of brothers to remain faithful to their distinctive vocation and mission in the church.[44] As Doris Gottemoeller has noted in the previous chapter, some large institutes of brothers did not opt to ordain members.

The pope singled out those so-called mixed institutes, which in the founder's original plan were envisaged as a brotherhood in which all the members, priests and those not ordained to the priesthood, were considered equal among themselves. He advised that the members of such institutes should evaluate, on the basis of a deeper understanding of the founder's charism, whether they should return to their original inspiration. He observed that the members of the 1994 Synod of Bishops expressed a hope that in mixed institutes all the members would be recognized as having equal rights and obligations, with the exception of those that derive from ordination. The pope noted that a special commission had been established to examine and resolve the problems connected with this issue.[45] As has already been noted, the principal issue is whether brothers may be elected superiors in such religious institutes.

Clearly, jurisdiction in an institute of consecrated life is not an end in itself. It is a means to promote the life of the institute and its service to the larger church and world. Hence, it should be conferred on those members of the institute best qualified to exercise legislative, executive, and judicial governance in the community.

ORDINATION RITES AND OTHER LITURGICAL MATTERS

The Second Vatican Council's Constitution on the Sacred Liturgy, *Sacrosanctum Concilium,* decreed that the rites for the conferral of the sacrament of orders were to be revised.[46] The council also restored the diaconate as a permanent and independent order of the Western church; that decree was carried out by Pope Paul VI in a *Motu Proprio, Sacrum diaconatus ordinem,* dated 18 June 1967. The document was issued only three days after the pope had made public his encyclical upholding the Latin church's tradition of priestly celibacy.[47] In his *Motu Proprio,* he maintained that the diaconate must no longer be considered as "a pure and simple step to ascent to the priesthood." The document asserted that two types of deacons would exist: single men, for whom the minimum age for ordination is twenty-five, and married men, who must have their wives' consent in writing and for whom the minimum age is thirty-five. The bishops of the United States used an option allowed by the pope in his *Motu Proprio* and chose thirty-five as the minimum age for all permanent deacons.[48] In this country, institutes of consecrated life have rarely opted for ordination of any of their members to the permanent diaconate; in most communities the diaconate is simply a transitional step on the way to ordination to the presbyterate.

On 18 June 1968 Pope Paul VI, in his apostolic constitution *Pontificalis Romani,* announced a major revision of the rites of ordination to the diaconate, priesthood, and episcopate.[49] The new rites, promulgated on 15 August 1968,[50] were severely criticized from various liturgical and theological points of view, but the most telling critique came from members of institutes of consecrated life. They objected to the language of the rites, with its emphasis on honor, status, and dignity rather than humble service, and its propensity for the hierarchical sacralization of ministry.[51]

On 29 June 1989 the Congregation for Divine Worship and the Discipline of the Sacraments published a second edition of the rites for ordination; the publication containing this *editio typica altera* carries a copyright date of 1990. Several aspects of the new edition deserve comment. In the ordination of religious to the diaconate, the candidates are required to make a public profession of their commitment to celibacy, even though they have already made a public profession of perpetual chastity in their proper religious institute.[52] One might make a technical distinction between chastity and celibacy, but in the minds of religious superiors and their subjects, a public profession of a vow of chastity certainly implies a public commitment to a life of celibacy.

Experience has already shown that the bishop's questioning of the religious candidate for the diaconate regarding his commitment to celibacy is both embarrassing and awkward because it gives the clear impression that the previous profession of chastity has not been taken seriously. To avoid embarrassment, bishops usually try to contextualize the promise in terms of the commitment to chastity that the candidate has already made, with the result that the new profession appears to be redundant.

The other significant change in the new edition of the ordination rites for the diaconate and presbyterate occurs in the language of the consecratory prayers.[53] As already noted, in the 1968 edition the language emphasized the honor and status being conferred upon the candidates. Instead of God being addressed as the giver of honors, the distributor of orders, and apportioner of offices, the 1990 edition praises God as the giver of graces. Hence, the orders of diaconate and presbyterate are no longer imaged as superior ranks in the church. The emphasis on status elevation has generally been eliminated from the text. This is certainly an improvement, one that should be appreciated by religious as well as diocesan ordinands. However, although the 1990 text does correct the status elevation of the ordinands, it continues to speak exclusively of the hierarchical sacralization of ministry. The revised texts do not in any way address the serious problem of identifying, designating, and empowering other ministers who are called to serve the church. One gets the impression that only the ordained are ministers in the church. The image that is projected in the 1990 rites is exclusively that of a pyramidal church.[54]

For institutes of consecrated life, perhaps the most controversial change and the one most fraught with difficulties in the 1990 ordination rites occurs in the promise of obedience that is made by religious. The new text now requires that the promise of respect and obedience on the part of religious being ordained to the diaconate and the presbyterate be made to both their religious superiors and the diocesan bishop.[55] This change deserves extended comment.

The first extant ritual requiring a promise of obedience occurs in the tenth-century Romano-Germanic Pontifical.[56] The origins of such a promise seem to go back to the time of Boniface, who on 30 November 722 was ordained a bishop by Pope Gregory II. At that time he made the same promise of obedience that the suffragan bishops of the Roman province made to the pope. The following year, Pope Gregory III made Boniface an archbishop and conferred upon him the pallium as a symbol of authority delegated by the pope. Boniface subsequently attempted a reform in the church by requiring the subordination of the bishops in his area to himself and the subjection of the clergy to their proper diocesan bishop. He wanted both bishops and presbyters to be able to work independently of the civil authorities in their area. In the ninth century the promise of obedience was looked upon as an external manifestation granting freedom and security both to the institutional church and to the bishops and presbyters as leaders of the church. It was a sign of the church's efforts to free itself from secular control of any kind.[57]

In the tenth-century Romano-Germanic Pontifical we find an explicit promise of obedience inserted into the rites for the ordination of presbyters and bishops. In both instances it concludes the examination of the candidate in order to affirm his suitability for ordination. In the case of the presbyter, the promise was meant to assure a personal and responsible relationship of the priest to the bishop; in the case of the bishop, it was meant to ensure proper allegiance of the bishop to the pope.[58] In later texts the promise was removed from the examination of the candidate and inserted after the reception of Communion.[59]

The Council of Trent dealt with the sacrament of orders in its twenty-third session, which formulated its basic teaching on the sacrament on 15 July 1563.[60] Canon 7 deals with the examination of the one to be ordained a presbyter. Although the conduct, doctrine, and faith of the ordinand are all to be investigated, there is no specific mention of his obedience, probably because obedience was not seen as an issue separate from the good order required of ordained ministers in the church. In the *Pontificale Romanum* issued after the Council of Trent (1596), the actual ordination of deacons to the presbyterate takes place after the first reading and the tract but before the gospel. After the newly ordained presbyters have received Communion, there is a second imposition of hands and the conferral of the Holy Spirit for the forgiveness of sins. This is followed by a promise of obedience. Distinct forms are given for diocesan presbyters and for the members of exempt religious orders.[61] The issue is one of jurisdiction, not priestly power. Hence, the primary concern is with the jurisdiction that is needed for the forgiveness of sins. The promise of obedience is thus placed in a juridical context, one in which the priest promises obedience to his diocesan bishop or major religious superior in order to have faculties to function as an ordained cleric.[62] In the 1596 rite for the ordination of bishops, the candidate promises that he will be both faithful and obedient to the pope and his successors.[63]

Note that in the Roman Pontifical promulgated after the Council of Trent there is a similarity in the vocabulary between the rites of religious profession and the blessing of abbots and the promises of obedience in the ordination rites of presbyters and bishops. The primary issues are those of jurisdiction and the consequences of exemption enjoyed by both monks and mendicants.[64] As we have seen in chapter 2 of this book, many monks were ordained presbyters in the Middle Ages. The privilege of exemption made them subject directly to the Roman pontiff, so that, in effect, they bypassed the control of the local bishops. The bishops, however, increasingly sought to gain control over exempt religious. For example, the First Lateran Council (1123) emphasized the authority of the local bishop over the ministry of all presbyters in his diocese.[65] Canon 12 of the Fourth Lateran Council (1215) required that the local bishop hold a general chapter every three years to be made up of all those abbots and priors who could not claim exemption. It also called for a visitation of the monasteries by the local bishop on a regular schedule. Canon 13 of the same council forbade the establishment of new orders with new rules because the great variety of religious orders was thought to cause confusion in the church.[66]

The emphasis on obedience continued with the establishment of the major mendicant orders. For example, in the rite of profession of the Dominicans, approved as an order by Pope Innocent III in 1216, special emphasis was placed on the promise of obedience to the master general. The promise was made while the candidate placed his hands in the hands of the ruling prior.[67] The hand ritual seems to have originated with the Cluniac reform, which required that the priors of dependent priories should take an oath of loyalty to the abbot of Cluny while placing their hands in the abbot's hands.[68]

As with the Dominicans, obedience was also emphasized by the Franciscans whose first rule was approved by Innocent III. According to the

Regula bullata of 1223, Francis himself promised obedience and reverence to the pope, and the brothers promised obedience to Francis and his successors.[69] It is significant that in 1331 the minister general of the Franciscans made several changes in the ritual, including the moving of the profession rite to Communion time so that it was linked to the Eucharist.[70] This change seems to have brought the profession rite into conformity with the rite for the ordination of presbyters in the thirteenth-century Pontifical of the Roman curia.[71] Hence, the mendicant promise of obedience and the promise of obedience in the ordination rites for presbyters seem to be mutually dependent. It also seems that the rite whereby the ordinand made his promise of obedience with his hands in the hands of the bishop was derived from the monastic and mendicant rites of religious profession.[72]

One of the remarkable aspects of the mendicant orders was the fact that they enjoyed papal exemption. Their exemption differed, however, from that of Cluny and the other monastic communities. Whereas the Benedictines and Cistercians were exempt from any episcopal control so that they could develop their monastic life, the mendicant orders were exempt so that they could exercise their external apostolates effectively. They were able to preach everywhere and teach without episcopal restriction; hence they contributed in very significant ways to the reform of the church.[73] This ministerial exemption did, however, result in tension between the mendicants and local bishops.

The Fifth Lateran Council (1512–1517) tried to alleviate the tension by insisting that the authority of the local bishop should be kept intact whenever there was a conflict with mendicants. The bishops were granted the right to make visitations of the parishes run by mendicants and also the right to examine the friars before they were ordained and given faculties to hear confessions. Mendicants needed the consent of the pastor to officiate at marriages in his parish and to carry out other liturgical rites. Finally, the friars were to give the bishops obedience since they are the successors of the apostles. Clearly, the council tried to strengthen the hierarchical structure of the church by subordinating the friars to the diocesan bishops.[74]

The Council of Trent continued the line taken by the Fifth Lateran Council. In session twenty-three it approved canon 10, which prohibited abbots and others enjoying the privilege of exemption from conferring minor orders on anyone not subject to them without dimissorial letters. Canon 12 insisted that the members of regular orders should not be ordained too young or without proper examination by the local bishop. Canon 15 required that the bishop examine and approve confessors, the privilege of exemption notwithstanding.[75]

These councils strengthened the juridical character of the church, with the result that local bishops gained more control of both monasteries and friaries in their dioceses. There was not much change in the juridical understanding of the church until the Second Vatican Council, apart from the fact that the

First Vatican Council strengthened the role of the papacy in the church so much that it overshadowed the episcopacy in many ways. In practice the life of exempt religious was governed mainly by the Roman dicasteries rather than by local bishops. This was above all the situation following the promulgation of the 1917 Code of Canon Law and the approval of the proper constitutions of religious institutes following the promulgation of the Code.

At the Second Vatican Council the issue of obedience was not prominent in discussions preceding the preparation of the documents dealing with the sacrament of orders; it was simply taken for granted. The theological under-standing of the sacramental relationship between the bishop and presbyters, however, was strongly emphasized in the texts of Vatican II. As has already been noted, the various documents of the council give a rather clear statement of the rights of local bishops over religious in their dioceses, but, unfortunately, the conciliar texts do not provide an equally clear statement of the rights of reli-gious vis-à-vis the local bishop. Especially lacking is a satisfactory statement clarifying the nature of that autonomy that is essential for the development of the life and service of institutes of consecrated life in the church.

Although the 1968 edition of the rites for the ordination of deacons, pres-byters, and bishops did not require a promise of obedience to the local bishop to be made by candidates from religious institutes, the 1990 revised edition does contain such a requirement. The *coetus* that was responsible for the work on the revised rites was under the direction of Reiner Kaczynski. The work of the committee was discussed by both the members and consultors of the Congregation for Divine Worship on 20–24 May 1985. The *coetus* continued its work and then included new wording for a promise of obedience, but noth-ing was said about religious making a promise of obedience to the local bishop.

The work of the committee was further discussed in plenary session of the Congregation for Divine Worship on 15–16 October 1985. The promise of obedience for religious was on the agenda, but no conclusion was reached. Finally, the matter was proposed, along with other concerns, to the secretary of the Congregation for the Doctrine of the Faith on 20 May 1986. Apparently, various members of the latter congregation wanted religious presbyters to make a promise of obedience to the local bishop. During a plenary session of the Congregation for Divine Worship on 29 November–3 December 1988, it was announced that the final text of *De Ordinibus sacris* was prepared and that, with the final approval of the Congregation for the Doctrine of the Faith, the text had gone to the pope at the end of June. It was given final approval by the pope on 10 May 1989 and promulgated by decree of the Congregation for Divine Worship on 29 June 1989, but its actual publication date was 31 May 1990.[76]

Leon Strieder summarizes the matter well:

In general, the promise of religious, of both deacons and presbyters, to the local diocesan bishop flows out of the basic teachings of *Christus Dominus* 35.1 and 4...and *Ecclesiae Sanctae*
22–26, both of which emphasize the need for harmony in the pastoral ministry of a diocese. Both state that religious are subject to
the local bishop in all aspects of their public ministry and worship.
This same basic understanding of the relationship between the
pastoral ministry of religious and the local bishop was codified in
the 1983 Code of Canon Law in canons 678 and 681. Thus, it
seems that this special promise of obedience made by religious to
the local diocesan bishop developed out of an ecclesiological
understanding of the diocese as the local church, and thus, the
need for the unity of all pastoral ministry in that diocese under the
authority of the local bishop.[77]

When the leadership team of the United States Conference of Major
Superiors of Men visited Rome and the various dicasteries after the 1990 edition of the ordination rites was promulgated, they were informed that neither the
Union of Superiors General of Men nor the Congregation for Institutes of
Consecrated Life had ever been consulted about the promise of obedience to the
local bishop to be made by religious deacons and presbyters. The nature of the
relationship of religious deacons and presbyters to the local diocesan church
certainly needs clarification. The issue is further confused by the requirement,
already noted, that religious deacons make a promise of celibacy in the ordination rite, a promise specifically required by Pope John Paul II, contrary to the
exemption provided by canon 1037 of the 1983 Code of Canon Law.

   This issue concerns not only the nature of the relationship between religious life and the sacrament of orders but also the nature of the relationship
between the charismatic and hierarchical dimensions of the church, both of
which are divinely instituted according to *Lumen Gentium*.[78] The institutional,
hierarchical model of the church has been so strongly emphasized by the Holy
See in recent years that the other models of the church that are either explicitly
or implicitly set out in the documents of the Second Vatican Council have
been overshadowed, if not repressed. More attention must be given to the
church as community, as prophetic people of God, as sacrament, as servant,
and as herald so that the distinctive role of religious in general and ordained
religious in particular might be enhanced rather than hindered.

   Needless to say, recent restrictive tendencies on the part of the hierarchical church are apt to increase rather than diminish the tensions between institutes of consecrated life and local ordinaries. During his pontificate Pope John
Paul II has appointed an increased number of religious as bishops of local dioceses. These bishops, with their background and formation in religious life,

should understand the difficulties that the developments have caused for religious. Diocesan priests who become bishops, however, are likely to be ignorant of the nature and rights of religious in their dioceses and, consequently, of the difficulties inherent in recent developments that tend to infringe upon the legitimate autonomy of institutes of consecrated life. Certainly the practical implications of the promise of obedience that religious ordinands make to the local ordinary will need to be clarified with fairness to all sides so that both religious life and ministry in the church will flourish in a climate of trust and encouragement.

A final issue related to ordination that needs to be addressed is the installation of ministers in the church provided for in Pope Paul VI's *Motu Proprio Ministeria Quaedam.*[79] That document concerned the reform of the discipline of first tonsure, minor orders, and subdiaconate in the Latin church. The orders of porter and exorcist were suppressed, and the acolyte took on the functions of the subdeacon. The minor order of lector became the ministry of lector.

Strictly speaking, Paul VI suppressed the minor orders altogether. We are to speak of "ministries" rather than "orders" when referring to the functions of lectors and acolytes, and these ministries are conferred by installation rather than by ordination. The ministries are conferred on laymen and do not imply that one has been admitted to the clerical state. Tonsure has been suppressed; admission to the clerical state takes place at the ordination to the diaconate.

Canon 1035 of the 1983 Code of Canon Law requires that all religious who are to be ordained to the permanent or transitional diaconate must have received the ministries of lector and acolyte and have exercised them for a suitable period of time. The canon also specifies that an interval of at least six months must exist between the conferral of the ministry of acolyte and the diaconate. These ministries may be committed to other Christian laymen; hence they are not reserved to candidates for the sacrament of orders.[80]

By reason of their religious profession, members of institutes of consecrated life commit themselves to serve the community in their liturgical celebrations under the superior's direction. That service normally includes exercising the role of reader and minister at the altar. It is inappropriate to institutionalize these or similar ministries in religious communities by formally installing religious according to approved liturgical rites, even when they are to be ordained deacon. Apart from the fact that the legislation is biased against women in that it precludes their installation in such ministries, application of the procedures in religious institutes would imply inadequate understanding of the meaning of religious profession and the implicit responsibilities assumed at that time. Hence, a formal installation is little more than empty ritualism because most of those installed have already been exercising those ministries in their communities ever since the time of their religious profession.

Another liturgical issue that needs to be addressed is that of preaching in institutes of consecrated life. In communities the superior has both the right and the responsibility to form the community in the Spirit of God's Word. Traditionally superiors have given conferences on religious spirituality or deputed others to do so. With the emphasis on the homily in both conciliar and postconciliar liturgical documents as well as in the 1983 Code of Canon Law, the celebration of the Eucharist has become a regular occasion during which the Word of God is effectively shared and broken open for religious, often on a daily basis. These homilies in religious institutes are often given not only by the priest presiding at the Eucharist or by a deacon but also by others whom the superior deems competent, including nonordained religious, both men and women. The practice has generally been very well received and has proved to be a wholesome way of enriching the spiritual lives of the community members. This has been the case especially in those communities where there are very few or often no members ordained to the priesthood or diaconate but where other members of the community have been trained in Scripture, theology, and liturgy and are in fact competent preachers.

The simple fact is that chaplains appointed to communities without priests have sometimes been incompetent from both theological and liturgical points of view and often have seemed to have little understanding of religious life in a contemporary world. A democratic approach has not been taken in response to this situation; not everybody in the community preaches, but only those authorized by the superiors. Hence, there is what might be called a licensing process whereby the superiors designate and delegate those who are to preach. The practice is really in keeping with the responsibility of professed religious to use their gifts and training generously for the good of the community under the direction of the superior.[81]

Canonical conflicts, however, have developed in the area of the homily since canon 767 has been interpreted in such a way that the breaking open of the Word after the gospel is reserved exclusively to a priest or deacon. The diocesan bishop may not dispense from this reservation. Canon 766 does, however, give lay people permission to preach even during the Eucharist, although such an address does not constitute a homily according to canon law. In some instances the address has been postponed to a position after Communion. That practice, however, violates the structure of the liturgy and should not be condoned.[82]

Canon 767 is a constitutive canon, defining the essential elements of a homily. It is a form of preaching that is an integral part of the liturgy and is reserved to a priest or deacon. Whatever does not fulfill these requirements is not a homily—call it a reflection, an exhortation, or an instruction. The point is that a rigorous interpretation of this legislation that would preclude the possibility of religious other than ordained priests or deacons from breaking open the Word of God for the religious community as need be is really unreasonable because it hinders the spiritual welfare of the religious community. It is for that reason that lay preaching in religious communities is in fact a common occurrence even at the Eucharist.[83]

The final liturgical issue that needs to be briefly addressed is that of legitimate customs that have developed among institutes of religious life, especially in the rites executed by ordained ministers. Throughout the centuries religious have developed what might be called a distinctive liturgical choreography. This has been so especially in such communities as the Benedictines, the Cistercians, the Carthusians, the Dominicans, and the Franciscans. The rightful autonomy of these communities and their long-standing traditions justify continuation of their rites and entitle the communities to develop them as they see fit. These traditions are regularly reflected in postures, special rituals, and distinctive celebrations and observances in the liturgical year. In other words, local bishops should not interfere in the sound liturgical practices of institutes of consecrated life.[84] Legitimate liturgical customs in religious institutes should not be imperiled by canon law or by directives issued by diocesan liturgical commissions.

CONCLUSION

Throughout history the relationship between institutes of consecrated life and the hierarchical dimension of the church has been extremely complex. That complexity has been specifically reflected in legislation designed either to protect the legitimate autonomy of religious institutes or to restrict their freedom and bring them under the surveillance and control of the hierarchy. Much of that legislation has been directed toward the ordained members of religious institutes and their ministerial service in the church. Antinomians might instinctively hold all such legislation in contempt; legalists might look upon it as the answer to all community and personal problems. Either attitude is unfortunate and irresponsible.[85] As Ladislas Örsy has written, what is most important is that both members of the hierarchy and members of institutes of consecrated life develop a sound hermeneutic of law. Basic to any such hermeneutic within the Christian community is the necessity of subordinating all human laws to the Spirit and the gospel. In the church human laws are apt to be misused if they are divorced from Christian faith, sound theology, and life in the contemporary world. They will be misused if they become a refuge from the responsibilities and challenges of Christian freedom for those who are insecure or immature. They will be misused if they provide easy, pragmatic solutions to difficult problems on the part of those who fail or do not even attempt to base their lives on sound principles derived from the gospel and theological reflection on the gospel.[86]

As this chapter has shown, legal norms pertaining to institutes of consecrated life and ordained ministry within those institutes all have a history. There have been developments, shifts, and even radical changes in the meaning of some of the norms. The norms concerning the relationship between ordained members of religious institutes and the hierarchy and between the ordained and nonordained members of institutes themselves cannot be properly understood and evaluated—and therefore correctly implemented—without a knowledge of the many factors that have shaped those relationships in the course of history. That history shows that meanings do not stand still. The Spirit of God continuously recreates the face of the earth, which means that both the hierarchical and the charismatic structures of the church must be constantly open to reformation according to the principles of the gospel. Presumably, both the members of the hierarchy and the members of institutes of consecrated life are searching for God. Both will come to know God only through the power of the Spirit, not through the mere observance of law. Canon law, however, when carefully formulated and wisely interpreted, can in fact modestly facilitate the search.

Only when a sound theology of the church as hierarchical and a sound theology of religious life as a prophetic manifestation of the charismatic dimension of the church are kept in tension with one another will the legislation concerning institutes of consecrated life and ordained ministry within those institutes benefit both the hierarchy and religious institutes. The ongoing challenge is not to eliminate the tension but to keep the tension poised.

NOTES

1. Frank J. Morrisey, "The Laity in the New Code of Canon Law," *Studia Canonica* 17 (1983): 135–48.

2. Ladislas Örsy, "General Absolution: New Laws, Old Questions," *Theological Studies* 45 (1984): 676–77. See Frank G. Morrisey, *The Canonical Significance of Papal and Curial Pronouncements* (Washington, D.C.: Canon Law Society of America, 1981).

3. Ladislas Örsy, "The Interpretation of Laws: New Variations on an Old Theme," *Studia Canonica* 15 (1983): 96–133; and idem, *Theology and Canon Law: New Horizons for Legislation and Interpretation* (Collegeville, Minn.: The Liturgical Press/Michael Glazier, 1992).

4. See Vatican Council II, Decree on Ecumenism *Unitatis Redintegratio*, no. 6, *Acta Apostolicae Sedis* 56 (1965): 96–97 (hereafter cited as *AAS*).

5. G. D. Ghirlanda, "Ecclesialita della Vita Consecrata," in G. D.

Ghirlanda, V. De Paolis, and A. Montan, *La Vita Consecrata, Il Codice del Vaticano II* (Bologna: Ed. Dehoniane, 1983), 3:16–23.

6. David J. Kay, *Exemption: Origins of Exemption and Vatican Council II* (Rome: Pontifical Gregorian University, 1990), 1–2; and "The Historical Origins of Canon 591 of the Code of Canon Law," *Studia Canonica* 25 (1991): 452–53.

7. *Conciliorum oecumenicorum decreta,* curantibus J. Alberigo, J. A. Dossetti, P.-P. Joannou, C. Leonardi, and P. Prodi, 3rd ed. (Bologna: Instituto per le scienze religiose, 1973), 89. See also Leo Ueding, "Die Kanones von Chalkedon in ihrer Bedeutung für Mönchtum und Klerus," in A. Grillmeier and H. Bacht, *Das Konzil von Chalkedon,* vol. 2, *Entscheidung um Chalkedon* (Würzburg: Echter Verlag, 1953), 568–676.

8. Kay, "The Historical Origins," 458.

9. C. Cipolla, *Codice diplomatico del monastero di S. Columbano di Bobbio fino all' anno 1208,* vol. 1, *Fonti per la storia d'Italia* (Rome: Tip. del Senato, 1918), 52; idem, *Diplomi,* sec. VI–XIII 102-03; and Kay, "The Historical Origins," 458–60.

10. Kay, *Exemption,* 11; and T. McLaughlin *Le très ancien droit monastique de l'occident* (Paris, 1935), 188.

11. Kay, *Exemption,* 12; T. Schaefer, *De Religiosis,* 4th ed. (Rome 1947), 757; and McLaughlin, *Le très ancien droit,* 189.

12. Kay, "The Historical Origins," 460.

13. *Ibid.,* 460–61.

14. *Ibid.,* 461.

15. Kay, *Exemption,* 15; *Consiliorum Oecumenicorum Decreta,* ed. Centro di Documentazione Instituto per le Scienze Religiose—Bologna (Freiburg: Herder, 1962), 752–60.

16. *Ibid.* See A. Gutierrez, "De gradibus libertatis et subiectionis religiosorum respectu ordinarii loci," *Commentarium pro Religiosis* 22 (1941): 28–37, 89–92, 133–43, 213–27, 305–13; 23 (1942): 30–41, 113–24, 292–98; idem, "Romanus Pontifex- Episcopi-Religiosi," *Commentarium pro Religiosis* 41 (1962), 139-59; J. D. O'Brien, *The Exemption of Religious in the Church* (Milwaukee: Bruce Publishing Company, 1943); and E. Fogliasso, *De extensione iuridici instituti exemptionis religiosorum logice, historice ac positive considerati* (Rome, 1947).

17. See canon 476.

18. *AAS* 57 (1965): 51–52. See Kay, *Exemption,* 20–84.

19. *AAS* 58 (1966): 690–92. David Kay's conclusion of his doctoral dissertation is very important: "Since *Christus Dominus* is a decree, it must take its main inspiration from the Dogmatic Constitution on the Church, *Lumen Gentium,* and it must be faithful to this constitution's ecclesiology. In the hierarchy of church documents a dogmatic constitution represents a much more

substantial pronouncement of the church in serious matters. The four constitutions of Vatican Council II determine how the decrees and other council documents are to be understood. Just as the new Code of Canon Law will not usually vary from the mind of Vatican Council II, so the decree on the bishops' pastoral office in the church, *Christus Dominus*, may not derogate from the dogmatic constitution on the church, *Lumen Gentium*. Lastly, the conciliar debate had made it patently clear that juridical matters could not be settled at the council. These were left to the revised Code of Canon Law. Canon 591 of the Code of Canon Law of 1983 clarified any remaining obscurities on the matter, and clearly enunciated the principle of exemption" (*Exemption*, 83–84).

20. *AAS* 70 (1978): 473–506.

21. See R. Kevin Seasoltz, "Benedictine Monasticism and the New Code: Some Reflections on Autonomy, Work and Worship," *American Benedictine Review*, 37 (March 1986): 12–13.

22. *AAS* 70 (1978): 478.

23. Seasoltz, "Benedictine Monasticism," 13.

24. *Ibid.*, 14.

25. *Ibid.*, 12.

26. *Ibid.* See also Daniel Rees and others, *Consider Your Call, A Theology of Monastic Life Today* (Kalamazoo: Cistercian Publications, 1980), 27–38.

27. See canon 576 of the 1983 Code of Canon Law.

28. The Italian original was published in a special supplement to *Informationes S.C.R.I.S.*, the bulletin published by the Sacred Congregation for Religious and Secular Institutes. English translations appeared in the English edition of the bulletin, in the English-language *Osservatore Romano*, and in *Religious Life Review* 20 (May-June 1981), 171–83, and (July-August 1981), 223–31.

29. Seasoltz, "Benedictine Monasticism," 24.

30. English translation in *Origins* 25, no. 41 (1996): 681–719.

31. No. 37, *Origins*, 693.

32. Nos. 36–37, *Origins*, 693.

33. No. 48, *Origins*, 697.

34. No. 49, *Origins*, 697.

35. *Ibid.*

36. No. 74, *Origins*, 706.

37. *Who Are My Brothers?* ed. Philip Armstrong (New York: Alba House, 1988).

38. "Canon Law: Rights and Relationships," in *Who Are My Brothers?* 97–108.

39. Elizabeth McDonough, "Clerical Institutes," *Review for Religious* 40 (January-February 1992): 145.

40. See canon 134.

41. Elizabeth McDonough, "The Potestas of Canon 596," *Antonianum* 63 (1988): 552-55. The most recent and complete treatment of this topic is by John P. Beal, "The Exercise of the Power of Lay People: State of the Question," *The Jurist* 55 (1995): 1–92. See also Myriam Wijlens, *Theology and Canon Law: The Theories of Klaus Morsdorf and Eugenio Corecco* (Lanham, Md.: University Press of America, 1992).

42. McDonough, "The Potestas of Canon 596," 576–77.

43. Justin Der, in *Who Are My Brothers?* 105–6.

44. No. 60, *Origins,* 701.

45. No. 61, *Origins*, 701.

46. No. 76, *AAS* 56 (1964): 119.

47. *Sacrum Diaconatus Ordinem*: *AAS,* 9 (1967): 697–704; and *Sacerdotalis Caelibatus, AAS* 59 (1967): 657–97.

48. Bishops' Committee on the Permanent Diaconate, *Permanent Deacons in the United States* (Washington, D.C.: United States Catholic Conference, 1971). See canon 1031.

49. *Notitiae* 4 (1948): 209–19.

50. *Ephemerides Liturgicae* 83 (1959): 4.

51. Jan Michael Joncas, "The Public Language of Ministry Revisited: *De Ordinatione Episcopi, Presbyterorum et Diaconorum* 1990," *Worship* 68 (September 1994): 386–87. See also Annibale Bugnini, *The Reform of the Liturgy 1948–1975*, trans. Matthew J. O'Connell (Collegeville, Minn.: The Liturgical Press, 1990), 721–23. Critiques by religious include Mary Collins, "The Public Language of Ministry," in *Official Ministry in a New Age*, ed. James H. Provost (Washington, D.C.: Canon Law Society of America, 1981), 7–40; and David N. Power, "Appropriate Ordination Rites: A Historical Perspective," *Alternative Futures for Worship*, vol 6, *Leadership Ministry in Community*, ed. Michael A. Cowan (Collegeville, Minn.: The Liturgical Press, 1981), 136.

52. *Pontificale Romanum ex decreto Sacrosancti Oecumenici Concilii Vaticani II renovatum auctoritate Pauli Pp. VI editum Joannis Paulis Pp. II cum recognitum "De Ordinatione Episcopi, Presbyterorum et Diaconorum,"* Editio typica Altera (Urbs Vaticana: Typis Polyglottis Vaticanis, 1990), 109.

53. See Joncas, 397–401.

54. Mary Collins, "Facing the Hard Issues," *Sung Liturgy: Toward 2000 A.D.*, ed. Virgil Funk (Washington, D.C.: Pastoral Press, 1991), 32–33.

55. *De Ordinatione*, nos. 125 and 201.

56. Leon Strieder, *The Promise of Obedience in Ordination Rites in the West* (Romae: Pontificium Institutum Liturgicum, 1994), 23–36.

57. *Ibid.*, 8–14.

58. *Ibid.*, 27–31.

59. *Ibid.*, 47–54.

60. N. Tanner, *Decrees of the Ecumenical Councils* (London: Sheed and Ward, 1990), 2: 681–83.

61. *Pontificale Romanum*, Pars Prima, Editio typica (Urbs Vaticana: Typis Polyglottis Vaticanis 1962), 57–58.

62. Strieder, 72.

63. *Pontificale Romanum*, Pars Prima, 60-61. See G. Alberigo, *Lo sviluppo della dottrina sui poteri nella Chiesa universale: Momenti essenziali tra il XVI e XIX secolo* (Rome: Herder, 1964); and S. Ryan, "Episcopal Consecration: Trent to Vatican II," *Irish Theological Quarterly* 33 (1966): 135–40.

64. Strieder, 104–6.

65. Tanner, 1:193.

66. *Ibid.*, 1:240–42.

67. Strieder, 89–92.

68. *Ibid.*, 90-91.

69. *Ibid.*, 94.

70. *Ibid.*, 95.

71. *Ibid.*, 95–96.

72. *Ibid.*, 96.

73. *Ibid.*, 101.

74. *Ibid.*, 102–4.

75. *Ibid.*, 103–4.

76. *Ibid.*, 140-56.

77. *Ibid.*, 150–571.

78. No. 12, *AAS* 57 (1965) 16–17. See R. Kevin Seasoltz, "Monastic Autonomy and Exemption: Charism and Institution," *The Jurist* 34 (1974): 321–24.

79. *AAS* 64 (1972): 529–34.

80. R. Kevin Seasoltz, *New Liturgy, New Laws* (Collegeville, Minn.: The Liturgical Press, 1980), 78–79. See also David N. Power, *Gifts That Differ: Lay Ministries Established and Unestablished* (Collegeville, Minn.: The Liturgical Press/Pueblo Books, 1985), 5–39.

81. Seasoltz, "Benedictine Monasticism," 27–28.

82, The Canon Law Society of Great Britain and Ireland, *The Canon Law: Letter and Spirit* (Collegeville, Minn.: The Liturgical Press/Michael Glazier, 1995), 425.

83. See John M. Huels, *The Pastoral Companion*, rev. ed. (Quincy, Ill.: Franciscan Press, 1995), 91–92; idem, *Disputed Questions in the Liturgy Today* (Chicago, Ill.: Liturgy Training Publications,1988), 17–25; and

Preaching and the Non-Ordained, ed. Nadine Foley (Collegeville, Minn.: The Liturgical Press, 1983).

84. Seasoltz, "Benedictine Monasticism," 27.

85. Elizabeth McDonough, *Religious in the 1983 Code: New Approaches to the New Law* (Chicago: Franciscan Herald Press, 1985), 6–7.

86. Örsy, *Theology and Canon Law*, 77–82.

7

Voices of Religious Priests: Data from the *FORUS* Study

Miriam D. Ukeritis, C.S.J., and David J. Nygren, C.M.

The previous chapters in this volume have dealt with theological, historical, and pastoral aspects of priesthood and the charism of religious life. The purpose of this chapter is to assess, as much as possible, the congruence between the ideals regarding religious priesthood discussed in previous chapters and the recent experience of the men who embrace this role in today's religious orders. It will present some of their beliefs about religious life in general, areas of similarity and difference among members of the apostolic, mendicant, and monastic traditions, how the men relate to their congregations, and how they themselves experience their lives as religious priests. In short, the voices of these men as they responded to questions regarding their beliefs and values concerning religious life and their experience of it will provide the content for this chapter.

Funded by the Lily Endowment Inc. and encouraged by our own religious congregations, we were privileged to conduct a major study of religious life in the United States. It was published in 1993 under the title *Futures of Religious Orders in the United States (FORUS)*.[1] The *FORUS* National Survey, from which most of the member-based empirical findings in this project are derived, was distributed to 9,999 women and men religious and yielded a usable database of 6,359 responses. Within this database, the subset of 1,556 priests who identified themselves as apostolic (872), mendicant (338), or monastic (346) provides the population that forms the statistical basis for the discussion in this chapter.

While the design of the survey was completed prior to the composition of the distinct chapters of this volume, the resulting data do provide significant information concerning the beliefs, lived experience, current status, and hoped-for futures of these ordained men who are also members of religious orders. In many cases, the data serve to support and corroborate the theory and reflections posed by other authors in this volume. They provide some behavioral verification of what would be expected in light of the traditions discussed, particularly as regards what may be unique to different traditions. They also point to some apparent departures from the "expected," highlighting what may be the often-found gap between theory and practice or between espoused and lived values. There is also some evidence of the increasing tendency toward parochial assimilation, for both men and women religious, discussed earlier in this volume and in the *FORUS* study.

ASSUMPTIONS

The purpose of this chapter is to examine the nature of the relationship between charism and the current reality of ordained members of religious orders. Because, as noted above, the data used to respond to this question find their source in a much larger database, a direct answer to the question posed is not possible. A close inspection of the findings of the *FORUS* research does, however, provide much information that is useful in addressing this question. In some ways, the methodology may appear parallel to the ancient story of four blind men who are set with the task of describing an elephant. As they go about exploring the trunk, the legs, the tusk, and the side of the animal, their descriptions vary greatly. In this instance, however, our "sight" has been enhanced by a body of literature, including that of the authors of the preceding chapters in this volume, that provides a basis for the assumptions that served to guide both the analysis of the data for the current chapter and subsequent discussion. Some of these assumptions follow.

• Religious life, as a gift to the church, is a social institution. That is, there are to be found broad-based beliefs, attitudes, and behaviors that are common to all religious orders. This assumption is shared and noted in the writings of John O'Malley, Doris Gottemoeller, Roland Faley, and David Power that appear earlier in this volume.
• Over the course of history, various traditions have emerged in religious life. As David Power notes, each has brought with it its own charism or set of gifts that highlights one or another facet of the Christian life.
• Within the various traditions, each of the different congregations has also brought to the church its unique charism. Charisms within a tradition are more related than those that "cross" traditions.
• Apostolic congregations typically have an external ministerial focus. This may include a history of sponsored institutions. While communal experiences of prayer are valued, the apostolate takes a primary place, and prayer is more likely to be individual.

- Mendicant congregations, while directed historically to the work of preaching, also have a history of fraternity that implies a greater value placed on the communal aspects of their life. David Power offers a description of mendicant "preachers, whose main purpose was to bring the discipleship of Christ to fruition among the faithful, through example, preaching, teaching, and hearing confessions."
- Monastic congregations have a clear order of life that strives to balance work and prayer. As John O'Malley notes, "*stability* gives form to the ministries... [in] that whatever ministry is performed [is] performed within the monastery or its environs."
- In face of shifting ecclesiologies as well as the statistical reality of the decreasing number of diocesan clergy available to staff parishes in many of the dioceses in the United States, there is an increasing pressure on religious orders of both women and men to provide personnel to undertake these duties.

THE VALUE AND CLARITY OF RELIGIOUS LIFE

Regardless of behaviors or differences between traditions, the value that the ordained members of religious orders place on religious life, particularly as it relates to their personal lives, is clear. These men not only express a value of religious life in the abstract, but also report its significance in their own lives. Among all religious, religious priests were strongest in their assertion that they have of an understanding of what it means to be a religious in the church today (75 percent) and in their agreement with the statement that "religious life is a permanent element in the church" (78 percent). In assessing its importance, the percentage of religious priests who believe that "religious life is as important as it once was to the church" matched the overall respondents' rate of 64 percent. When compared to sisters and religious brothers, role clarity of priests was the highest. Some, including Roland Faley in his earlier chapter, have speculated that the distinctiveness associated with the presbyteral role has some influence on this. Yet, 80 percent of all priests responding to the survey agreed with the statement that "being a religious gives meaning to my life in a way no other vocation can."[2]

SIMILARITIES AND DIFFERENCES AMONG THE APOSTOLIC, MENDICANT, AND MONASTIC TRADITIONS

Consistent with the assumption that religious life is a social institution, we found in the *FORUS* study more similarities than differences among members of religious congregations. David Power alluded to this same belief in his observation that, in the discussion of religious life, "there is little distinction made between female and male communities in what regards the essence of religious life and the works in which religious engage in virtue of their mission and charism." This held true across gender and tradition comparisons in the *FORUS* study, further affirming a belief that religious life is itself a "social institution," a single gift to the church.

It is also true that this gift is expressed in different ways at different times and in different settings. The image of a gem, with several facets, each of whose beauties come to the fore as light changes, may convey this notion. Each of the different historical traditions in religious life reveals a treasured aspect of the Christian life. Many of the responses to the questions do provide evidence regarding the distinctions among the traditions as described in the assumptions above. These differences appear in what might be considered the significant components of religious life: prayer, community life and living, and ministry.

Prayer. For all forms of religious life, how one's relationship with God is expressed in prayer and liturgical practices is key. In monastic communities, communal and personal prayer are clearly visible components of the daily life. In mendicant and apostolic groups, there is a need for more flexibility as demands of the apostolate temper schedules. The *FORUS* survey invited religious to respond to the following questions:

> *Over a typical week, how often is eucharistic liturgy a part of your routine?*
> *Over a typical week, how often is Liturgy of the Hours a part of your routine?*
> *How often do you pray or meditate privately?*
> *Other than celebration of the Eucharist, how often do you pray or meditate privately?*
> *In what context do you usually find yourself at eucharistic liturgy?*

As Tables 1 and 2 below indicate, there is great variation among the traditions in terms of their styles and frequency of prayer. One would assume, given their status as priests, that regular participation in the Eucharist is part of the routine of these men. Hence, the relatively high reports of participation in the Eucharist listed in Table 1 is not surprising. Yet, while few report participation in the Eucharist on a weekly-or-less basis, the apostolic priests selected this response more than twice as often as the monastic men (4.1 percent versus. 1.5 percent).

Table 1

Frequency of Participation in Eucharist and Liturgy of the Hours by Percentage of Respondents[a]

Group	Eucharistic Liturgy						Liturgy of the Hours					
	1	2	3	4	5	6	1	2	3	4	5	6
Apostolic	65.1%	18.8%	12.0%	3.8%	.3%	—	49.8%	14.1%	10.2%	2.2%	4.1%	19.6%
Mendicant	69.0%	18.2%	10.7%	1.5%	.6%	—	63.1%	21.1%	8.0%	1.2%	1.8%	4.8%
Monastic	78.7%	11.7%	8.2%	.9%	.6%	—	85.4%	7.6%	3.8%	.3%	1.5%	1.5%
Total	69.0%	17.1%	10.9%	2.7%	.5%	—	60.6%	14.2%	8.3%	1.6%	3.0%	12.3%

[a] *Frequency Codes*:   1 = Every day   2 = 5–6 times per week   3 = 2–4 times per week
4 = Once each week   5 = Less than once a week   6 = Almost never

Reviewing the responses for the Liturgy of the Hours, the difference is quite dramatic. Fewer than half of the apostolic men report praying Liturgy of the Hours on a daily basis, in contrast to 63 percent of the mendicant priests and 85 percent of the monastics. Even more significant, perhaps, is the fact that nearly 20 percent of the priest respondents from apostolic groups indicate that they "almost never" pray the Liturgy of the Hours. This should be read as indicative of the fact, not that apostolic clergy do not pray (consult Table 2), but that the form of their prayer is different. One possible interpretation of this is that apostolic religious are defining a form of prayer, particularly communal prayer, that is more distinctive of their tradition than the monastic style of the Liturgy of the Hours.

Differences among traditions also emerge when considering the tendency to pray alone or with a group. As can be found in Table 2, there are no real differences in the percentage of each group reporting that they pray or meditate privately daily or several times each week. Yet, when asked about the frequency of group prayer, responses for the monastic priests reflect their daily schedule and stand in contrast to the reports of the apostolic and mendicant respondents.

Table 2

Frequency of Private and Group Prayer by Percentage of Respondents[a]

Group	Pray or Meditate Privately						Pray with a Group					
	1	2	3	4	5	6	1	2	3	4	5	6
Apostolic	1.7%	2.8%	3.7%	25.9%	65.6%	.2%	12.5%	18.4%	13.3%	26.9%	27.1%	1.8%
Mendicant	2.2%	2.2%	1.9%	23.2%	70.2%	.3%	3.5%	9.3%	5.8%	32.1%	47.1%	2.2%
Monastic	2.1%	2.7%	2.7%	16.1%	75.8%	.6%	8.0%	6.4%	5.8%	10.1%	68.1%	1.5%
Total	1.9%	2.7%	3.1%	23.1%	68.9%	.3%	9.6%	13.7%	10.0%	24.3%	40.5%	1.9%

[a] *Frequency Codes*:   1 = Seldom or never   2 = On special occasions   3 = About once a week
4 = Several times   5 = Daily   6 = Other
each week

Also interesting is the 20 percent difference in the frequency of daily group prayer between the apostolic and the mendicant priests. This latter finding lends support to the assumption that communal life may be more significant in the lived experience of the mendicant priests than of the apostolic priests. David Power noted, in his description, the emphasis on example in calling the faithful to community. This may be an indication that this dynamic is operative in groups of the mendicant tradition.

It is noteworthy that 54 percent of the apostolic men do report praying with others several times a week, if not daily. It seems reasonable to assume that this response is a reflection of the significance and role of community life for these men as religious. While it seems unlikely that such a high percentage of diocesan priests would report praying with a group at this level of frequency, this cannot be assumed. The absence of comparable data from diocesan clergy is regrettable and poses possible directions for further investigations.

The typical context of celebration of Eucharist is indicative of values, lived experience, and locus of ministerial involvement. As presented in Table 3, nearly 60 percent of the monastic men report that they most frequently celebrate the Eucharist in the context of a religious congregation. Mendicants celebrate in the context of the local parish (42 percent) more frequently than with the religious congregation (33 percent). Of the three traditions considered, the apostolic priests are more likely than the others to celebrate Eucharist in an institutional (e.g., school, hospital) context (16.9 percent).

Table 3
Context of Eucharistic Participation[a]

Group	Frequency					
	1	2	3	4	5	6
Apostolic	32.3%	3.0%	37.0%	16.9%	2.7%	8.1%
Mendicant	42.2%	2.8%	33.2%	10.8%	3.7%	7.4%
Monastic	20.3%	1.2%	58.8%	8.5%	5.6%	5.6%
Total	31.7%	2.5%	41.1%	13.7%	3.6%	7.4%

[a] *Frequency Codes*: 1 = Your local parish 2 = Another parish
3 = A religious congregation 4 = Institution (e.g., school, hospital)
5 = Covenant community 6 = Other

Community Life and Living. As seen in Table 4, the living situations of religious priests are typically to be found in the context of their own religious communities. The few differences that do exist are in terms of living alone. Such circumstances are more likely to be the case for apostolic and mendicant priests. Once again, this is consistent with the thrust of the ministerial involvement and the already frequently cited descriptions of religious priests who find themselves pursuing individual ministries, often as parish ministers.

Table 4
Current Living Situation by Percent

Descriptions of Living Situation	Percents			
	Apostolic	Mendicant	Monastic	Total
Alone	12.9%	12.4%	9.8%	12.1%
In a community with more than one other person of my congregation	71.2%	72.0%	73.2%	71.8%
With member(s) of other congregation(s) (same sex)	6.5%	7.1%	7.1%	6.8%
In a mixed community of men and women religious	3.7%	4.3%	4.3%	4.0%
In a community that includes men and women, married and celibate	1.2%	1.9%	1.2%	1.4%
With an elderly or ill parent/relative	.1%	.3%	.3%	.2%
Other	4.0%	.9%	3.4%	3.2%

Overall, religious priests express a high degree of satisfaction with their present living situation, rating it beyond 4.0 on a 5-point Likert scale. The most striking difference in priests' responses to the series of questions concerning living situation involves the role of ministry in determining the respondent's living situation. Members of apostolic groups reported the highest level of agreement with the statement that "ministry is the primary factor in determining my living situation." Mean scores of the mendicant and monastic priests were lower and statistically significant ($p < .01$). Once again, we see evidence in the lived experience of apostolic religious priests that ministerial concerns supersede those of community.

Table 5
Satisfaction with Living Situation

Item	Means[a]			
	Apostolic	Mendicant	Monastic	Total
33. I am satisfied with my present living situation.	4.11	4.07	4.19	4.12
34. My congregation allows me sufficient freedom in determining my living situation.	3.88	3.92	***3.67***	3.84
35. My present living situation detracts from my prayer life.	1.90	1.95	1.85	1.90
36. My present living situation enhances my sense of belonging to my congregation.	3.77	3.76	3.86	3.78
37. Ministry is the primary factor in determining my living situation.	3.94	***3.62***	***3.14***	3.70

[a] Means based on Likert-scale ratings: 1 = Strongly disagree to 5 = Strongly agree.
    Bold italics indicates significant difference between that group and apostolic group (at least $p < .01$).
    Underline indicates significant difference between monastic and mendicant groups (at least $p < .01$).

Ministry. The survey asked respondents to identify both their current primary ministry and the ministry they intend to pursue in the future. Results appear in Table 6. Pastoral ministry is the most frequently cited current and anticipated ministry. Interestingly, mendicant priests, currently involved in pastoral ministry at nearly twice the level of monastic clergy, show nearly a one-third drop in their indication of involvement in pastoral ministry in the future. Higher education, education, retreat ministry, and "other" account for the greatest proportion of their increase among mendicants. Mendicants were also the group strongest in their agreement with the statement that "religious life is so tied to institutions that its prophetic role is almost snuffed out" (difference of their means between both apostolic and monastic groups significant at the $p < .01$ level). Concern with this issue, and, perhaps, the decision to act on this concern, is consistent with the mendicant and monastic traditions.

Table 6
Current and Anticipated Area of Ministry by Percentage of Respondents

Area of Ministry	Current				Anticipated			
	Apostolic	Mendicant	Monastic	Total	Apostolic	Mendicant	Monastic	Total
Parish Ministry	27.6%	39.0%	20.8%	28.6%	28.6%	30.3%	19.1%	27.0%
Hospital Administration	.2%	.9%	.3%	.4%	.3%	.7%	.4%	.4%
Congregation/Prov. Leadership	.8%	1.2%	4.3%	1.7%	.1%	.3%	1.1%	.4%
Congregation/Prov. Adm.	2.5%	2.4%	4.3%	2.9%	1.4%	1.0%	1.5%	1.3%
Social Service	.5%	—	—	.3%	.8%	.7%	.7%	.8%
Educational Administration	3.9%	1.2%	5.9%	3.7%	2.7%	1.4%	4.4%	2.8%
Higher Education	11.5%	7.9%	10.6%	10.5%	11.0%	9.2%	9.9%	10.4%
Education	10.2%	4.0%	17.4%	10.4%	8.3%	6.1%	14.3%	9.0%
Health Care	3.0%	3.7%	.6%	2.6%	2.4%	2.0%	.7%	2.0%
Communications	1.5%	.6%	.3%	1.0%	3.1%	.7%	.4%	2.0%
Pastoral Visiting	2.3%	4.9%	3.4%	3.1%	3.4%	2.0%	4.0%	3.2%
Agriculture	.1%	—	.6%	.2%	.1%	—	.7%	.2%
Eucharistic Ministry	.7%	.6%	—	.5%	.7%	1.7%	1.5%	1.1%
Business and Finance	1.5%	.6%	4.7%	2.0%	.5%	1.4%	2.9%	1.2%
Art	.1%	—	—	.1%	.4%	—	1.8%	.6%

Continued on p. 178

Table 6 *continued*
Current and Anticipated Area of Ministry by Percentage of Respondents

Area of Ministry	Current				Anticipated			
	Apostolic	Mendicant	Monastic	Total	Apostolic	Mendicant	Monastic	Total
Retreat Ministry	5.6%	3.7%	1.6%	4.3%	6.5%	7.8%	4.4%	6.4%
Prison Ministry	.5%	.6%	.9%	.6%	.4%	.7%	.4%	.5%
Social Work	.2%	.6%	.3%	.3%	.4%	.7%	.7%	.5%
Apostolate of Prayer	.5%	—	2.5%	.8%	.7%	2.0%	3.3%	1.5%
Counseling	1.8%	.6%	.3%	1.2%	3.7%	2.7%	2.6%	3.2%
Pastoral Counseling	1.0%	2.4%	.9%	1.3%	3.0%	1.4%	2.6%	2.5%
Retired	4.0%	3.4%	5.3%	4.1%	6.0%	7.1%	11.8%	7.4%
Formation/Vocation	6.8%	8.8%	3.1%	6.4%	2.8%	3.7%	2.9%	3.1%
Peace and Justice	1.0%	.9%	—	.7%	2.4%	2.4%	.4%	2.0%
Other	12.3%	11.9%	11.8%	12.1%	10.2%	13.9%	7.4%	10.4%

While parish ministry is the most frequently noted involvement of priests across all traditions, the percentages (current and anticipated) account for less than one-third of these ordained ministers. Current and anticipated involvement in education, retreat, and other spiritual ministries comprise the bulk of their ministerial commitments. Admittedly, the question may be posed as to the necessity of priesthood to accomplish these ministries. Remember, however, the high degree of consensus around the question "being a religious is important to the job I hold." It could be instructive to pose the accompanying question, "Is being a priest important to the job I hold?" Again, regrettably, this information is not available.

While seemingly not related directly to the question of priesthood and religious charism, the issue of the interest of members in ministries is critical to the continuance of the congregation. Internal ministries, such as congregational leadership and formation/vocation work hold little interest for members of any of the groups. While some may be relieved that the power struggles that marked earlier periods in church history are not blatant today, this lack of interest is most unfortunate. Leaders who will ensure the accomplishment of the mission of the congregation and members willing to be responsible for the integration of new members into a culture that is able to transmit the charism to the next generation are central to the life of any group. While one might assume that humility drives the reluctance of members to aspire to such positions, the lack of interest in assuming such positions (and presumed concomitant absence of preparation) can be a sign of more significant distress.

Finally, there is the question of commitment to the poor. This issue has generated more heat than light in chapter rooms and around dinner tables of religious houses in recent years. The pattern of religious priests in responding to their own inclination to work directly with the poor mirrors what would be expected in terms of tradition: to a degree of difference that is significant when compared to both apostolic and mendicant priests, monastics indicate the least inclination (consistent with their tradition). Mendicant and apostolic priests are nearly equal in their articulation of their moderate willingness to work directly with the poor.

Connections with Their Own Congregations. There is no doubt concerning the reality of fraternal bonds that exist between these members of religious congregations. Across traditions, respondents report that they look forward to "being with members of my congregation" (mean = 4.02) and that they "are personally involved in my congregation" (mean = 3.87).

There is much less clarity as to the awareness of "agreement as to what our congregation's goals are" (mean = 3.00), but members report being willing to "contribute more than is normally expected to help my congregation fulfill its mission" (mean = 3.94). The fact that members are eager to expend energies on behalf of the congregation, even though they may not be clear on the congregation's goals, is quite striking and an issue to which leadership may wish to attend. These men are committed to their congregations, interested in their workings, and eager to be involved—though, as noted above, not to the point of embracing an internal ministry. Organizational clarity and focus beg for attention from leaders and decision makers, as does the challenge to invite the members to, colloquially, "walk the talk" they voice with reference to the significance of their congregations.

Regarding members' own commitment to their congregations, there is high level of agreement with the statement "I intend to remain a member of my congregation for the rest of my life" (mean = 4.4). The fact that members rate their agreement with the statement "I care about the future of my congregation" even higher (mean = 4.5) again speaks to the connection and care that members have for their congregations. Even should "social desirability" be influencing this response, note that other items that might have a similar pull for the "correct" answers do not have the same high level of agreement.

As regards the experience of a sense of increased significance of religious life, already noted by Roland Faley in his autobiographical reflection on life as a Franciscan, monastics are strongest in their agreement with the statement that "my life as a religious is more meaningful to me today than it was in the past." They agree at nearly the 68 percent level with the statement that "my awareness of the significance of religious life is more than when I took vows." Level of agreement for apostolic and mendicant groups was only slightly lower (64 percent).

In rating their "level of satisfaction as religious today," barely 49 percent of the members of the mendicant groups indicated it was "more than when I took vows." This differed from both the apostolic and monastic groups, whose ratings approached 55 percent.

Religious Life and/or Priesthood. A full 83 percent of the respondents indicated that "if I had to do it all over again, I would still choose to become a religious." Unfortunately, the survey did not pose the contrasting question, "if I had to do it all over again, I would still choose to be ordained." Hence, those data are not available. As Roland Faley noted in his review of the history of religious priesthood in Chapter 4, some members of religious orders opted for priesthood in light of the career opportunities available to them. Others were encouraged in this direction because of other personal or intellectual gifts. Anecdotal accounts gleaned during the course of the *FORUS* study provided some confirmation for this speculation. Interviews also surfaced the fact that some currently ordained members of religious orders have questioned whether they would pursue ordination were they to enter their congregation at this point in time. In recent conversations, vocation directors of some Benedictine congregations have noted a decrease in the percentage of their candidates who are seeking ordination This is in line with Kevin Seasoltz's development of ordination within monasticism in Chapter 2.

In rating the relative importance of priesthood and religious life ("religious priests regard their priesthood as more important than they regard membership in their congregation"), the mean for members of apostolic groups was highest, and the mean for the monastic respondents (2.87) was lowest. While this may not appear numerically large, the difference is statistically significant and in a direction that reflects Kevin Seasoltz' discussion of the lesser emphasis on priesthood in the monastic community as well as the other authors' reflections on the increasingly traditional priestly roles that members of apostolic communities, in particular, have been encouraged to assume. Doris Gottemoeller's speculation regarding the effect of ordination on communities of women seems very appropriate based on the experience of communities of men.

SUMMARY: CONCLUSIONS AND CHALLENGES

Based on the data just reviewed, what can we conclude about the relationship between priesthood and religious life as it is experienced today? If the voices of the men who are members of religious orders are to be believed (and there is no reason they should not), it is clear that

• they perceive religious life, in the abstract, as a gift to be valued;
• religious life, as experienced by these men, is a significant factor in their ministerial life and happiness;
• religious priests have great interest in the future of their religious congregations;
• differences do exist among the apostolic, mendicant, and monastic traditions as evidenced by prayer styles, ministerial preferences, and the role of ministry as related to living situation;
• currently, approximately one-fourth to one-third of religious priests are involved in pastoral ministry;
• apostolic priests give some indication that they do experience some conflict between the roles of religious and of priest.

Role of Leadership. Inevitably, the role of the leader of the religious congregation surfaces in such considerations. The role of the leader in enabling the members of the congregation to accomplish the mission of the group has already been noted. When reviewing questions from the leadership section of the *FORUS* national survey, the apostolic leaders received the highest ratings of "inspiring loyalty." Monastic leaders, in contrast, received the lowest. Given the different governance structures among monastic and apostolic congregations, this difference may indeed be an artifact of the varying length of terms. Research in the area of leadership tends to support the hypothesis that six years is an optimal term, and in monastic communities the term of abbot frequently exceeds this. Assessments of the leader's ability to challenge members to spiritual growth and to function in a charismatic role were less than striking.

Table 7
Statements About Leaders (Selected Items)

Item	Means[a]			
	Apostolic	Mendicant	Monastic	Total
256. Makes me aware of strongly held values, ideals, and aspirations that are shared in common.	2.47	2.46	2.57	2.48
263. Inspires loyalty to the congregation.	2.27	2.46	*2.57*	2.38
267. Challenges me to spiritual growth.				
	2.68	2.74	2.75	2.71

[a] Ratings based on a 5-point Likert scale with 1= Frequently, if not always; 2 = Fairly often; 3 = Sometimes; 4 = Once in a while; 5 =Not at all. ***Bold italics*** indicates the significant difference between that group and apostolic group (at least p< . 01).

Parochial Assimilation. As noted by the earlier authors, religious orders have arisen classically in the midst of the church to serve emerging or unmet human needs. They have been historically quite independent of, yet complementary to, the hieratic order of the church. As David Power observed, the "consecrated life," as it has been known in the past, today is being assimilated into either the lay state for brothers and sisters or the clerical state for religious priests. The complementary structures of the hierarchy and the charisms of the church are being blended into a predominantly parochial view. This is due, in part, to the absence of a vibrant declaration by Vatican II about the clear role of members of religious orders in the church. The decline of sponsored institutions among religious orders has also altered the independence of their members. Moreover, the decreased numbers of diocesan clergy, at a time when the parish is defined as the primary locus of ecclesiology, has led to an increasing dependence and pressure on religious orders to staff diocesan operations.

The increasingly widespread insertion of members of religious orders into diocesan and parochial positions, to the point where such commitments take precedence over involvements in the lives of their congregations, is a growing phenomenon in the United States. It easily can lead to a compromise of the prophetic role of members of religious life.

Some vital congregations have chosen not to be assimilated into the exclusively parochial context. They tend to exact a higher cost among their members as regards belonging and are characterized by a focused mission that clearly serves the church. The cost for clerical congregations may be even greater as they face both the struggle and the consequences related to resisting pressure from the institutional church.

It is, therefore, incumbent upon all members of religous orders to come to new understandings of both religious life and priesthood—and of their combination in the religious priest. This critical issue is to be pursued not only by theologians and historians of religious life but also particularly by religious themselves. David Power devoted a significant portion of his chapter to praxis. This content is not to be ignored. As religious life negotiates the paths of renewal—and use of the plural is intentional—theological reflection based on a review of experience and the stretching input of scholars and practitioners together will enable the voices of the members of religious orders to echo more clearly the voice of the Spirit of God who calls.

NOTES

1. Results of this project are reported in David J. Nygren, C.M., and Miriam D. Ukeritis, C.S.J., *The Future of Religious Orders in the United States: Transformation and Commitment* (New York: Praeger, 1993).

2. A listing of selected items from the *FORUS* National Survey may be found in the appendix. Means for the apostolic, mendicant, and monastic priests, as well as for the total sample studied in this chapter are included. A lengthier discussion of this data appears in the Nygren and Ukeritis volume cited in note 1.

Conclusion:
Road Signs at a Crossroads

Paul J. Philibert, O.P.

Although for more than a decade many bishops have been in denial about the critical situation brought about by the lower number of priests available for a growing Catholic population in the United States, more commonly today bishops and priests admit that we stand at a dramatic crossroads in ministry in this country. Evidence points to a 40 percent loss in the population of diocesan priests in the last four decades of this century. This is accompanied by a 65 percent growth in the Catholic lay population (which was forty-five million in 1965 and is projected to be roughly seventy million in the year 2005). Priestly services as we knew them in 1965 will be cut in half.

The immediate causes of this crisis have been poor recruitment and poor retention for twenty-five years. From 1960 to the year 2000, ordination rates dropped 10 percent each decade. In the '70s and '80s, more priests left priesthood than were ordained. The next period of mass exodus, however, will be perhaps the most dramatic of all. It will come about through attrition, since the largest cohort of priests were ordained in the 1940s and 1950s and will soon reach retirement age. So the full impact of the priest shortage is just around the corner.[1]

At present, about one parish out of twenty is without a resident priest. Furthermore, the context surrounding Catholic priesthood has changed dramatically. The socioeconomic status of Catholics has increased significantly since the 1960s. In addition, along with the rest of the American culture, Catholics have been strongly influenced by the individualism, materialism, and consumerism that are hallmarks of these last decades of the century. Feminism is another strong factor in shaping Catholic attitudes. Perhaps the most significant difference in the thirty years between 1965 and 1995 is the notable changes in the role of laypeople in church ministries. Altar boys would have been found in the sanctuary in 1960, but not adult laymen and -women. But today, one is surprised at a parish Sunday mass if one does not find laymen and -women in the sanctuary, assisting at the altar as readers, servers, and eucharistic ministers. The expectations for priestly ministry are likewise in transition.

A first response to the priest shortage in some places where it is most keenly felt has been to import foreign clergy to supply for a lack of American-born priests. In addition, where priests become unavailable, the bishops have arranged for Communion services to replace mass when no priest can be found for Sunday services. The most ancient pastoral norm of the New Testament, celebration of the Lord's Day with the breaking of the bread, is being relativized by the Vatican's insistence on its present norms for ordination. These and other consequences are evident to us. We can anticipate that there are yet others, less evident, that will gradually emerge as consequences of the present situation. It seems clear, then, that it is not an exaggeration to speak of a "crisis" or a "crossroads" in the ministry of the Roman Catholic Church in the United States.

THE STUDY OF RELIGIOUS WHO ARE PRIESTS

In 1988 Roland Faley, then the executive director of the Conference of Major Superiors of Men (CMSM), took the initiative to form the Task Force on Religious Priesthood to examine what response regular clergy needed to make to these conditions. What would be the likely consequences of this new pastoral situation for priests who were ordained as members of religious institutes? That initiative has continued through almost ten years of sustained effort to lead to the present publication.

What began as an effort to interpret the sign of the times has become an assessment of a new age of ecclesial life. In the mid-1980s it was clear that significant transitions were at work that would change our ways of thinking about our roles as religious. At the time, the major motive for concern, I think, was somewhat defensive. While many bishops and the Vatican congregations continued to insist that the diminution of clerical vocations was far from critical, most American major superiors saw evident signs of the church's entering a definitively different situation.

One instinct that emerged immediately was the desire to safeguard the autonomy of clerical religious in the face of already grave pastoral deficiencies in many dioceses with regard to their capacity to provide an adequate and steady supply of priests for parish leadership. Thus, the first step in our reflection on the shortage of priests was for major superiors to insist on the primacy of the collegial life and typical ministries of their institutes. Along with the defensive movement to forestall larger numbers of religious priests from being co-opted into service to supply diocesan parishes came the parallel recognition that, for a century, most American regular clergy had already compromised their charisms or their autonomy by becoming too deeply involved in parishes.

In response to the critical need for evangelization in the first century of the American church, many clerical religious devoted their energies for two generations or more to establishing and staffing parishes from coast to coast.[2]

In 1989 the CMSM Task Force issued its report, which reviewed major theological, cultural, and pastoral factors that face regular clergy in this critical moment of transition.[3] Subsequently, this document was taken to all the regions of the conference in a workshop. Most major superiors expressed sincere appreciation for the achievements of the task force and the contribution of CMSM in highlighting the issues. The board of CMSM expressed the desire to continue research on this topic, however. It became clear that more information of a historical, theological, and cultural nature was needed to help put the issues in perspective.

Additional sources of reflection were available in the edited volumes of Robert Wister and Donald Goergen, who, with their colleagues, articulated some important steps toward understanding a theology of priesthood.[4] As to origins, they made it clear that twentieth-century understandings of the office of presbyter are the result of a gradual and slow evolution of awareness and reflection on Sacred Scripture and protohistoric data revealing the nature of the apostolic generation's conceptions of Christian life and ministry.

Recent study of the origins of Christian ministry promotes a kind of reversal of field imagery (as in imagery experiments in Gestalt psychology) whereby what was initially dominant imagery moves into the background and the former background moves forward. (The typical Gestalt field experiment challenged the observer to find either two faces or a vase—or, perhaps better, *both* the two faces and the vase.)

In the case of ecclesiology, we have been accustomed to look for prototypes of contemporary church offices as we know them (bishop, priest, deacon) and have failed to pay attention to the background against which these protoministries were expressed. That background, many scholars would argue, is both as important and likely more expressive of the consciousness of the apostolic generation than the articulations of church offices that we find. But, here again, the desired end result of our research (as in the Gestalt experiment) is to render both field and ground mutually significant.

This means that we need to develop the freedom to move back and forth in perspective as well as to recognize the importance of context in both directions of interpreting the ground, namely, the importance of an apostolic and charismatic "body" as the context for analyzing the protoministries, as well as the importance of the nurture and leadership of the protoministries as the context for interpreting the apostolic/ministerial élan of the "body."

Donald Senior, Thomas O'Meara, Nathan Mitchell, and others have remarked that today's postconciliar church is perhaps more like the Corinthian church described by Paul than any other moment in the intervening history between the first century and our own.[5] As in the first century, we are a generation inventing, naming, and institutionalizing new ministries. As at that time, we are confronted with new needs, which we impulsively try to understand in terms of categories that arose in another context.

Paul insisted that the gift of the Spirit in baptism was a dynamic and charismatic gift to every Christian. Today the apostolic teaching of John Paul II in *Christifideles Laici, Redemptoris Missio,* and elsewhere likewise insists upon the apostolic fruitfulness of baptismal grace.[6] One of the principal themes of the "new evangelization" is the dynamic involvement of ordinary Christians in the work of proclaiming the faith—all people becoming heralds of a gospel experience.

Quite clearly the privileged context for laity to express this evangelizing mission is in their own secular frame of reference, transforming their family life and their professional work into expressions of the Spirit's ferment in the world. At the same time, this allows us to recognize the refocusing of attention away from an exclusive preoccupation with the rights and duties of hierarchical figures toward the rights and duties of laity. In addition, the involvement of laity in catechetical, social, and liturgical ministries is conspicuous. In many cases, lay associates have become the personnel for most of what was done fifty years ago by the ordained or by vowed religious in education, social ministry, and works of compassion. Scott Appleby has expressed this transition in terms of describing the priest in this new ecclesial context as an "orchestra leader" whose principal responsibility is to call, train, and coordinate the ministerial energies of the laity.[7]

THE PAROCHIAL PREDICAMENT

It would be simplistic, then, to suggest that the present state of affairs could be described exclusively in terms of a crisis of available minister power for the parish. Especially if one imagined the pre-Vatican II model of priestly ministry (in which the priest was the only one recognized to be doing "ministry" in any real sense), we clearly have entered a period of new understanding. Few would consider it ideal to return to that preconciliar model. What troubles people most, of course, are the implications of the present shortage of priests, namely, that parishes will be bereft of the celebration of the Eucharist on Sunday more and more frequently.

But the role of the parish was an issue for the ministry of religious even before the present personnel crisis came to be the focus of our attention. As the authors of this volume have indicated in various places, the issue of the "parochialization of ministry" has been a concern for some decades. It is not related exclusively to the crisis over a shortage of presbyters. For example, Doris Gottemoeller indicates that one effect of the ministerial reorientation of sisters after Vatican II was for many religious women who had previously been involved in education or healing ministry to enter parish work in cate-chetical or associate administrative positions. As a consequence of their almost total investment in the apostolic exigencies of their parishes, many of them invested less in their religious communities. Roland Faley points out that, in a similar way, religious priests who become involved in parish admin-istration easily find themselves overtaken by the pastoral demands and the social attitudes of the diocesan clergy. The lay parish community often becomes more significant and more satisfying as a relational context than one's religious community for regular clergy serving in parochial ministry. As he notes above, "Although our parish residences may carry a distinctive name, how much different are they from the diocesan rectory?"

John O'Malley provides helpful critical insight into other problems related to parochialization of ministry. As he points out, *Presbyterum Ordinis* desired to root presbyteral ministry in the ministry of the Word and ministry to the baptized community. It had as its goal the illumination of the evangelizing dynamics that occur within the context of the parish. Its effect, however, was to create the impression that the parish is the normative context for all min-istry. As a consequence, the Second Vatican Council's teaching on priesthood did not esteem sufficiently the exercise of priesthood in ministries of evange-lization, missionary preaching, healing, and administrative ministries coordi-nating works for justice and peace.

John O'Malley articulates thoughtfully another parallel issue that must be taken very seriously, namely, the empowerment of the charisms of religious institutes in guiding the ministries of their members. One of the key insights gleaned from this discussion is the recognition that the call to ministry for reli-gious flows from the charism of the institute, not only from ordination. It is part of one's call to a gospel fraternity and an apostolic mission as a member of a group such as the Jesuits, the Benedictines, the Dominicans, the Franciscans, or other institutes to participate in the apostolic works that are the ministerial tasks of the institute and a charismatic leaven within the church.

Finally, relative to questions concerning the parish, it should be noted that the parish as such is an institution in a state of flux. Although the very con-cept of parish is territorial, that is, a division of a governmental jurisdiction like a county, today the parish no longer maintains this orientation too suc-cessfully. Forty years ago, Catholics would have felt themselves obliged to worship within the territorial parish in which they found their residence. Today, many Catholics relate to a parish not in terms of territory, but rather as an elective assembly. This is common knowledge. Few are the places where the old territorial relationship is rigidly maintained in force today.

As a result, the tendency of religious (men and women) in the 1960s and 1970s to acquiesce to the dominant force of the parish as their ecclesial center of gravity is changing. As parishes become more and more "elective assemblies," the taken-for-granted canonical force of the territorial parish is diminished. This may lead to a reemergence of the importance of other locales for worship and ministry. In any case, changes would clearly be expected in coming years as a result both of the diminished number of available priests to lead parish structures and also of the new elective attitude of Catholics toward the place where they exercise their weekly worship. It is, at present, a "buyer's market."

In summary, the issues surrounding the dominant influence of parishes in the past century will deserve careful attention from religious in coming years. Priests in religious orders and congregations will have the responsibility to verify that their deployment in parochial supply ministries (or as pastors of parishes) is truly coherent with the charism of their institutes. Nonclerical religious will measure the degree to which their communities need or deserve the development of liturgical offices within their local establishments as an integral part of their life-style as well as a means of extending hospitality to the laity in their circle of influence. The oratories of religious houses have served through the centuries as places of spiritual refuge for the laity. This should remain a valid and welcome expression of Christian life as religious continue this tradition into the future.

AUTONOMY AND EXEMPTION

Kevin Seasoltz has made a number of points that are important in helping us assess the autonomy of religious institutes in a canonical framework. He reminds us that monastic life began as a precanonical experience. The first monks did not seek orders; rather, they saw themselves outside the hierarchical structure of the church. They understood themselves as laity. Only gradually, as they exercised the leadership of holiness and prudential wisdom, did they come to draw to themselves large numbers of followers, some of whom became members of cenobitic monastic structures, others of whom sought out monks as spiritual guides.

The abbot's role as prelate is symbolic of the autonomy of the monastic community as an entity with its own integrity, standing alongside the bishop and the diocese. There were centuries during which the monasteries were, in some places, the central educative and organizing structures for the majority of people in rural areas. Monasteries generally maintain today this same kind of independence or autonomy for the sake of their spiritual ecology—community and spirituality organized around a routine of regular common prayer, contemplative environment, and hospitality.

Kevin Seasoltz points out that the apostolic exhortation *Vita Consecrata* recognizes the special quality of priestly identity for those living vowed religious life. A deeper examination of the intent of the papal text will be needed to verify its exact significance, but it seems to affirm the interpretation articulated in recent years that the office or function of presbyter is at the service of the charism of the religious institute of regular clergy.[8] Bishops are asked to respect and honor the orientation of the religious institute's charism in accepting religious priests into their dioceses. The good of the church as a whole requires the fidelity of regular clergy to their institute's apostolic/ministerial orientation.

The cautionary dimension is evident as well. Not only are institutes deprived of spirit, but the church as such is also when religious priests ignore the directive power of their institute's charism or succumb too easily to being siphoned off to supply for absent diocesan clergy in parishes. This issue, however, remains neuralgic—one that will require careful deliberation. For example, a major superior mused recently in conversation with me: "How can I rest easy with forty-two men in my priory when I am surrounded by small dioceses where many parishes go without priests on Sunday?" (This conversation took place abroad, but it will soon be replicated in our own country as conditions worsen for the availability of priests for Sunday services.)

There are other neuralgic issues touching religious autonomy, as Kevin Seasoltz has pointed out. Perhaps the most visible and painful of these at present is the requirement in the new ordination rite for deacons and priests who are religious to promise obedience to the bishop. As Seasoltz points out, it is to one's own religious ordinary (the major superior) that religious have already promised obedience. The good functioning of the church's ministry requires benevolent cooperation between religious priests and the bishops of the places where they will exercise ministry. But the present structure of the revised ordination rite suggests a parity between the claim of the bishop and the claim of the regular clergy's religious superiors. This, given the history so carefully sketched by Seasoltz, suggests a misunderstanding of the nature of the relationship of religious with diocesan ordinaries.

This last point may be an example of a tendency that was evident in the *Lineamenta* preparatory to the 1994 synod. There certain texts suggested that religious life was a generic phenomenon with distinct institutes as various species marked by differences that only lightly modify the fundamental orientation of a generic vocation to gospel service. Many American religious found this to be generally unsatisfactory in articulating their understanding of their form of life.[9] The tendency toward centralization evident in many actions of the present Vatican administration, both acts of the papal office and acts of the Roman congregations, indicates a perspective that is inclined to treat all apostolic activities as simply various departments of one ecclesiastical bureaucracy.

The imagination of most religious runs in another direction. It is rooted in concrete images of the founders, the historical context and origins of the institute, the spirituality and writers of the religious family, and the great moments of apostolic experience of each institute. While there is fellow feeling among religious of distinct congregations and orders, there is not really the sense that we are all the same with but very minor historical or pastoral differences.

Autonomy and exemption (much under threat in recent decades) is an area of discussion that will require ongoing attention. The lines of debate have not yet been fully drawn. The attempt here has been to give historical perspective to both the concept of autonomy and the concept of exemption. For this, we are grateful to Kevin Seasoltz for his careful analysis. The most pressing question, however, is posed to the institutes themselves: How do they interpret their need for autonomy to express both the apostolic life-style and the ministerial expression of their institute's charisms? This key question cannot be answered for them by others. This is homework for each institute to attend to. Failing to do this needed work risks leaving open future co-optation by bishops or Vatican congregations of decisions concerning ministry or life-style that ought to be the responsibility of the religious institutes themselves.

THE ONGOING WORK OF SUPERIORS AND COMMUNITIES

The objective of this volume has been to raise consciousness about a number of issues that will be extremely important for the viability of religious priesthood in coming years. The strong tendency of Vatican II in its statements on priesthood was to presuppose the near uniformity of all priestly ministry and place it essentially in the context of the parish as the normative locus for all ministerial expression. The historical retrieval elaborated here is an attempt to reclaim the variety of ministerial expressions of the priesthood, which, as noted, includes educational, healing, evangelizing, and social ministries.

It is significant that the warrant for ministry for regular clergy is rooted first of all, not in ordination, but in the apostolic orientation of the institute's charism. As an ecclesiological principle this helps to illuminate the question of the source for ministerial mandates for the nonordained as well. How do those who enter in various ways into sharing the charism of a religious institute derive from such an affiliation a call or a claim to participate as well in the ministries of the institute? We should examine how this dynamic is already in force and judge carefully how we imagine it to serve as a principle for the future.

THEOLOGIES OF PRIESTHOOD

David Power's chapter on theologies of priesthood makes it clear that only gradually did the variety of theological understandings of priestly ministry come to be elaborated. Catholics today commonly understand ordination as the primary phenomenon in the life of regular clergy. The Sulpician theology that presents the priest as a figure conformed to Christ as mediator provides a strong warrant for priestly spirituality, but at the price of separating the priest from the laity to a degree that is unrealistic in the light of contemporary ecclesial experience. If, as mentioned above, priesthood functions for regular clergy in the service of the charism of the institute, then final or solemn vows are the key moment in the development of apostolic commitment for the religious priest, not ordination. This is an area where institutes of regular clergy need to give serious reflection and to articulate their understanding of the relationship of orders to their lifelong commitment to the institute's charism.

Other theologies of priesthood place either contemplation (monastic/contemplative life) or the *vita apostolica* (the apostolic ecology of contemplation and ministerial action that Aquinas called the "mixed life") as primary.[10] Both of these are valid expressions of religious priesthood, long honored and recognized in the life of the church. It is important to assure that their validity is respected and the integrity of their forms of life is maintained.

REGULAR CLERGY IN PARISHES

Since many regular clergy are involved in parochial service, a key question that needs serious attention is the following: how do these individuals see themselves fulfilling the "original inspiration" or charism of their institutes in the pastoral service that they provide to the diocese? Experience clearly shows that the majority of religious priests working in parishes feel confident that they are well placed, doing good work coherent with the spirit of their institutes. Legend has it that there is a distinctive way of creating ministerial experiences that mark a certain place as a good "Jesuit parish" or "Franciscan parish" or "Oblate parish," and the like. It is important, however, to ask for the accountability of those doing such service to interpret their work in terms of their charism so as to illuminate for the other members of the institute the apostolic potential of parochial work.

As times continue to change, the potential for religious working in parochial structures may very well offer more rather than fewer opportunities for the distinctive exercise of the charism of the institute to be well expressed. The development of lay groups, base communities, sodalities, third orders, and the like are all aspects of associate membership that have existed in monastic and mendicant traditions for many centuries. This seems to be a time that would favor the reinvigoration of such lay associations that are commonly rooted in a parish setting.

What may be decisive about this question, however, is the critical issue raised by David Nygren and Miriam Ukeritis in their 1993 publication summarizing their research on American religious.[11] They claimed that religious in the United States had a threshold of ten years to reclaim and refound their institutes. They saw as the biggest hazard for recruitment and successful growth of religious institutes their lack of role clarity. Ambiguity about just what the committed life and the apostolic mandate of a community may be is corrosive of both the internal well-being of the members of the province or congregation as well as of the external opportunities to draw new members.

An uncritical continuation of placing religious priests in diocesan pastoral settings without articulating the relation of this ministry to the institute's mission and charism would likely produce increased confusion of role expectations for the future. For institutes with very definite apostolic missions, repossessing the claim of that charism is the path toward increased clarity. Vibrant community life and satisfying internal relations within religious life are affected strongly by the esprit de corps of the group as a whole, which depends in significant ways on its satisfaction and pride in the fact that it is indeed expressing its true nature within the church. Doing this, whether the apostolic objectives involve preaching, missionary endeavor, teaching, healing, theological research, or social ministries, revives the corporate sense of identity as a whole. This revival lies at the heart not only of survival, but also of the kind of "greening" of the institute that will make it attractive to new members.

A CONCERT OF CHARISMS

The image used for the title of this book evokes one of the fundamental turns that the church has taken since Vatican II. Looked at from the perspective of the century as whole, the most decisive transformation of ecclesial life has been the way in which we imagine the agency of the Holy Spirit in engaging vessels of ministering grace. At the beginning of this century, before the documents of Vatican II brought the Pauline category of *charism* into widespread use, we inhabited an ecclesiology in which the ordained were "active" vessels of ministering grace and the laity were "passive" clients of the same. Now we see things quite differently.

Lumen Gentium speaks of the special vocation of the laity, "to make the Church present and fruitful in those places and circumstances where it is only through them that she can become the salt of the earth" (no. 33).[12] This, and many other conciliar statements that clearly impute to the nonordained an "active" role in ministering grace, make it clear that we have entered a new period of practical ecclesiology. In referring to a "concert of charisms," we have in mind the new frame of reference that emerges from this conciliar teaching linked to the new pastoral realities of the church.

Among these pastoral realities, as noted above, is the disproportion (in terms of recent expectations) between a growing Catholic lay population and a diminishing number of ordained clergy to serve their sacramental life. The decisive turn of imagination here will be to remember that all those in question—all of the baptized, clergy and laity alike—possess charisms of service for the mission of Christ. "Whether these charisms be very remarkable or more simple and widely diffused, they are to be received with thanksgiving and consolation since they are fitting and useful for the needs of the Church" (*Lumen Gentium,* no. 12).[13]

The particular focus of our discussion, however, is the coordination of the ministry of regular clergy with the warrants for ministry arising from the charisms specific to their religious institutes. We have just noted here the wider sense of charism as a phenomenon universally applicable to all the baptized. It seems appropriate, therefore, to conclude with some remarks that clarify what we mean by charism in this more focused context. There are three points to be noted: (a) The prescriptive quality of charisms for religious is not easily described or summarized. (b) The church has a right to expect religious congregations and orders to articulate how they envisage their contribution to its mission. (c) The ministerial charisms of all institutes are ordered toward the blossoming of communion and the integration of charisms of all Christians in a common effort of proclaiming and inaugurating the kingdom preached by Jesus.

First, let us briefly note that the concept of charism as a description of the original inspiration of the founder and of the historically developed patrimony of a religious institute is not easily or succinctly articulated. For older orders, the matter is made complex by centuries of apostolic decisions and pastoral experience. In addition, the dramatic evolution of the church as a whole in the present century will make its claim upon the evolution of religious charisms. Institutes whose foundations were linked to particular historical circumstances may have to transpose the meaning of their original inspiration into a vastly different cultural world or (perhaps) acknowledge that their contribution to the life of the church may expire at some point in the future. This leads to the second point.

Given that regular clergy, in large part, were introduced into the United States at a time of territorial expansion, most institutes became involved in missionary activities and in staffing the first new parish communities of an emerging republic. For some generations, we took for granted the integrity of continuing business as usual (which in this case meant the substitute missionary and pastoral work into which mendicants, monks, and apostolic priests with a prophetic portfolio were directed by reason of pastoral urgency in the nineteenth century).

A decade ago, Howard Gray, S.J., articulated a call to recognize the responsibility to discern between "maintenance" and "mission" in the administration of religious life.[14] This remains a challenging insight. Placing mission above maintenance will involve, among other difficult decisions, being able to discern the demands of the institute's mission (in this case, little different from what we are describing as charism) as prescriptive of how we invest the primal energies of our personnel. Already formed habits of involvement will complicate response to this challenge, but so also will the growing urgency for priestly ministry in parishes lacking assigned resident priest-pastors. Yet the argument of this book has been consistent across the spectrum of issues and authors, namely, that the principal responsibility of religious in the troubled pastoral situation of today is to remain true to the life-style and pastoral orientation of the institute that arises from its foundation and its patrimony. This difficult challenge leads to the third and final point.

In evoking the imagery of a concert of charisms in the title of this book, the authors harken back to the ecclesiology of Paul in First Corinthians, where we learn that "there are varieties of gifts...because we are all made to drink of one Spirit" (1 Cor 12:4,12). At one stroke, we find ourselves today faced with a plurality of new phenomena: a diminishing number of the ordained, a growing number of lay people in pastoral service, a growing and increasingly diverse and sophisticated laity, and a variety of new pastoral accommodations to the resulting needs. Nostalgia for a settled past (be it 1950 or 1940 or 1930...) will not provide the key for the future whose vague delineation we surmise from these changing circumstances. Rather, faith, openness, fidelity to our commitments, and generosity of spirit seem the appropriate response.

What is the best way for religious—and in particular for regular clergy—to contribute most positively to this moment? The argument of this book is that their best response is to be themselves—to retrieve as honestly and as deeply as they can their ecclesial significance in the light of the church's present pastoral needs. In doing this, they will contribute most fully the characteristic influence that is their charism—their blessing—for the church, for which reason the Spirit of God called them into existence at their beginning. In so responding, they will maximize the possibilities for the charisms of others—religious and laity, bishops and diocesan clergy—to establish themselves in a climate of graced life and pastoral cooperation.

History is full of surprises. No one can really judge where our present moment of possibilities will be leading us. But if we can imagine a new church that will overcome the potential divisiveness of ethnic tensions and ideological polarities, so we can also imagine a new pastoral moment in which the full expression of ministerial compassion and passion for justice blossom because the door closed on the past has led us toward a more universal experience of the graced agency of the Spirit. This is the concert of charisms of which we wished to speak. Regular clergy will have a special role to play in this pastoral moment. It is theirs to claim, to exercise, and to contribute.

NOTES

1. Richard A. Schoenherr and Lawrence A. Young, *Full Pews and Empty Altars: Demographics of the Priest Shortage in United States Catholic Dioceses* (Madison: University of Wisconsin Press, 1993). See also, William V. D'Antonio et al., *Laity: American and Catholic—Transforming the Church* (Kansas City: Sheed and Ward, 1996), v–24.

2. John A. Grindel, "Understanding Ourselves as a People: The Context of Our Religious Priesthood," in *Religious and Priest: Examining the Questions* (Silver Springs, Md.: Conference of Major Superiors of Men, 1990), 3ff.

3. "Religious Priesthood Task Force: A Working Paper," in *Religious and Priest: Examining the Questions,* 16ff.

4. Robert Wister, ed., *Priests: Identity and Ministry* (Wilmington: Michael Glazier, 1990); and Donald J. Goergen, ed., *Being a Priest Today* (Collegeville: Minn.: The Liturgical Press/Michael Glazier, 1992).

5. See Donald Senior, "Living in the Meantime: Biblical Foundations for Religious Life," in Paul Philibert, ed., *Living in the Meantime: Concerning the Transformation of Religious Life* (Mahwah, N.J.: Paulist Press, 1994), 55f: Thomas O'Meara, *Theology of Ministry* (New York: Paulist Press, 1983); and Nathan Mitchell, *Mission and Ministry History and Theology in the Sacrament of Order* (Wilmington: Michael Glazier, 1982).

6. John Paul II, *Redemptoris Missio: On the Permanent Validity of the Church's Missionary Mandate* (Washington, D.C.: United States Catholic Conference, 1990); and John Paul II, *Christifideles Laici: The Vocation and the Mission of the Lay Faithful in the Church and in the World* (Washington, D.C., 1989).

7. R. Scott Appleby, "Present to the People of God: The Transformation of the Roman Catholic Parish Priesthood," in Jay Dolan et al., *Transforming Parish Ministry* (New York: Crossroad, 1989), 1ff.

8. John Paul II, *Vita Consecrata: On the Consecrated Life and Its Mission in the Church and in the World* (Vatican City: Libreria Editrice Vaticana, 1996), see esp. nos. 30, 48, and 49. See, e.g., Paul Philibert, "Priesthood Within the Context of Religious Life," in Goergen, 73ff.

9. CMSM, "Religious Orders Amid Cultural Realities." *Origins* 22, no. 42 (1993): 724ff.

10. *Summa Theologica*, IIa IIae, 188, 6, c.

11. David J. Nygren and Miriam D. Ukeritis, *The Future of Religious Orders in the United States: Transformation and Commitment* (New York: Praeger, 1993).

12. Dogmatic Constitution on the Church in Austin Flannery, ed.,

Vatican Council II: The Conciliar and Post Conciliar Documents (Northport, N.Y.: Costello, 1975), 390.

13. *Ibid.,* 363.

14. Howard J. Gray, "The Challenge to Religious Leadership: Maintenance or Mission," in Philibert, *Living in the Meantime*, 39ff.

Appendix:
Means for Selected Questions
from FORUS National Survey

Item	Means[a]			
	Apostolic	Mendicant	Monastic	Total
61. I know what it means to be a religious in the church today.	3.80	3.84	*3.97*	3.85
63. Religious priests regard their priesthood as more important than they regard membership in their congregation.	3.18	3.11	*2.87*	3.10
64. My life as a religious is more meaningful to me today than it was in the past.	3.55	3.54	3.71	3.58
66. I think being a religious is important to the job I hold.	3.88	3.96	3.91	3.90
67. If I had to do it all over again, I would still choose to become a religious.	4.22	4.18	4.25	4.22
95. I look forward to being with members of my congregation.	4.02	4.01	4.04	4.02
96. I am personally involved in my congregation.	3.87	3.86	3.87	3.87
98. Members of my congregation agree on what our congregation's goals are.	3.00	2.93	3.08	3.00
100. Although there is increasing talk about religious working with the poor, I feel little commitment to that.	2.61	2.56	*3.05*	2.70
101. I am willing to contribute more than is normally expected in order to help my congregation fulfill its mission.	3.93	3.95	3.94	3.94
102. I feel little loyalty to my congregation.	2.02	2.10	1.94	2.02
103. I find that my values and my congregation's values are similar.	3.78	3.71	3.70	3.75
105. I intend to remain a member of my congregation for the rest of my life.	4.41	4.36	4.42	4.40
111. I care about the future of my congregation.	4.51	4.47	4.52	4.50
114. My closest friends are members of my religious congregation.	3.44	3.34	3.56	3.45
115. The mission of my congregation is clear.	3.77	*3.54*	3.65	3.70
116. I would prefer to work outside the corporate commitment of my congregation.	2.16	2.35	_1.98_	2.16
117. I know what is expected of me as a religious.	4.00	4.00	4.11	4.02

Item	Means[a]			
	Apostolic	Mendicant	Monastic	Total
120. Being a religious gives meaning to my life in a way no other vocation can.	3.93	3.98	*4.13*	3.99
154. Church institutions provide a conduit for the effective exercise of ministry by religious.	3.66	<u>3.54</u>	3.76	3.66
159. Religious life has been a major factor in my ministerial happiness and success.	4.06	4.04	4.19	4.08
161. In my experience as a religious, I see that there is seldom, if ever, any real conflict for men religious between being a member of a congregation and being an effective priest.	3.71	*3.32*	*3.32*	3.54
166. In its efforts toward renewal, my congregation has not recaptured the original spirit of our founder/ress.	2.45	2.64	2.61	2.52
170. Religious life is so tied to institutions that its prophetic role is almost snuffed out.	2.64	*<u>2.87</u>*	2.57	2.68
171. Renewal in my congregation has been marginal.	2.41	2.56	2.58	2.48

[a] Means based on Likert-scale ratings: 1 = Strongly disagree to 5 = Strongly agree.

Bold italics indicates significant difference between that group and apostolic group (at least $p < .01$).

<u>Underline</u> indicates significant difference between monastic and mendicant groups (at least $p < .01$).

Bibliography on Ordained Ministry in Consecrated Life

Auther, John P., "Apostolic Congregations' Monastic Roots," *Review for Religious* 54 (1995): 389-98.

Buckley, Michael, "Jesuit Priesthood: Its Meaning and Commitments," *Studies in the Spirituality of the Jesuits* 8, no. 5 (1976).

————, "Mission in Companionship," *Studies in the Spirituality of the Jesuits* 11, no. 4 (1979).

Canals, Salvador, *Secular Institutes and the State of Perfection, and the Priesthood and the State of Perfection* (Dublin: Sceptre, 1959).

Carpentier, René, "Priestly Vocations and Religious Vocations," in *Today's Vocation Crisis*, ed. G. Poage and G. Lievin (Westminster, Md.: The Newman Press, 1962).

Carr, A. M., "Religious Priests as Military Chaplains: Instruction of the Congregation of Religious," *Homiletic and Pastoral Review* 55 (May 1955): 674-77.

Catholic Priesthood [Papal Documents: Pius X to Pius XII], ed. Pierre Veuillot, 2 vols. (Westminster, Md.: The Newman Press 1958–64).

Chapelle, Albert, *Pour la vie du monde: le sacrement de l'ordre* (Brussels: Institut d'Études Théologiques Editions, 1978).

Coleman, John A., "The Future of Ministry," *America* (March 28, 1981), 243–49.

Comyns, J. J., "Relation of the Religious Pastor to the Local Ordinary," *The Jurist* 15 (April 1955): 186–204.

Cooke, Bernard, *Ministry to Word and Sacraments: A History and Theology* (Philadelphia: Fortress Press, 1976).

Coppens, Joseph, ed., *Sacerdos et célibat: études historiques et théologiques* (Gembloux: Duculot, 1971).

Crehan, Joseph, "Ministerial Priesthood: A Survey of Work Since the Council," *Theological Studies* 32 (1971): 489–99.

Daley Brian, "In Ten Thousand Places," *Studies in the Spirituality of the Jesuits*, 17, no. 2 (1985).

————, "Ordination: The Sacrament of Ministry," *America* (December 11, 1982).

————, "The Ministry of Disciples: Historical Reflections on the Role of Religious Priests," *Theological Studies* 48 (1987): 605–29.

Daniel, E. Randolph, *The Franciscan Concept of Ministry in the High Middle Ages* (Lexington: University of Kentucky, 1975).

Diego, Luis de, *La opción sacerdotal de Ignacio de Loyola y sus compañeros 1515-1540* (Rome and Caracas, 1975).

Dulles, Avery, "Imaging the Church for the 1980s," *Thought* 56 (1981): 121–37.

―――, "St. Ignatius and the Jesuit Theological Tradition," *Studies in the Spirituality of the Jesuits*, 14, no. 2 (1982).

Dunne, Edmundus, *Canonical Fitness for the Religious Priesthood* (Mayfield, N.S.W., 1952—Angelicum dissertation).

Euart, Sharon, "Religious Institutes and the Juridical Relationship of the Members to the Institute," *The Jurist* 51 (1991): 103–18.

Fink, Peter, "The Other Side of Priesthood," *America,* April 11, 1981, 291–94.

―――, "The Priesthood of Jesus Christ in the Ministry and Life of the Ordained," in *Priests: Identity and Mission*, ed. Robert Wister (Wilmington: Michael Glazier, 1990), 71–91.

Flannan, Mark, "Religious Priesthood: A Time for Re-Appraisal?" *Religious Life Review* 27, no. 131 (Mar.-Apr. 1988): 97-99.

Fleming, David, "Commitment in Priestly Community," *Review for Religious* 41, no. 4 (1982): 616–18.

Franciscan OFM English-Speaking Conference, *Religious Priesthood within the Franciscan Tradition: An Initial Statement and Theological Outline* (Chicago: Croatian Franciscan Press, 1991).

Galot, Jean, *Theology of Priesthood* (San Francisco: Ignatius Press, 1984).

Garrigou-Lagrange, Reginald, *The Priesthood and Perfection* (Westminster, Md.: The Newman Press, 1955).

Goergen, Donald J., ed., *Being a Priest Today* (Collegeville, Minn: The Liturgical Press/Michael Glazier, 1992).

Goggins, Ralph, *Towards the Clerical Religious Life* (Milwaukee: Bruce, Publishing Company 1933).

Harmless, J. William, and Donald Gelpi, "Priesthood Today and the Jesuit Vocation," *Studies in the Spirituality of the Jesuits* 19, no. 2 (1987).

Havener, Ivan, "Monastic Priesthood: Some Thoughts on Its Future in America," *Worship* 56, no. 5 (1982): 431ff.

Hemrick, Eugene, *A Survey of Priests Ordained Five to Nine Years* (Washington, D.C.: National Catholic Educational Association, 1991).

Hill, Richard A., "Departure of a Religious Priest or Deacon," *Review for Religious* 46, no. 6 (1987): 135–38.

Huels, John M., "The Demise of Religious Exemption" *The Jurist* 54 (1994): 40–55.

―――, "Loss of Clerical Status Revisited," *Review for Religious* 48, no. 4 (1989): 617–18.

————, "The Universal Faculty to Hear Confessions," *Review for Religious* 46, no. 2 (1986): 302–4.

Jaer, André de, "Ignace de Loyola et le ministère des prêtres," *Nouvelle Revue Théologique* 109 (1987): 540–53.

Kay, David J., *Exemption: Origins of Exemption and Vatican Council II* (Rome: Pontifical Gregorian University, 1990).

Knowles, David, *From Pachomius to Ignatius*, (Oxford: Clarendon Press, 1966).

Landini, Lawrence C., *The Causes of Clericalization of the Order of Friars Minor, 1209–1260, in the Light of Early Franciscan Sources* (Chicago, 1968).

Leclercq, Jean, "On Monastic Priesthood," *Studia Monastica* 3 (1961): 141ff.

————, "La sacerdoce des moines," *Irénikon* 36 (1963): 5–40.

Lonergan, Bernard, "The Response of the Jesuit, as Priest and Apostle," *Studies in the Spirituality of the Jesuits* 2, no. 3 (1970).

Madigan, F., "Life Table for Religious Priests, 1953–1957," *Review for Religious* 18 (July 1959): 225–31.

Marliangeas, Bernard-Dominique, *Clés pour une théologie du ministère* (Paris: Cerf, 1978).

Marmion, Dom Columba, *Christ: The Ideal of the Priest* (St. Louis: Herder, 1952).

Martelet, Gustave, *Deux mille ans de l'église en question: Théologie du sacerdoce* (Paris: Cerf, 1984).

Martin, Dennis D., "Popular and Monastic Pastoral Issues in the Later Middle Ages," *Church History* 56 (1987): 320–32.

McDonough, Elizabeth, *Religious in the 1983 Code: New Approach to the New Law* (Chicago: Franciscan Herald Press, 1985).

Meersseman, G. G., "Il tipo ideale di parroco secondo la riforma tridentina," in *Il Concilio di Trento e la riforma tridentina* (Rome, 1965), 1:24–77.

Merton, Thomas, *The School of Charity: The Letters of Thomas Merton on Religious Renewal and Spiritual Direction* (New York: Farrar, Straus and Giroux, 1990).

Mitchell, Nathan, *Mission and Ministry: History and Theology in the Sacrament of Order* (Wilmington: Michael Glazier, 1982).

Mohler, James, *The Origin and Evolution of Priesthood* (New York: Alba House, 1970).

Olivares, Estanslao, "Aportación de la Compañía de Jesús a la vida religiosa en su época," *Manresa* 56 (1984): 229–59, 345–64.

O'Malley, John W. "Diocesan and Religious Models of Priestly Formation: Historical Perspectives," in *Priests: Identity and Mission,* ed. Robert Wister (Wilmington: Michael Glazier, 1990), 54–70.

————, *The First Jesuits* (Cambridge, Mass.: Harvard University Press, 1993), esp. 157-59.

————, "The Fourth Vow in Its Ignatian Context," *Studies in the Spirituality of the Jesuits* 15, no. 1 (1983).

————, "The Houses of Study of Religious Orders and Congregations: A Historical Sketch," in Katarina Schuth, *Reason for the Hope: The Future of Roman Catholic Theologates* (Wilmington: Michael Glazier, 1989), 29–45.

————, "Priesthood, Ministry, and Religious Life: Some Historical and Historiographical Considerations," *Theological Studies* 49 (1988): 223–58.

————, "Spiritual Formation for Ministry: Some Roman Catholic Traditions–Their Past and Present," in *Theological Education and Moral Formation*, ed. Richard John Neuhaus (Grand Rapids: William B. Eerdmans Publishing Company, 1992), 79–111.

————, "To Travel to Any Part of the World," *Studies in the Spirituality of the Jesuits* 16, no. 2 (1984).

O'Meara, Thomas, *Theology of Ministry* (New York: Paulist Press, 1983).

O'Reilly, Michael, "Recent Developments in the Laicization of Priests," *The Jurist* 52 (1992): 684–96.

Osborne, Kenan B. *Ministry: Lay Ministry in the Roman Catholic Church, Its History and Theology* (New York: Paulist Press, 1993).

————, *Priesthood: A History of Ordained Ministry in the Roman Catholic Church* (New York: Paulist Press, 1988).

Padberg, John, "The Society True to Itself [GC 32]," *Studies in the Spirituality of the Jesuits* 15, no. 34 (1983).

Philibert, Paul, "Priesthood Within the Context of Religious Life" in *Being a Priest Today*, ed. Donald J. Goergen (Collegeville, Minn.: The Liturgical Press/Michael Glazier, 1992), 73-96.

————, ed., *Living in the Meantime: Concerning the Transformation of Religious Life* (New York: Paulist Press, 1994).

Power, David N., *The Christian Priest: Elder and Prophet* (London: Sheed and Ward, 1973).

Provost, James H., *Official Ministry in a New Age* (Washington, D.C.: Canon Law Society of America, Catholic University of America, 1981).

Rahner, Karl, "Bemerkungen zur Eneuerung des Ordenslebens," ed. H. Vorgrimler, in *Ordensnachrichten* 27, no. 6 (1988): 17–28.

————, *Theological Investigations* (Baltimore: Helicon, 1963–, esp. vol. 12, 39–60; vol. 14, 203–19; and vol. 19, 57–72, 73–86, and 117–38.

Rausch, Thomas P., *Priesthood and Ministry: From Küng to the Ecumenical Debate* (Ann Arbor: University Microfilms, 1976).

————, *Priesthood Today: An Appraisal* (New York: Paulist Press, 1992).

Rees, Daniel, "Monasticism and the Priesthood" in *Consider Your Call* (Kalamazoo: Cistercian Publications, 1980), 318ff.

Religious and Priest: Examining the Questions (Silver Spring, Md.: Conference of Major Superiors of Men, 1990).

Ridder, Todd, "The Clericalization of Monasticism," *Review for Religious* 49 (1990): 227–42.

Schillebeeckx, Edward, *The Church with a Human Face: A New and Expanded Theology of Ministry* (New York: Crossroad, 1985).

————, *Ministry: Leadership in the Community of Jesus Christ* (New York: Crossroad, 1981).

Schneiders, Sandra M., *New Wineskins: Re-imagining Religious Life Today* (New York: Paulist Press, 1986).

Schwartz, Robert M., *Servant Leaders of the People of God: An Ecclesial Spirituality for American Priests* (New York: Paulist Press, 1989).

Seasoltz, R. Kevin, "Benedictine Monasticism and the New Code: Some Reflections on Autonomy, Work, and Worship," *American Benedictine Review* 37 (March 1986): 1–33.

"Spirituality and Priesthood," *The Way: Supplement* 47 (1983)—an entire issue on the subject.

"Study of U.S. Diocesan Priesthood Statistics," *Origens* 20 (1990): 206.

Tavard, George, *A Theology for Ministry* (Wilmington: Michael Glazier, 1983).

Thurian, Max, *Le prêtre configuré au Christ: identité et spiritualité du sacerdoce* (Paris: Mame, 1993).

Tugwell, Simon, "Introduction" in his *Early Dominicans* (New York: Paulist Press, 1982).

Van Hoye, Albert, *Old Testament Priests and the New Priest According to the New Testament* (Petersham, Mass.: St. Bede's Publications, 1986).

Vicaire, M.-H., "Sacerdoce et prédication aux origines de l'ordre des prêcheurs," *Revue des sciences philosophiques et théologiques* 64 (1980): 241–54.

Walsh, Eugene, *The Priesthood in the Writings of the French School: Bérulle, de Condren, Olier* (Washington, D.C.: Catholic University of America Press, 1949).

Wister, Robert, ed., *Priests: Identity and Mission* (Wilmington: Michael Glazier, 1990).

Zipfel, Paul A., "Priesthood, Listening, and the Music," *Review for Religious* 51 (1992): 733–35.